CONTEMPORARY LANGUAGE STUDIES

GENERAL EDITOR: Professor F. M. Willis

Based on an original plan, this series is a new venture, in publishing for modern language students, and aims to promote the inter-disciplinary study of language and of the sociocultural context in which language is used and evolves.

Its predominant concern at present is with French studies, and this governs the selection of themes. At the outset, however, the programme provides for a general text on linguistics designed for students not only of French but of other European languages also.

The books are of an introductory nature and devised, with appropriate adjustments in each case, on the following general plan:

- a section, in English, with chapters of description and analysis
- illustrative texts, in French, at the end of each chapter, and bearing directly on it
- a section, in French and English, of linguistic exercises followed by bibliographical guidance

The series is addressed to all who are concerned with the study of France and its language, and is of special value to two broad categories:

1. Modern language students who are engaged in a new discipline (e.g. economics, politics, business studies) involving new concepts and requiring them to acquire a new technical lexis and a new style of writing or speech.
2. Students of social sciences and business studies taking a modern language course requiring application of the principles or theory already acquired in their primary discipline.

PUBLISHED

Linguistics for Language Learners by Anthony F. Hartley
Contemporary French Society by Linda Hantrais
The Contemporary French Economy by Graeme M. Holmes and Peter D. Fawcett
Contemporary French Politics by Malcolm Slater

Contemporary French Politics

Malcolm Slater

MACMILLAN

First published 1985 by
Higher and Further Education Division
MACMILLAN PUBLISHERS LTD
Houndmills, Basingstoke, Hampshire, RG21 2XS and London
Companies and representatives throughout the world

Filmset in Great Britain by
CK Typesetters Ltd, Sutton, Surrey

Printed in Hong Kong

British Library Cataloguing in Publication Data
Slater, Malcolm
Contemporary French politics. —
(Contemporary language studies)
1. French language — Readers — France —
Politics and government   2. France —
Politics and government — 1945–
I. Title   II. Series
448.2′421   PC2117
ISBN 0–333–33989–4
ISBN 0–333–33990–8 Pbk

Contents

List of Tables

List of Figures

List of Abbreviations

BAS	*Bureau d'Aide Sociale*
CAD	*Centre d'Action Démocratique*
CD	*Centre Démocrate*
CDS	*Centre des Démocrates Sociaux*
CEDEP	*Centre National d'Etudes et de Promotion*
CERES	*Centre d'Etudes, de Recherche et d'Education Socialistes*
CFDT	*Confédération Française Démocratique du Travail*
CFTC	*Confédération Française de Travailleurs Chrétiens*
CGC	*Confédération Générale des Cadres*
CGT	*Confédération Générale du Travail*
CGT–FO	*Confédération Générale du Travail – Force Ouvrière*
CIR	*Convention des Institutions Républicaines*
CNJA	*Centre National des Jeunes Agriculteurs*
CNPF	*Conseil National du Patronat Français*
CODER	*Commission de Développment Economique Régional*
DATAR	*Délégation à l'Aménagement du Territoire et à l'Action Régionale*
DDE	*Direction Départementale de l'Equipement*
FEN	*Fédération de l'Education Nationale*
FGDS	*Fédération de la Gauche Démocrate et Socialiste*
FNSEA	*Fédération Nationale des Syndicats d'Exploitants Agricoles*
FSD	*Fédération des Socialistes Démocrates*
GAM	*Groupe d'Action Municipale*
HLM	*Habitation à Loyer Modéré*
INC	*Institut National de la Consommation*
MDSF	*Mouvement Démocrate Socialiste de France*
MRG	*Mouvement des Radicaux de Gauche*
MRP	*Mouvement Républicain Populaire*
OAS	*Organisation de l'Armée Secrète*
PCF	*Parti Communiste Français*

PR	*Parti Républicain*
PS	*Parti Socialiste*
PSA	*Parti Socialiste Autonome*
PSU	*Parti Socialiste Unifié*
PTT	*Postes, Télégraphes et Téléphones (Postes et Télécommunications)*
Rad.	*Parti Radical*
RI	*Républicains Indépendants*
RPF	*Rassemblement du Peuple Français*
RPR	*Rassemblement pour la République*
SAC	*Service d'Action Civique*
SFIO	*Section Française de l'Internationale Ouvrière*
SIVOM	*Syndicat Intercommunal à Vocation Multiple*
TPE	*Trauvaux Publics de l'Etat*
UCRG	*Union des Clubs pour le Renouveau de la Gauche*
UDF	*Union pour la Démocratie Française*
UDR	*Union des Démocrates pour la République*
UDSR	*Union Démocratique et Socialiste de la Résistance*
UFC	*Union Fédérale des Consommateurs*
UFD	*Union des Forces Démocratiques*
UGCS	*Union des Groupes et Clubs Socialistes*
UGS	*Union de la Gauche Socialiste*
UNM	*Union pour la Nouvelle Majorité*
UNR	*Union pour la Nouvelle République*
URP	*Union des Républicains pour le Progrès*

Acknowledgements

My gratitude is to Professor F.M. Willis for his helpful advice and generous encouragement as series editor, to friends and acquaintances on both sides of the Channel, to Mrs Linda Rose, who typed most of the manuscript, and especially to Mr Tony Hartley and Dr Claire Laudet, colleagues in the University of Bradford, for their indispensable counsel.

MALCOLM SLATER

Glossary

An explanation or translation of some of the French words and phrases which the student of contemporary French politics will encounter most frequently is given on the page or pages indicated:

adjoint 193; alternance 74, 95; aménagement du territoire 197; apparenté 170; arbitrage 87, 125; arrondissement 193; l'audiovisuel 64; autogestion 37; ballotage 168; bilan social 227; blancs et nuls 69; bloc de la constitutionnalité 225; bulletin de vote 167; cabinet ministériel 124; candidat à la candidature 97; candidat fantaisiste 97; canton 193; chargé de mission 100; cogestion 227; commission 170; commune 193; conseil général 73, 193; Conseil des Ministres 125; conseil municipal 73, 193; conseil restreint 125; conseiller technique 100; contentieux électoral 222; contre-pouvoirs 142, 204; contreseing 87; courant 153; cumul des mandats 72, 197; décrispation 93, 179; démagogie 238; département 193; désistement réciproque 152; discipline républicaine 152; domaine de la loi 175; domaine réservé 253; droits de l'homme 5; la durée 117; électeur inscrit 69; élections anticipées 73, 117; élections cantonales 193; élections partielles 168; élus locaux 196; élus sociaux 204; énarque 101; exode rural 197; filière 130; force de dissuasion 90; force de frappe 90; forces vives 73; grands corps 129; groupuscules 40; irrecevable 127; incompatibilité 129, 166; intéressement 227; intergroupe 170; interlocuteurs 204; interpellation 179; investiture 87; isoloir 168; loi de finances 176; loi d'habilitation 176; loi organique 176; majorité présidentielle 96; marketing politique 66; Médiateur 224; motion de censure provoquée 173; motion de censure spontanée 172; navette 177; non inscrit 170; notable 34, 71; panachage 194; parlementarisme rationalisé 85, 165; parrain 97; parti attrape-tout 148; politique politicienne 74; pouvoirs publics 5; préfet 193; projet de loi 127; projet de société 74, 227; proposition de loi 127, 176; quinquennat 237; rassemblement 27, 41; rééquilibrage 153; remaniement ministérielle 123; sans étiquette 195; septennat 97; la société civile 204; suffrages exprimés 168; suppléant 167; troisième tour 73; tutelle 197, 199; vote préférentiel 194

xiv

General Editor's Foreword

This book is one of a series designed primarily to meet the needs of two types of students – modern linguists and social scientists with an interest in contemporary France. It is assumed that both will be seeking to acquire a deeper understanding of various aspects of French society and at the same time to improve their command of the language used by members of that society.

Accordingly, while the descriptive and analytical sections of the book are in English, each is illustrated by suitable texts in French aimed at providing examples of an appropriate technical vocabulary as well as an appreciation of the various approaches adopted by French authors who write in different language varieties and for different readerships. Based on these texts are the linguistic exercises which have been constructed not only to develop competence in the foreign language, but also to involve students in a critical appraisal of the arguments and the ways in which they are expressed. The selected and annotated bibliographies at the end of each chapter are intended to give useful guidance to authoritative and specialised works and also to up-to-date source material; here the aim is to provide readers with the stimulus and help to undertake further independent study in areas of particular interest to them.

This presentation of interlinked descriptive, analytical and illustrative materials and their linguistic exploitation is the means by which the authors of the books in the series attempt to promote an interdisciplinary study of French and certain facets of French civilisation which form part of the indivisible sociocultural context in which the language is used and developed.

As an introductory work the present volume should be invaluable to modern linguists who are seeking to understand the unfamiliar concepts of a new discipline and to social scientists who, already familiar with the conceptual framework of their discipline, wish to extend its field of reference to another European society. It is hoped, however, that the book will be of interest and help to more general readers wishing to increase their knowledge of French life and institutions.

FRANK M. WILLIS

1

The Constitutional Background

Introduction

France is among the most long-established, powerful and enduring nation states in Europe. From the seventeenth century, and with a national history going back many centuries before, France has been a force in European and world politics. As a sovereign nation state, she has survived the effects of international conflict and internal dissension, where others have been profoundly affected in the past, or now face an uncertain future. And yet, certainly until quite recently, France had the reputation among students of its political affairs as a country characterised by tension, conflict and instability. It was commonly said that Frenchmen were incapable of agreeing on effective solutions to fundamental political questions, but were subject to what General de Gaulle called a *'perpétuelle effervescence politique'*.

These two elements – durability and instability – combined to give a picture of French politics as a uniquely paradoxical phenomenon, providing valuable material for comparative study, and affording the opportunity, particularly to Anglo-Saxon observers, of vaunting the relative merits of their own political systems. It is a picture which was thought to provide a framework not only to describe the most important features of contemporary French politics, but also to explain how they had developed historically.

To explain politics in terms of history seemed natural to commentators on French political affairs. The idea of an enduring State and a politically 'effervescent' people, which together made French politics unique, was a frequent theme of General de Gaulle. French Presidents since his departure from the political scene fall easily into historical references when, for example, they address the French people on television, knowing that chords will be struck and points understood if not always accepted by a nation imbued,

1

perhaps more than others, with a heightened sense of the past.

There is no denying that the French state is long established: it was forged over many centuries into a coherent political unit. It is also true that France is a powerful nation state. She was among those states which had a dominant role in the Europe of medieval and early modern times; in the eighteenth and nineteenth centuries, and in the first half of the twentieth, France was one of the great powers which supervised the balance of power in Europe and helped to manage a Eurocentric global system. In the post–1945 world of superpowers, France has sought to be in the forefront of the category of 'middle powers', exerting significant political and economic influence in the international system. Moreover, the French nation state has been an enduring one: in the course of its political modernisation, the political system has survived internal upheavals such as revolutions involving a high level of violence (in 1789–99; 1830; 1848) and limited civil war (in 1870–1; and the threat of it as recently as 1958). It has also surmounted crises caused by international events such as defeat in European wars; military occupation of a significant part of national teritory; enforced cession of territory; and the evacuation of overseas territories in troubled circumstances.

This picture of France as a long-established powerful state, whose national unity has survived intact despite the buffetings to which it has been subjected, must be completed by the idea of the French nation as the embodiment of cultured Western values, of a civilisation manifesting itself in an artistic and literary flowering, which reinforced – and by the seventeenth century had already merged with – the nascent idea of a French state. And yet, against the notion of a unifying protective state, and a humanising, progressive body of cultural achievements, it has always been necessary to set the idea that French politics could be understood adequately only by making significant reference to aspects of political behaviour, individual and collective, especially when these seemed to be more conflictual than cooperative.

Despite the pre-eminence of their nation state in many fields, Frenchmen, according to the received wisdom of commentators, are incapable of compromise and collaboration on the fundamental elements of political life, but instead have inherited a political system characterised by defects which prevent its efficient functioning and which call for diagnosis and remedies. Alleged imperfections have been identified in various fields of political activity, but they can conveniently be grouped under the headings of constitutional evolution, ideological conflict, and political culture.

Constitutional evolution

Since 1789 there has been in France a multiplicity of constitutions, with an average life of about 13 years. This average figure however encompasses extremes of duration from the 70 years of the Third Republic (proclaimed 1870, overthrown 1940) to the two months of the *Acte additionnel* (April–June 1815) which reflected in constitutional terms the brief 'Hundred Days' reappearance of Napoleon as Emperor. Moreover, problems of definition are inherent in any discussion of French constitutions: some constitutions were drafted but the conditions for their lawful application never met – the Constitution of the Vichy regime was drawn up by virtue of powers given to the Head of State Marshal Petain in July 1940, but never officially promulgated, and the first of the Fourth Republic draft Constitutions was rejected by voters in the May 1946 referendum. One constitution was legally enacted but never applied – that of June 1793, because of the exigencies of the worsening war with Austria. Some constitutional acts, while making significant changes in the nature of the regime, fall in the category of modifications to an existing constitution, rather than of new constitutions – a declaration by the Senate in November 1852 transformed a Republic into an hereditary Empire, without major revision of the Constitution, by making the incumbent President of the Republic into the Emperor Napoleon III. In 1870, a further *'sénatus-consulte'* purported to infuse a greater measure of legitimacy, through parliamentary control of the executive, into an authoritarian Empire which was fast losing what support it had, and which was to meet its downfall only months later, following military defeat by Prussia and its allies.

Apart from times when some form of legal constitution was in operation, the picture is further complicated in that there were periods when, strictly speaking, France had no constitution, but was governed by *de facto* regimes such as the Vichy Regime of 1940–4, or regimes provisional upon the drawing up and enacting of a constitution. Examples of this latter, semi-constitutional regime are those of the 1944–6 transitional period before and after the end of the Second World War, and the changeover from the Fourth to the Fifth Republic in the second half of 1958.

Despite uncertainties of definition, what is incontrovertible is not only the existence of a large number of different constitutional arrangements in French political history, but also the wide range of political orientation reflected in these arrangements. Using the Left–Right representation of political orientation, French constitutions have provided the institutional framework for regimes stretching from democratic, quasi-revolutionary Republics on the Left, to absolutist, authoritarian dictatorships on the Right.

Any attempt to understand modern French politics with the help of an overall picture of two centuries of constitutional evolution since the French Revolution must be prefaced by a description of the institutional arrangements – the *'ancien régime'* – which that momentous chain of events begun in 1789 purported to improve upon. These arrangements had developed over a span of eight centuries, during which a coherent nation state progressively established itself and spread towards the so-called 'natural frontiers' of the Alps, the Pyrenees, and the Rhine, although the presence of considerable numbers of non-Frenchmen west of the latter always vitiated the claim.

But the only solution to the inherent geographical diversities of the expanded territory (which however contributed to the economic strength of the new nation state) and to religious quarrels in the sixteenth and seventeenth centuries (which nearly destroyed it) was to intensify the process of adminstrative centralisation. Centralisation implies that all levels of local administration are subordinate to the central government – under the *ancien régime*, the King – or to local agents appointed by it. These latter, however, can possess a significant amount of power to make decisions themselves: there was in the *ancien régime* an administration which had at the same time a high degree of centralisation and a high degree of deconcentration of power. Moreover the *ancien régime* never totally succeeded in suppressing regional and provincial identities often associated with deeply-felt ethnic sub-nationalisms – Brittany is the prime example of this.

And yet the dominant political figures to emerge from the first years of the Revolutionary period – commonly subsumed under the term Jacobins, still used to denote the supporters of strong centralisation – were happy to take over the centralised administrative system as the means to put their political principles into effect, and as the only practical solution to the basic problems of the geographical and cultural diversity of French territory. What the French Revolutionaries objected to was less the existence of a centralised bureaucratic administration than the abuses inherent in its application. The absolute monarchy of the *ancien régime* concentrated sovereign power in the hands of the King, who was at the same time warlord, supreme law-giver, and ultimate arbiter of the fate of all his subjects, and, after the defeat of Protestantism, of their spiritual orientation. The King possessed all the powers associated with sovereignty:

1 legislative power: the power to make laws;
2 executive power: the power to govern, with ministers to advise him;
3 judicial power: the power to decide legal disputes;
4 spiritual power: the power (and the responsibility) to direct the spiritual welfare of his subjects.

It was essentially the concentration of powers in the hands of the King to which the French Revolutionaries objected, and it was the principle of the separation of powers which they espoused. In this they were the heirs to a European intellectual tradition of political liberalisation which had manifested itself, particularly in the eighteenth century, in serious attempts to theorise about relationships in political life. The spiritual power such as the French kings possessed soon ceased to be a central concern, as individual freedom of conscience was progressively established in most of Europe. But the *pouvoirs publics* – legislative, executive and judicial – and the relationships between them, were one of the main preoccupations of those emerging forms of government which were inspired by democratic ideals, however broadly interpreted.

In addition, the Revolution of 1789 abolished in the name of equality a whole series of discriminatory rights and privileges which had accrued to certain groups of the King's subjects. It was particularly the aristocracy who, far from being the vehicle of political modernisation as was generally the case in Britain, had become the repository of rights and privileges during the development of the Bourbon nation state. The French Revolutionary leaders, of whom a large proportion were lawyers, were generally agreed on the fundamental aim and on the method of achieving it. The arbitrary and abusive exercise of overweening power, denying human and civil rights, had to be replaced by a Republican system of rationally evolved, legally entrenched principles. There was a need to define, and ensure the protection of, what Anglo-Saxons still call in the context of French constitutional history 'the Rights of Man', but which in most other contexts are referred to as 'Human Rights' –*les droits de l'homme*. However, not only was it necessary to separate public powers and abolish privilege by making rights a function simply of being human, but also to establish firmly the principle that sovereignty belonged inalienably to the people, and that the concentrated expression of this was in and through an elected legislature – a Parliamentary Assembly.

The most practicable method of achieving these goals was by a written constitution, which purported to enshrine a whole new political value system based upon the principles of popular sovereignty, and freedom and equality. The third element of the Republican tryptych – fraternity – may be equally emotive, as well as effective in terms of political mobilisation (the motto has appeared in all Republican constitutions since 1848) but has always been the least amenable to legislation.

Such a written constitution, however, as well as achieving the correct 'mix' with regard to these principles, had to have a capacity for its own organic transformation to meet changing social and political circumstances, and for the creation of political institutions which a substantial proportion of citizens supported. Figure 1.1 shows the succession of regimes since the French Revolution. Commentators who have analysed the more strictly institutional aspects of constitutional developments in France have stressed two points in particular.

Firstly, the large number and wide variety of French constitutions have led commentators to try to impose a logical pattern or cycle of constitutional development on what might appear to be a chaotic historical picture. This cyclical interpretation of French constitutional history rests on the view that there has been, since the first constitution in 1791, a succession of phases of regimes (Figure 1.2). Analysis of this nature represents an attempt not only to put order into an apparently chaotic picture, but also the exploit the predictive aspects of such a model. When General de Gaulle, in the early years of the Fifth Republic, was seen to be interpreting in an extreme, personalised fashion those aspects of the 1958 Constitution which emphasised executive dominance, some writers saw this as possible proof that the cyclical pattern still operated; and no doubt a future President who behaves like, and rules as long as, a constitutional 'monarch', or a future 'radical' French republic will see the notion of constitutional cycles exhumed. The objection to the theory is that the socio-economic environment of any constitutional change, as well as its political actors, their objectives and achievements, are hardly likely to be reproduced with any exactitude for any subsequent modifications.

A second approach to the more properly institutional aspects of instability is to say that although the separation of powers has been a central concern of most written constitutional arrangements since 1791, the precise place and function of each 'branch' has never been satisfactorily delineated. Of the three 'powers', the place of the judiciary has not really been at issue: its neutral position, free from formal government interference, has always been accepted as a basic principle of liberal democracy (which is not to say there are

Figure 1.1
Regimes since the French Revolution

	CONSTITUTION (DATE UNDERLINED)	TYPE OF REGIME ESTABLISHED	REASON FOR DEMISE
	1791 – 1792	limited 'constitutional' monarchy	fall of monarchy
FIRST REPUBLIC	1793 (year I)	'democratic' republic	never applied, because of war
	1795 (year III) – 1799	'bourgeois' republic	coup d'etat by Napoleon Bonaparte
CONSULATE	1799 (year VIII) –1802	dictatorship by Napoleon as 'First Consul'	superseded by more stringent dictatorship
	1802 (year X) – 1804	reinforcement of existing régime	superseded by more Imperial regime
FIRST EMPIRE	1804 (year XII) –1814	dictatorship by Napoleon as Emperor	abdication of Napoleon
RESTORATION	1814 – 1830 (interrupted briefly by:	quasi-constitutional monarchy	change of dynasty to Orleanist
	1815	return of Napoleonic Empire, somewhat liberalised)	second abdication of Napoleon
	1830 – 1848	constitutional monarchy	revolution of 1848
SECOND REPUBLIC	1848 – 1851	'democratic' republic, but Right-leaning	coup d'état by Louis-Napoleon
	1852 (Jan 14) 1852 (Nov 7) – 1870	personalised republic, then authoritarian Empire	superseded by more liberal Imperial régime
SECOND EMPIRE	1870	somewhat liberalised Napoleonic Empire	military defeat
THIRD REPUBLIC	1875 – 1940	parliamentary republic	
	1940 – 1944	authoritarian dictatorship: 'Vichy régime' – no Constitution in force	invasion of France by Western Allies
FOURTH REPUBLIC	1946 – 1958	democratic parliamentary republic	inability to solve acute political crises, esp. over Algeria
FIFTH REPUBLIC	1958 –	democratic parliamentary republic	

Figure 1.2
Constitutional cycles

CYCLES	CONSTITUTIONAL MONARCHY	'RADICAL' REPUBLIC	'CONSERVATIVE' REPUBLIC	STRONG EXECUTIVE
First	Constitution of 1791	Republic of 1792 (Constitution of 1793)	Constitution of 1795	First Empire and Bourbon Restoration
Second	July Monarchy 1830-48	(note A)	Constitution of 1848	Second Empire
Third	Liberalised Second Empire 1870 (note B)	(note A)	Third Republic	Vichy Régime
Fourth	(note C)	Fourth Republic 'tripartisme' 'immobilisme'		Fifth Republic

NOTE A: There were no 'radical' republics as such in these cycles; but there were in both cases examples of strong revolutionary movements, especially in Paris, which posed serious threats to the emerging 'conservative' republics: the workers' movement culminating in the 'June days' of 1848, and the Paris Commune of 1871.

NOTE B: To this brief interlude might be added the period 1871–5, which can be described as a 'monarchy without a monarch', or a 'republican monarchy' since MacMahon, the President, was a Royalist, as were the majority of deputies in the Assembly.

NOTE C: There was no monarchy as such, but detractors of de Gaulle might plausibly argue that de Gaulle's behaviour was 'monarchical' in his domination, after Giraud was ousted, of the *Comité français de Libération nationale*. In 1944, this became the Provisional Government, held in check only by a Consultative Assembly. When a Constituent Assembly was elected in October 1945, de Gaulle quickly found the constraints on his freedom of action unacceptable, and resigned in January 1946.

no political implications in judicial recruitment or in individual judicial decisions). A fundamental problem in the elaboration of constitutional arrangements has always been the relationship between the executive (the Government and its administrative machinery) and the legislature (the parliamentary assembly).

Commentators point out that in France the problem has plagued political life for two centuries, a fact which has to be admitted even by those who claim that the Fifth Republic, after nearly three decades of existence, has finally solved the problem, and established (or caused to evolve) institutions with a high degree of legitimacy and a strong chance of survival. It is argued that the problem of conflict between the idea of executive dominance and that of legislative dominance is not only of long standing, but also important in understanding some of the constitutional preoccupations of present-day French politics. Figure 1.3 indicates how constitutional development has seemed to oscillate like a pendulum between the two extremes of executive dominance and legislative or parliamentary dominance.

In any constitution, the number of Articles devoted to executive power and legislative power is a useful guide to how the framers approached the problem of the relationship between them. In the 1958 Constitution, half of the 92 Articles address themselves to

Figure 1.3
The 'pendulum' of constitutional development

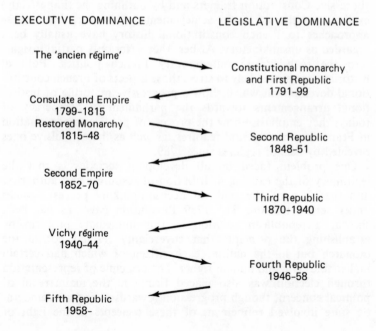

EXECUTIVE DOMINANCE   LEGISLATIVE DOMINANCE

The 'ancien régime'

Constitutional monarchy
and First Republic
1791–99

Consulate and Empire
1799–1815
Restored Monarchy
1815–48

Second Republic
1848–51

Second Empire
1852–70

Third Republic
1870–1940

Vichy régime
1940–44

Fourth Republic
1946–58

Fifth Republic
1958–

these preoccupations. The order in which matters are dealt with can also broadly reflect the importance placed on each element by those who draw up a Constitution. Some indication of the relative power of the executive and the legislative can be gained from the position of the section (*titre*) dealing with, for example, the President of the Republic and the Government on the one hand, and the legislature and individual rights on the other. The 1958 Constitution lays down Presidential powers in Section II; the Fourth Republic Constitution had relegated this aspect to Section V and an earlier draft – rejected by referendum – to Section VI, after listing civil and human rights, and considering the modalities of legislative power. These latter had similar prominence in the Constitutions of 1791, 1793, 1795, 1799 and 1848 (that of 1875 was in reality a series of separate enactments, which however, with subsequent revisions, constitute a coherent set of constitutional dispositions). On the other hand, the texts of 1804, 1814, 1830, 1852 (November) and 1940 gave pride of place, by dealing with them before any mention of the legislature, to the concepts of 'imperial dignity', or 'royal government', or 'governmental function'.

It may be that the dynamic tensions of post-Revolution French politics are better understood by reference to the preoccupations of successive Constitution framers and by outlining the (imperfectly) cyclical pattern of their achievements. However, both these approaches to French constitutional history have usually been regarded as unsatisfactory. At best they offer only partial insights into the realities of contemporary French politics. Political historians are more likely to stress those aspects of French constitutional development which show a progressive maturing of institutional arrangements towards the parliamentary democracy of today: they emphasise how the process of political modernisation in France has incremental features, as well as the convulsive ones revealed by lists of regimes since 1789.

One problem faced by all developing societies is that the legitimacy of the existing distribution of resources and authority, and therefore of the political decision-making process, comes under severe tension. The 1789 Revolution gave, as has been shown, a republican solution to this immediate problem by establishing the principle that sovereignty resided not in the monarch but in the nation, each citizen of which had certain inalienable civic and human rights. The principle of representation through election was also placed firmly in the mainstream of political concern, though progression towards a modern democratic state involved refinement of these concepts in the light of changing social and economic circumstances. However, on the basis of the accepted idea of popular sovereignty, even though it could be entrusted, with the nation's approval, to a temporary keeper, the notion of a parliamentary regime was able to emerge. Even the 'Caesarism' of Napoleon Bonaparte and the restored Bourbon monarchy, which denied popular sovereignty, did not dispense totally with a legislature, one Chamber of which was elected by limited suffrage. It was paradoxically under the latter regime (1814–30) that the idea of a balance, rather than a total separation, of powers appeared. Although in the last resort the King held ultimate legislative and executive power, this was in practice limited, and the regime relied on quite close collaboration between King, his Ministers and the two Chambers – the Chamber of Peers, including life peers, and the Chamber of elected departmental deputies. The legitimate existence of an elected parliamentary assembly was complemented by a development of supreme importance: that Ministers of the Government should feel obliged to account for their policy to a Parliament which would assess its acceptability. Parliament thus shared the King's powers, by placing a constraint on his Ministers' application of them. Since it was the Ministers who acted for the King in making laws and in deciding how money should be spent, it was desirable, even necessary, that they should not be implacably opposed to majority views in the Assembly. It was better still, in the interests of the smooth running of increasingly complex affairs, if Ministers were close to these views, and even better if they shared them. This was the basis of parliamentary sovereignty, which implied that the people's will was located in an institution, and that the latter had meaningful powers.

The basic problems faced by Republican constitutions from 1848 onwards were not only the degree to which a President of the Republic should have the executive powers formerly held by the monarch or the Emperor, but also the extent of the electorate from which the legislature derived its legitimacy. Universal male suffrage was introduced by the Second Republic in 1848, but did not stop the establishment of Louis Napoleon's dictatorship, or prevent the election under the Second Empire (1852–70) of Government-sponsored candidates. Indeed, universal suffrage in the guise of plebiscites was used by the Emperor Napoleon III to give legitimacy to his regime, based, initially at least, on popular support, and bypassing the legislature. However, by leaving to the *Corps législatif* prerogatives that were real, if not realised, the Second Empire prepared for a final conciliation between universal suffrage and representative government, once the Third Republic became established in the 1870s, and the paradox of a conservative republic became a reality.

The Third Republic was stable in that it lasted seventy years, despite occasional political and constitutional crises. But its durability has been attributed to one particular development: an initially quasi-monarchical regime was eventually taken over by the Republican 'opposition', which made it its own, and successfully established political practices and conventions which were so far removed from the text of the 1875 Constitutional dispositions that it is possible to speak of a 'violation' of the Constitution. In contemporary France, it has been possible to apply this analysis to the 1958 Constitution, and argue that:

1 the first decade of the Fifth Republic was one where developing political practice often involved behaviour which can reasonably be considered unconstitutional;
2 the stability of the Fifth Republic became a reality only when in 1981 the Left opposition occupied and operated the existing institutional system, thus establishing an 'institutional synthesis'.

However, it is necessary to complement the constitutional aspects of contemporary French politics which still reveal the preoccupations of the last two hundred years, by a study of ideological conflict and an examination of political culture.

Bibliographical guidance

The first chapter, or chapters, of the following general studies of French politics will normally reveal each author's approach to the idea of understanding contemporary French politics by reference (with varying degrees of emphasis) to aspects of French history.

J.S. Ambler, *The Government and Politics of France* (Houghton Mifflin, 1971)
P. Avril, *Le Régime politique de la Ve République*, part II (LGDJ, 1967)
S. Berger, *The French Political System* (Random House, 1974), reprinted from part 3 of S.H. Beer and A.B. Ulam (eds) *Patterns of Government*, 3rd ed. (Random House, 1973)
H.W. Ehrmann, *Politics in France*, 3rd ed. (Little, Brown & Co., 1976)

F. Goguel and A. Grosser, *La Politique en France*, 9th ed. (A. Colin, 1981)

J.E.S. Hayward, *The One and Indivisible French Republic* (Weidenfeld and Nicholson, 1973). 2nd edition retitled *Governing France - the one and indivisible republic* (1983)

D. Pickles, *The Fifth French Republic*, 3rd ed. (Methuen, 1965)

D. Pickles, *The Government and Politics of France*, 2 vols. (Methuen, 1972-3)

W. Safran, *The French Polity* (Mackay, 1977)

P. Williams, *Politics in Post-war France*, 2nd ed. (Longmans, 1958), renamed for 3rd edition *Crisis and Compromise* (1964). Translated as *La Vie Politique sous la 4e République* (A. Colin, 1971)

Several commentators adduce, some more explicitly than others, the notion of explanation of contemporary French politics, and the problems which it raises. Examples can be found in:

P. Avril, 'Signification de la V République', *Pouvoirs*, no. 4 (1978)

M. Crozier, *Le phénomène bureaucratique* (Seuil, 1963)

J. Fauvet, *La France déchirée* (Fayard, 1957)

D. Johnson, 'The Two Frances: the Historical debate', *West European Politics*, vol. 1, no. 3, reprinted in V. Wright (ed.), *Conflict and Consensus in France* (Frank Cass, 1979)

D.-G. Lavroff, introduction to *Le Système politique français - la Ve République* 2nd ed. (Dalloz, 1979)

E.M. Lipransky, *L'âme française ou le national-libéralisme* (Anthropos, 1979)

Of the many books by French constitutional experts with '*institutions politiques*' and '*droit constitutionnel*' in the title, the following are recommended:

G. Burdeau, *Droit constitutionnel et institutions politiques*, 19th ed., vol. 2 (LGDJ, 1980)

C. Debbasch *et al. Droit constitutionnel et institutions politiques* (Economica, 1984)

M. Duverger, *Institutions politiques et droit constitutionnel*, 16th ed., vol. 2 (PUF, 1982)

A. Hauriou and J. Gicquel, *Institutions politiques et droit constitutionnel*, 7th ed. (Montchréstien 1980, also Addendum published annually from October 1981)

M. Prélot and J. Boulouis, *Institutions politiques et droit constitutionnel*, 8th ed. (Dalloz, 1981)

Less juridically oriented approaches can be found in the following books, as well as in the appropriate parts of some of the general works listed in the first section:

R. Barrillon *et al. Dictionnaire de la Constitution*, 3rd ed. (Cujas, updated 1983)
C. Debbasch and J.-M. Pontier, *Les Constitutions de la France depuis 1789* (Garnier-Flammarion, 1970) has all the constitutional texts, as well as enlightening introductions to each.
J. Godechot, *Les grandes étapes du régime républicain en France* (Cujas, 1970)
S. Rials, *Textes politiques français* (PUF, 1983)
G. Richard, *Les Institutions Politiques de la France de Louis XV à Giscard d'Estaing* (Flammarion, 1979)
D. Thompson, *Democracy in France since 1870*, 5th ed. (OUP, 1969)

Illustrative texts and linguistic exercises

Texte 1.1   Notre vieille propension aux divisions

Mise en situation
Le General de Gaulle, chef de la France Libre pendant la deuxième guerre mondiale, et des régimes provisoires après la Libération, se retira brusquement de la politique en janvier 1946. Mais, inquiet quant à l'évolution politique de la France et hostile aux conceptions constitutionnelles des trois principaux partis politiques – surtout les socialistes et les communistes –qu'il jugeait trop 'parlementaires' et que le peuple français venait de rejeter au référendum de mai 1946, de Gaulle se rendit à Bayeux, en Normandie, en juin 1946, et à l'occasion des cérémonies du deuxième anniversaire du débarquement allié en France, prononça devant la sous-préfecture une allocution importante. Avant d'expliciter ses idées sur la constitution qu'il jugeait appropriée à la République naissante, le Général s'étendit sur une explication de l'évolution politique récente et une évocation des dangers qu'il croyait menacer la France.

                    *   *   *

C'est ici que sur le sol des ancêtres réapparut l'Etat; l'Etat légitime, parce qu'il reposait sur l'intérêt et le sentiment de la Nation; l'Etat dont la souveraineté réelle avait été transportée du côté de la guerre, de la liberté et de la victoire, tandis que la servitude n'en conservait que l'apparence; l'Etat sauvegardé dans ses droits, sa dignité, son autorité, au milieu des vicissitudes du dénuement et de l'intrigue; l'Etat préservé des ingérences de l'étranger; l'Etat capable de rétablir autour de lui l'unité nationale et l'unité impériale, d'assembler toutes les forces de la patrie et de l'Union française, de *porter la victoire à son terme*, en commun avec les Alliés, de traiter d'égal à égal avec les autres grandes nations du monde, de préserver l'ordre public, de faire rendre la justice et de commencer notre reconstruction.
Si cette grande oeuvre fut réalisée en dehors du cadre antérieur de nos

institutions, c'est parce que celles-ci n'avaient pas répondu aux nécessités nationales et qu'elles avaient, d'elles-mêmes, abdiqué dans la tourmente. Le salut devait venir d'ailleurs.

Il vient, d'abord, d'une élite *spontanément jaillie des profondeurs de la Nation* et qui, bien au-dessus de toute préoccupation de parti ou de classe, se dévoua au combat pour la libération, la grandeur et la rénovation de la France. Sentiment de sa supériorité morale, conscience d'exercer une sorte de sacerdoce du sacrifice et de l'exemple, passion du risque et de l'entreprise, mépris des agitations, prétentions, surenchères, confiance souveraine en la force et en la ruse de sa puissante conjuration aussi bien qu'en la victoire et en l'avenir de la patrie, telle fut la psychologie de cette élite partie de rien et qui, malgré de lourdes pertes, devait entraîner derrière elle tout l'Empire et toute la France.

Elle n'y eût point, cependant, réussi sans l'assentiment de l'immense masse française. Celle-ci, en effet, dans sa volonté instinctive de survivre et de triompher, n'avait jamais vu dans le désastre de 1940 qu'une *péripétie* de guerre mondiale où la France servait d'avant-garde. Si beaucoup se plièrent, par force, aux circonstances, le nombre de ceux qui les acceptèrent dans leur esprit et dans leur coeur fut littéralement infime. Jamais la France ne crut que l'ennemi ne fût point l'ennemi et que le salut fût ailleurs que du côté des armes de la liberté. *A mesure que se déchiraient les voiles*, le sentiment profond du pays se faisait jour dans sa réalité. Partout où paraissait la croix de Lorraine s'écroulait l'échafaudage d'une autorité qui n'était que fictive, bien qu'elle fût, en apparence, constitutionnellement fondée. Tant il est vrai que les pouvoirs publics ne valent, en fait et en droit, que s'ils s'accordent avec l'intérêt supérieur du pays, s'ils reposent sur l'adhésion confiante des citoyens. En matière d'institutions, bâtir sur autre chose, ce serait bâtir sur du sable. Ce serait risquer de voir l'édifice crouler une fois de plus à l'occasion d'une de ces crises auxquelles, par la nature des choses, notre pays se trouve si souvent exposé.

Voilà pourquoi, une fois assuré le salut de l'Etat, dans la victoire remportée et l'unité nationale maintenue, la tâche par-dessus tout urgente et essentielle était l'établissement des nouvelles institutions françaises. Dès que cela fut possible, le peuple français fut donc invité à élire ses constituants, tout en fixant à leur mandat des limites déterminées et en se réservant à lui-même la décision définitive. Puis, une fois le train mis sur les rails, nous-même nous sommes retiré de la scène, non seulement pour ne point engager dans la lutte des partis ce qu'en vertu des événements nous pouvons symboliser et qui appartient à la Nation tout entière, mais encore pour qu'aucune considération relative à un homme, tandis qu'il dirigeait l'Etat, ne pût fausser dans aucun sens l'oeuvre des législateurs.

Cependant, la Nation et l'Union française attendent encore une Constitution qui soit faite pour elles et qu'elle aient pu joyeusement approuver. A vrai dire, si l'on peut regretter que l'édifice reste à construire, chacun convient certainement qu'une réussite quelque peu différée vaut mieux qu'un achèvement rapide mais fâcheux.

Au cours d'une péroide de temps qui ne dépasse pas deux fois la vie d'un homme, la France fut envahie sept fois et a pratiqué treize régimes, car *tout se tient* dans les malheurs d'un peuple. Tant de secousses ont accumulé dans notre vie publique des poisons dont s'intoxique notre vieille propension gauloise aux divisions et aux querelles. Les épreuves inouïes que nous venons de traverser n'ont fait, naturellement, qu'aggraver cet état de choses. La situation actuelle du monde où, derrière des idéologies opposées, se confrontent des Puissances entre lesquelles nous sommes placés, *ne laisse pas d'introduire* dans nos luttes politiques un facteur de trouble passionné. Bref, la rivalité des partis revêt chez nous un caractère fondamental, qui met toujours tout en question et sous lequel *s'estompent* trop souvent les intérêts supérieurs du pays. Il y a là un fait patent, qui tient au tempérament national, aux péripéties de l'Histoire et aux ébranlements du présent, mais dont il est indispensable à l'avenir du pays et de la démocratie que nos institutions tiennent compte et se gardent, afin de *préserver le crédit des lois*, la cohésion des gouvernements, l'efficience des administrations, le prestige et l'autorité de l'Etat.

C'est qu'en effet, le trouble dans l'Etat *a pour conséquence inéluctable* la désaffection des citoyens à l'égard des institutions.

SOURCE: Charles de Gaulle, 'Discours prononcé à Bayeux', *Discours et Messages*, vol. 2, 1946–58 (Plon, 1970)

Exploitation du texte

1 Expliquez en quelques mots les expressions en italique.

2 Faites une analyse textuelle générale, en vous appuyant éventuellement sur l'approche suggérée dans l'Annexe A (p. 23).

3 Justifiez grammaticalement chaque usage du subjonctif dans le texte.

4 A partir de votre analyse générale, faites une étude plus détaillée du rôle de la structure des phrases dans la mise en relief des idées.

5 Le général de Gaulle fait référence (paragraphe 2) à la Troisième République. Décrivez brièvement les raisons pour lesquelles ce régime n'aurait pas 'répondu aux nécessités nationales'.

6 L'auteur donne ses idées personnelles sur la Résistance et aussi sur la situation politique au lendemain de la guerre. Essayez de déterminer dans quelle mesure la conception gaullienne de cette dernière s'accorde avec la réalité historique en examinant un ou plusieurs des aspects suivants:

la démission du Général (paragraphe 5);
l'acceptation d'une nouvelle Constitution par le peuple (paragraphe 6);
'la rivalité des partis' (paragraphe 7).

Texte 1.2 Un peuple de contradictions

Mise en situation

Jean-Denis Bredin, né en 1929, universitaire, avocat et vice-président du Mouvement des Radicaux de Gauche, dans son livre *Les Français au pouvoir?* (1977), fit des propositions pour humaniser la politique et réduire l'indifférence des Français à l'égard de la politique. Pour lui, le tempérament du 'cher et vieux pays', et 'une histoire trop lourde' expliquent peut-être cette indifférence.

*   *   *

Peuple léger, versatile. Capable, dans les grandes tempêtes de se montrer héroïque; dans les eaux calmes, irrésolu, presque inconsistant. Fait pour des circonstances extrêmes, qui découvrent en lui le meilleur et le pire, mais inapte à l'exercice des vertus quotidiennes. Inapte surtout à la démocratie tranquille; toujours prêt à s'offrir au sauveur du moment, à détruire ses lois, *à brader ses libertés* pour suivre un chef victorieux. Étonnant dans le combat et l'aventure; dénué de maturité politique. Semblable à ses produits, et à ses plaisirs: le champagne, la haute couture et *le théâtre de boulevard*. Ce portrait cliché, fait et refait, est-il ressemblant? Le tableau organise des morceaux d'histoire éclatée, des comportements disparates, d'où surgissent des traits préfabriqués. Ce que décrivent nos portraitistes nationaux, c'est une nation apparemment incohérente: sérieuse et futile, *pusillanime* et courageuse; ce qu'elle a été, aux différents moments de son histoire, selon les circonstances, et les hommes qui la menaient. Mais toutes les nations ont montré, dans des événements différents, des caractères opposés. Les Français aiment regarder leurs luxurieuses contradictions; les Anglais pourraient en faire autant. Ces belles fresques qui rassemblent tous les traits d'un peuple, elles sont incapables de rendre compte de toute la vérité; car ce peuple prétendument héroïque a été, naguère, lamentable dans la guerre. Ce peuple dit aventureux, il s'est gardé avec prudence de plusieurs révolutions. On pourrait tout aussi bien, sans le trahir, le décrire sage et timoré.

Ce qui est sûr, c'est que cette nation a derrière elle une longue tradition monarchique. La démocratie n'y est qu'une expérience récente – un siècle –et plusieurs fois interrompue. Seule parenthèse démocratique de longue durée: la IIIe République, morte de la guerre, et qui céda la place à Pétain-roi. La IVe République n'a pas duré treize ans. De Gaulle-roi en a organisé et liquidé la faillite. La Ve République, si République il y a, n'a pas encore vingt ans d'âge. L'histoire de la liberté n'est pas plus constante, en France, que celle de la démocratie. Périodiquement menacée, confisquée, rétablie, engloutie dans les guerres, *domestiquée par les sauveurs*, elle est pour nous non pas une grande tradition nationale, une habitude immémoriale, ce qu'elle est, sans doute, pour les Anglais, mais un mode de vie épisodique, superficiel, sans cesse remis en question, et qui n'a pas réussi à s'acclimater. Dans les circonstances exceptionnelles de leur histoire, les Français se hâtent de *mettre leurs libertés au placard*. Ce produit d'importation anglo-saxonne, dont nous ne mésestimons pas en période faste les avantages, semble toujours nous embarrasser dans l'épreuve; nous le bradons au profit du premier venu, qui nous promet la lune, pourvu que nous nous mettions en rang par deux. Depuis quarante ans l'histoire de ce pays a été sans cesse bouleversée, plus qu'il ne convient pour affermir une démocratie fragile: trois républiques, la guerre, l'occupation étrangère, les profondes issues de la résistance et la collaboration, et dont nous supportons encore les effets, l'épuration, les guerres coloniales, et surtout la guerre algérienne séparant à nouveau les Français, le coup d'Etat de 1958, la révolution manquée de 1968, l'écrasante présence de De Gaulle, puis son retour à Colombey, et depuis lors la vague menace d'une guerre civile suspendue sur chaque consultation électorale. Nous avons vu les constitutions jetées aux ordures, les prisons se remplir et se vider, un sauveur condamné à mort, un autre renvoyé chez lui, l'armée renversant la République, puis menaçant le chef qu'elle avait installé: en gros l'histoire d'une nation d'Amérique latine, où les moments de démocratie ne sont que des parenthèses entre les coups d'Etat et les régimes d'exception. Il n'est pas impossible que tant de remue-ménage ait fatigué les Français, usé leur confiance dans la démocratie, nourri leur indifférence à la vie politique. A trop voir défiler les régimes, les constitutions, à trop souvent vérifier que *le Capitole et la roche tarpéienne* sont si proches, on peut se retrouver sceptique. En tout cas fatigué; la nation française est peut-être comme les personnes d'âge, qui en ont trop vu. Dans l'épreuve, l'indignation et l'enthousiasme se sont émoussés. Qu'il faut survivre, manger, et tâcher de se distraire, voilà la douce philosophie d'un peuple qu'a vieilli une histoire trop lourde.

SOURCE: Jean-Denis Bredin, *Les Français au pouvoir?* (Grasset, 1977)pp. 56–9.

Exploitation du texte

1 Expliquez en quelques mots les expressions en italique.

2 Faites une analyse textuelle générale, en vous appuyant éventuellement sur l'approche suggérée dans l'Annexe A (p. 23).

3 A partir de votre analyse générale, faites une étude plus détaillée de l'usage d'adjectifs et de phrases adjectivales.

4 L'auteur fait mention de deux personnages importants dans l'histoire moderne de la France – Pétain et de Gaulle – qu'il qualifie de 'rois', et dont il reproche la chute politique ('un sauveur condamné à mort, un autre renvoyé chez lui') en quelque sorte au peuple français. Faites un bref résumé biographique de ces deux hommes, en soulignant l'importance qu'ils revêtent pour l'histoire politique de la France.

5 Par quels actes, au niveau tant des individus que des organisations, pourraient se caractériser:

   la Résistance?

la Collaboration?
l'Epuration?

6 Résumez en 500–750 mots les événements principaux

de la guerre algérienne
du 'coup d'Etat de 1958'
de la 'révolution manquée de 1968'

Texte 1.3   Le mal français

Mise en situation

Alain Peyrefitte est en même temps écrivain et homme politique: né en 1925, ancien élève de l'Ecole nationale d'Administration, il fit carrière dans l'enseignement, la diplomatie et l'administration avant d'être élu à l'Assemblée Nationale en novembre 1958 et réélu depuis. Placé à la tête de plusieurs ministères depuis 1962, il fut nommé en mars 1977 Garde des Sceaux, Ministre de la Justice. Ses livres, qui traitent de la dynamique des sociétés et des maladies de civilisation, sont un mélange d'exemples concrets et d'analyses. De son oeuvre *Le Mal Français* (1976) il dit: 'J'ai mêlé passé et présent. On ne trouvera ici ni des Mémoires, ni une étude historique, ni un traité de sociologie ou de psychologie collective, ni un manifeste politique, mais une tentative d'échapper à la loi des genres.' La question fondamentale qu'il pose est: 'Pourquoi le peuple des Croisades et de la Révolution, de Pascal et de Voltaire, ce peuple vif, généreux, doué, fournit-il si souvent le spectacle de ses divisions et de son impuissance?'

*   *   *

Le changement fut si réel et profond, que ce qui nous semblait, au début de 1958, hors d'atteinte, presque hors de rêve, nous apparaît comme allant de soi ...

Le retournement n'était-il pas suffisant pour que l'on pût déclarer guéri le mal dont la France souffrait avant 1958, et qui faisait la dérision du monde? Ce n'était pas un mince mérite, si l'on songe qu'avant la IVe, il avait miné la IIIe République; et pas seulement celle de l'entre-deux-guerres. Déjà, en 1914, la France avait connu, en quarante ans, soixante gouvernements: simplement, la volonté de revanche avait masqué l'instabilité. Ainsi, les Français guérissaient d'une maladie institutionnelle qui avait duré deux Républiques. Mais n'est-ce pas trop peu dire? Ne les accablait-elle pas en fait depuis la monarchie absolue?

Réussir là où dix-sept régimes avaient échoué. *Reprendre les aiguillages de l'histoire* – où tant de fois la France avait déraillé – à partir du premier d'entre eux, cette réforme de l'Ancien Régime, dont l'insuccès avait rendu la Révolution inévitable. Bref, guérir un 'mal français' qui durait depuis trois siècles: je crois bien que c'était l'ambition suprême de Charles de Gaulle, bien qu'il ne l'eût jamais proclamée.

'Je n'ai pas fondé une nouvelle république,' me dit-il un jour. 'J'ai simplement donné des fondations à la république, qui n'en avait jamais eu.'

Et une autre fois: 'Ce que j'ai essayé de faire, c'est d'opérer la synthèse entre la monarchie et la république.'

'Une république monarchique?' fis-je. Plutôt une monarchie républicaine.'

'Si vous voulez. Plutôt une monarchie républicaine.'

Pendant *son premier septennat*, de Gaulle n'eut pas d'autre souci que de refaire un État et une nation. L'État pour la nation. La nation par l'État. Un État qu'il voulait arracher aux luttes des partis et des intérêts, en conférant à son chef la stabilité, la continuité, l'indépendance. Une nation qu'il voulait arracher à l'emprise étrangère, en lui fournissant les moyens militaires, diplomatiques et financiers d'une souveraineté oubliée.

A la longue, il s'attaqua à une troisième dimension: la société. Sans doute, sa passion de l'unité avait toujours su qu'il faudrait *trouver une issue* au conflit absurde du 'capital' et du 'travail'. Il trouvait inacceptable qu'un Français sur quatre ou cinq, en votant communiste, fût un exilé de l'intérieur. Mais il reconnaissait qu'en ce domaine, il marchait 'à tâtons'. Et comme il n'aimait pas tâtonner, il préféra longtemps ne pas s'engager dans cette voie obscure.

Jusque vers la fin de son premier mandat, il pensa que, s'il accentuait l'autorité de l'État, tout le reste serait donné de surcroît. *Il fallut déchanter*. Il y avait bien quelque chose d'essentiel qui avait changé à la tête de l'État et, en écho, dans les profondeurs de la conscience nationale; mais tout l'entredeux restait terriblement semblable, terriblement immuable ...

Depuis trois siècles, les Français sont obsédés par la nature, le pouvoir, la composition de leur gouvernement. Pourtant, le changement des gouvernements et même des régimes est loin de donner les résultats qu'ils en escomptaient. Et ils chantonnent, comme dans 'la Fille de Madame Angot': 'Ce n'était pas la peine de changer de gouvernement.'

Force est de se demander si la maladie des institutions n'est pas elle-même un simple symptôme d'une maladie secrète, plus enracinée, que la meilleure santé de l'État ne saurait, à elle seule, guérir; et si l'un des traits caractéristiques du mal profond n'est pas, justement, notre obsession institutionnelle.

Le 'siècle des Lumières', cherchant à échapper à l'absolutisme, se persuada qu'il suffirait d'importer d'Angleterre le parlement et la monarchie surveillée. Cette illusion s'imposa après un demi-siècle de convulsions tragiques; le régime politique finit par adopter la forme que lui souhaitaient les philosophes. Mais les réalités profondes se perpétuaient: la hiérarchie administrative mise en place par Richelieu, Mazarin et Colbert demeurait, semblable à elle-même.

Pendant un siècle encore, l'obsession institutionnelle ne lâcherait pas sa prise sur nos esprits: monarchistes et bonapartistes, légitimistes et orléanistes, républicains conservateurs et républicains radicaux, modérés et socialistes, se sont affrontés pour savoir quelle étiquette on donnerait au régime, quelle couleur au drapeau. Pas un programme électoral qui ne proposât sa réforme constitutionnelle. Comme si ce débat allait trancher tous les débats.

En réglant enfin – au moins pour un temps – la question de l'Etat, la Constitution de 1958–1962 *nous a soulagés de cette obsession.* Du coup, la maladie profonde a pu commencer d'apparaître dans notre champ de conscience. C 'est le succès de la Ve République, mais *il bute sur sa propre limite.* Ce qu'elle a fait de mieux reste insuffisant. *Sous la couche, maintenant décapée,* du mal visible, qui affectait les institutions politiques, perce le mal caché, qui affecte la société.

Très vite, malgré l'État restauré, les désordres dans la rue sont venus attester que les 'pleins pouvoirs' n'avaient pas suffi à établir solidement le pouvoir. Notre Etat solide, dirigé et directif, nous l'avons vu en combien d'occasions *déraper, s'enliser!* Presque jamais quand il parlait pour la France; mais souvent quand il parlait aux Français. Chaque fois qu'il tentait d'*embrayer sur la société*; de toucher à cette 'société dans la société' qu'est le secteur public; de déranger les habitudes.

Le pouvoir ne recule pas; avance-t-il vraiment? Il dresse plus haut sa tête; mais il est investi de toutes parts. Comme si la société, instinctivement, automatiquement, cherchait à compenser tout pouvoir par un pouvoir égal et de sens contraire – par un contre-pouvoir; le pouvoir exécutif, par la conjonction vigilante de la minorité parlementaire et de la majorité des organes d'information, ou des notables, ou de la caste politique, ou des syndicats; le dynamisme d'une équipe, par son absence de moyens. Comme si la règle suprême du jeu politique était que les partenaires se réduisent mutuellement à l'impuissance.

Chaque Français, au fond de lui-même, reste prêt à se dresser contre l'État. Jamais autant que depuis 1958, ne se sont épanouis l'incivisme –sous couleur d'individualisme – *le goût du persiflage et de la fronde,* la nostalgie des révolutions ou en tout cas des révoltes, la mythologie anarchiste, l'horreur de l'ordre – du 'flic', du 'poulet' – et sa compagne indissociable, la revendication de l'ordre – expéditif, impitoyable – pour les autres … Bref, un Etat puissant mais ligoté, tel Gulliver à Lilliput. Une société qui réclame des réformes, mais réagit avec violence dès que vient le temps de les appliquer.

SOURCE: Alain Peyrefitte, *Le Mal Français* (Plon, 1976) pp. 56 ff.

Exploitation du texte

1 Expliquez en quelques mots les expressions en italique.

2 Faites une analyse textuelle générale, en vous appuyant éventuellement sur l'approche suggérée dans l'Annexe A (p. 23).

3 A partir de votre analyse générale, faites une étude plus détaillée du contraste entre niveaux de langue, par exemple, anecdotal et analytique.

4 Quelle fut la réalité de 'la hiérarchie administrative mise en place par Richelieu, Mazarin et Colbert' au dix-septième siècle, et qu'on prétend survivre, essentiellement, jusqu'à nos jours?

5 Qu'est-ce qui différenciait au juste, au dix-neuvième siècle:

monarchistes et bonapartistes?
légitimistes et orléanistes?
républicains conservateurs et républicains radicaux?
modérés et socialistes?

6 Selon l'auteur, en quoi consiste 'le mal français'?

Exercices de comparaison et d'application

1 Après avoir fait une analyse textuelle de chacun des textes, comparez entre eux les résultats, éventuellement en fonction des éléments suivants:

(i)   Les données de la "mise en situation" en tête de chaque texte.
(ii) Caractéristiques de l'auteur/l'orateur (sexe, âge, profession, etc.).
(iii) Caractéristiques du public visé (spécialistes, grand public, intellectuels, etc.).
(iv) But visé par l'auteur/l'orateur (convaincre, évaluer, décrire, etc.).

2 Préparez un débat sur les prétendus défauts et mérites du peuple français, en vous appuyant tant sur les propos des trois auteurs que sur vos expériences et lectures personnelles.

3 Ecrivez une dissertation d'environ 1500 à 2000 mots sur un des sujets suivants:

(i) Le concept de 'tempérament national' a-t-il une signification réelle?
(ii) Peut-on vraiment dire que les Français ont 'une obsession institutionnelle', par rapport, éventuellement, aux habitants d'autres pays?

4 Les auteurs de ces trois textes soulignent l'importance dans le domaine politique de facteurs qui ne relèvent pas directement des institutions politiques proprement dites, mais qui sont des facteurs plutôt 'sociétaux'. Préparez un exposé susceptible de convaincre un groupe d'étudiants français que l'étude du droit constitutionnel de leur pays ne saurait permettre à elle seule une bonne appréciation de la politique française.

5 Faites une liste, avec éventuellement un bref commentaire, des cas où la France a:

subi une défaite dans une guerre européenne

subi l'occupation militaire d'une partie considérable du territoire national
dû céder obligatoirement une partie de son territoire
dû évacuer certains de ses territoires d'outre-mer ou de ses colonies dans des circonstances troubles.

Annexe A

Analyse textuelle – cadre général

Questions: point de départ éventuel
1 *Quel impact* le texte fait-il sur vous?

2 *Comment* cet impact est-il réalisé?

Vocabulaire
1 Quelle est votre impression d'ensemble du vocabulaire employé (familier, argotique, technique, abstrait, affectif, soutenu)?

2 Regardez de plus près substantifs, adjectifs, adverbes et verbes:

quel genre d'action s'exprime à travers les verbes?
s'agit-il surtout de l'usage des verbes 'être' et 'avoir'?
est-ce que la voix passive s'emploie souvent?
quels temps verbaux sont utilisés? Sortent-ils de l'ordinaire?
retrouve-t-on beaucoup de modaux (devoir, falloir, il se peut, certainement ...)?

3 Est-ce qu'il s'en dégage plusieurs champs sémantiques?

4 Quel est le rapport entre champ sémantique et 'contenu' du texte?

Structures
1 Est-ce que les phrases sont (en général, ou dans des cas spécifiques dans un but précis):

longues ou courtes?
simples ou complexes?
complètes ou inachevées?

2 Relève-t-on beaucoup de questions ou de commandes?

3 Constate-t-on beaucoup de cas:

d'une répétition?
d'un ordre peu normal des mots?

4 Est-ce que le texte se lit facilement (ou est facilement assimilé par un auditeur)?

Liaisons, subordination, conclusion

1 Par quels moyens l'agencement de parties de phrases, de phrases et de paragraphes est-il assuré?

2 Quels sont les moyens de subordination, d'isolement et de mise en relief des idées?

la répétition (des mots, des structures, des idées ...)
les pronoms relatifs (qui, dont, auquel ...)
les pronoms démonstratifs ou adverbiaux (il, y, celui-ci ...)
la conjonction et la subordination (et, mais, bien que, donc, si, parce que, avant que ...)

3 Quels sont les moyens de conclure le texte et chacun de ses parties composantes?

4 Comment la cohérence de l'ensemble du texte est-elle réalisée?

le thème?
la chronologie?
l'espace?

2
Ideological Conflict

Behind any institutional arrangement in a state, behind any set of constitutional practices, lie unspoken influences on, and fundamental assumptions concerning, the nature of political relationships. These assumptions are typically subsumed in an ideology, which can best be understood as the way in which reality is represented and conceptually organised.

In most Western countries there exist a number of different ideological divides. These occur typically in the political context where the Catholic Church and the State are in conflict concerning the controlling influence over education, family, or information. The centre and the periphery are often in conflict concerning the degree to which State and Nation coincide, or the degree to which cultural homogeneity is a reality and administrative centralisation desirable. In the economic context, a crucial division would be between workers and owners or employers over the relationship of labour and capital to the means of production. No less important has been the clash between rural and urban interests over the appropriate degree of urbanisation and industrialisation.

Such basic conflicts can be seen in West European states, with varying levels of intensity and at different periods of history. They led to the development of political parties in the twentieth century, but before that (a process culminating in the eighteenth, and especially the nineteenth, century) to a pattern of competing doctrines which served as frames of reference for political thought and action. These are the '–isms' of nineteenth- and twentieth-century politics.

The –isms of French politics

In France in the last two centuries the '–isms' would include:

Monarchism	Liberalism	Socialism	Nationalism
Bonapartism	Republicanism	Syndicalism	Gaullism
Catholicism	Radicalism	Communism	

Any survey of the ideologies and doctrines of contemporary French politics will recognise the importance of the French Revolution as the beginning of a century or so of social and political upheaval. Chapter 1 dealt with the constitutional turbulence to which the Revolution gave rise, as Frenchmen tried to find agreement on the basic rules for the organisation of political life. The French Revolution will be used also as the reference point for an analysis of the various doctrines, ideologies and belief systems prevalent in France over the last two centuries, and an assessment of their importance in contemporary French politics.

Monarchism

Since the Monarchy was the institutional victim of the 1789 Revolution, it is hardly surprising that its supporters were strong in their opposition to the political and social changes that it brought about. But the Restoration of the Bourbon dynasty in 1814–15 raised the question of exactly what had been restored. Were the Church, aristocracy and other privileged elements back in place, unchanged? What was the status of the Charter which Louis XVIII issued to the French people, and which purported to establish responsible government? Monarchists realised that the limitation of the King's power by charter or constitution was necessary, but in the end, by 1830, an insufficient body of 'moderate' monarchist opinion supported the Bourbons, and the Revolution of that year brought to the throne Louis Philippe who was a member of the Orleanist branch of the Royal family; the fatal flaw of nineteenth century French monarchism was that no king, from any part of the Royal family, satisfied the political aspirations of a sufficiently large group of Frenchmen. Orleanism tried to establish a synthesis of the pre-1789 Royal heritage and the legacy of the Revolution, but it always rejected the more egalitarian aspects of the latter. Its attempt to build a consensual regime round the person of Louis-Philippe ended as narrow conservatism based on the political aspirations of the bourgeoisie.

Internal divisions between Orleanists and Bourbon 'Legitimists' were responsible for the missed opportunity to restore the Monarchy after the fall of the Second Empire in 1870. Whereas a majority of members of the new National Assembly were royalists or strong sympathisers, influential politicans supported a Republic, and this became accepted as the least divisive framework. Royalism in France never recovered from the events of the early 1870s, after which a constitutional monarchy in France became impossible. It was weakened by the extinction of the Bourbon (Legitimist) line in

1883 and the lack of a suitable Orleanist candidate, then discredited by association with the clumsy attempts of General Boulanger in 1889 to establish a quasi-military dictatorship. More importantly, it was tainted with the new Right-wing nationalist, anti-parliamentary cult exemplified in the 'Action Française' movement from the time of the Dreyfus affair in the 1890s to the 1930s. In the political uncertainty of May–June 1958, a few hastily-printed posters appeared saying *'Le Roi – pourquoi pas?'*, but although the present Royal pretender accepts the concept of a constitutional monarchy, his followers are few, only occasionally vociferous, and located largely on the French Riviera.

Bonapartism
Bonapartism was the product less of doctrine or systematic thought about political life, than of the military and political actions of one person – Napoleon Bonaparte. Those actions, however, made such a mark on France and on French sensibilities during the fifteen years of Napoleonic rule (1799–1814, plus a 'Hundred Days' in 1815) that Bonapartism became a force influencing French politics during significant periods of the nineteenth century. It also carried on to provide a point of reference in the analysis of certain aspects of Fifth Republic France. Napoleon's achievements were dramatic: he was able by military and dynastic means to make France the dominant power on the European continent, on the pretext of freeing other States from 'oppression'; he gave France a judicial system and a brand-new local administrative system (plus an improved central one) the basic features of which remain to this day; and above all he had a remarkable degree of success in pacifying conflicting factions and calming collective tempers unleashed during the turbulent decade from 1789.

It is to this latter aspect that the survival of Bonapartism and its later political impact can be mainly attributed, as well as to its association with the achievements of one man. Bonapartism therefore is characterised by:

1 The mobilisation of people of different ideological persuasions (often latent and unarticulated), around the ideal of national unity. This is the concept of *rassemblement*.
2 The central importance of one man, whether as Emperor or President, as the symbol of the glory of the State and the unity of the Nation, which itself is regularly asked to renew its support for its chief. This is the concept of a plebiscitary regime.

The Napoleonic achievement of 1799–1815, however, never had the advantage of a period of peace to consolidate an internal consensus, and Napoleon's exile destroyed the personal foundations of Bonapartism, which had to recreate itself by attaching the Napoleonic legend to Napoleon's descendants. During the period of the restored Monarchy (1815–48) Bonapartism became almost part of the anti-system (often Republican) Left, operating in a clandestine manner and inspired by a dwindling legend. After the death of Napoleon's son in 1832, the banner was carried by his nephew Louis-Napoleon, who, however, was something of an adventurer, and was imprisoned in the 1840s for an ill-prepared and clumsily executed attempt at a *coup d'état*.

It was Louis-Napoleon's comparative political immaturity which ensured his election as President of the Republic proclaimed in 1848, easily manipulated, it was thought, by conservative politicians – the *'parti de l'ordre'* – who returned triumphant in elections in 1849. But Bonapartism soon established its hold as a separate, dominant force, drawing on the latent emotional support of a predominantly rural France, nine million of whose inhabitants had the vote as the result of a significant extension of the suffrage.

The Second Empire which Louis-Napoleon was able to establish without difficulty in 1851 was revolutionary in many respects, combining a desire for modernisation, an emphasis on authority, and the pursuit of national glory. This gained the support of the peasantry, but the Church in the end turned hostile, and Louis-Napoleon's anti-democratic stance alienated those for whom basic liberties were more important than a spectacular, but far from successful, foreign policy. Bonapartism was discredited by the military defeats of 1870, and changed political circumstances and the absence of a suitable dynastic successor around whom the legend could be resuscitated both meant that Bonapartism swiftly declined with the consolidation of the Third Republic in the 1870s.

The modern significance of Bonapartism, however, lies in its alleged affinities with the characteristics of Gaullism, or at least of the Gaullism which emerged to dominate French political life in the 1960s under de Gaulle's presidency.

Catholicism
Since the revocation of the Edict of Nantes, which had given some degree of freedom of worship and of individual conscience to Catholic dissenters and to Protestants, the Catholic Church in France had been the highly organised official body of a national

religion. Its authoritarianism in religious affairs made it the natural ally of the Monarchy, which had the same approach in political and social matters, though there was a tension between the State's view that it should retain ultimate political control (Gallicanism) and the Church's desire that the will of Rome should prevail (Ultramontanism). Even if the Church was not always united or harmonious, it successfully prevented the development of dissenting groups, but could not stop the rise of intellectual innovators (the *philosophes*) who particularly in the eighteenth century emphasised individual liberty and whose influence was crucial in the preparation of the Revolution of 1789.

The Catholic Church led the attack on the social and political reforms of the Revolution. Against the principle of Reason, it pitted traditional dogma; against individual human rights, it set a divinely-inspired authority. It was the inspiration behind attacks on the new Jacobin-dominated state which the Revolution brought into being; it often, together with the privileged class which had fled abroad, allied with France's enemies in the European wars of the 1790s. However, under Napoleon, it had to accept limitations on its political and financial freedom which remained even when the counter-Revolution finally triumphed in 1815 with the Restoration of the Bourbon dynasty. Even though the dominant conservative element in the Church rejected constitutional monarchy in favour of a regime little different from the pre-1789 one, the fundamental relationship between the Church and the State had altered in favour of the latter. The nineteenth century French state, increasingly in the hands of the bourgeoisie, and finally adopting a Republican form, refused to share political power with the Catholic Church. But in a country where the majority of people were Catholics, the Church still hoped to control basic agencies of socialisation in the shape of the family and the education system. State involvement in the former, on any significant scale, did not being until after the First World War, and in any case ran parallel to an increasing secularisation of French society. But the struggle between Church and State for control of education provision is one of the central themes in the political history of France since the Revolution, and still has echoes in present-day France.

Napoleon had been concerned only with the educational meritocracy which provided the personnel to carry out policy – groups of highly-qualified specialists whose training was a State monopoly. He, and subsequent regimes up to 1870, were content to leave elementary education in the hands of the Church, usually the Order of Jesuits, mainly because the State lacked the resources for a comprehensive system at this level. Napoleon's nephew, Louis-Napoleon, Emperor from 1852 to 1870, confirmed the Church's dominant position in doctrinal and educational matters, and its own doctrine of Papal infallibility was a reaffirmation in 1868 of the theory of absolutism. It was the final establishment of a Republic in the 1870s which undermined the influence of the Church in education, by setting up from 1881 a comprehensive system of free and secular public education. The anti-clerical elements in the new Republic triumphed, and Church and State reached a compromise of sorts in a Law of Separation in 1905. But the relationship of the State to those private schools which remained in Church hands remained a political issue.

The nature of this relationsip was a bone of contention during the Fourth Republic (1946–58), between partners in governing coalitions upon which the survival of that regime depended. In the early years of the Fifth Republic agreement was reached on providing State financial aid for private schools (over 90 per cent of which are Catholic), which in return would teach to the State curriculum. And yet the issue did not disappear. It was resuscitated in the Socialist–Communist Programme for Government in the 1970s and more recently, François Mitterrand's declared aim was to transform education into a 'public service, unified and secular'. The religious aspects of the quesiton, and its political urgency, appeared to be diminished when polls in 1982 suggested that less than 10 per cent of parents chose the private sector for predominantly religious reasons, a fact reflected in the discourse of private education 'defence groups'. In 1983–4, however, proposals by the Education Minister, Alain Savary, for greater State control over private education were vigorously contested by both sides.

In the wider context, political Catholicism in the first two decades after 1945 was marked by the emergence of a political party, the *Mouvement Républicain Populaire* (MRP), professing Christian Democracy – the equivalent of movements in West Germany and Italy – which was the heir to a specifically liberal, or 'social' Catholicism (not necessarily the same thing) whose roots go back to Lamennais and Maritain. But the internal ambiguities of this movement, and then the remodelling of the party system during the 1960s led to its eventual incorporation into a wider, rather amorphous grouping of supporters of President Giscard d'Estaing (1974–81), after an unsuccessful attempt to establish a separate 'Centrist' identity. Many progressive Catholic elements, moreover, joined Left-wing groups in the late 1960s and 1970s and the new-style Socialist Party attracted activists and voters to an extent which suggested that the previous link between Catholicism and political conservatism was less close.

Liberalism

The growth of Liberalism in nineteenth-century France follows closely the major changes of regime and can often be defined only in the context of the political situation at any time, rather than by reference to a pre-existing doctrine or set of beliefs. Liberalism during the Restoration (1815–30) was the view of those who were denied political power, or even freedom of criticism, by the restored regime. But it was an affirmation for liberty which owed little to the revolutionary tradition of 1789; it was essentially the demand of the emerging bourgeoisie to be given the role in public affairs which Napoleon's Empire had been prepared to grant. And insofar as they would have preferred a regime which was not absolutist, they were supported by those sections of the population for whom the principles of 1789 did have some meaning.

The Orleanist regime of 1830–48 was the apotheosis of Liberalism – the achievement of political power after fifteen years of opposition (often clandestine) to an authoritarian monarchy. The newly-powerful group was a heterogenous category of lower, middle and upper bourgeoisie, but the dominant position of the latter meant that the policies of Liberalism in power were characterised by caution: a cautious anticlericalism and foreign policy, a reluctance to intervene in social life and in economic life except to protect a sector from foreign competition, and opposition to any significant extension of the right to vote. The result was that the Liberal and Orleanist bourgeoisie in power from 1830 until 1848 lost any support from proletarian and egalitarian sources which it might have had during the common opposition to the authoritarian monarchy before 1830.

The underlying doctrine of Liberalism, which is still identifiable in the contemporary context, was the belief that, faced with the advance of technology, human beings should show a sense of individual moral responsibility, and that this should be the main regulating influence on political relationships (as market forces should be in the case of economic relationships) rather than the State, which should content itself with safeguarding basic liberties.

While some of the bourgeoisie rallied after the end of the July Monarchy to Louis-Napoleon's Second Empire, Liberalism as a separate creed had to bide its time. It accommodated itself to the Third Republic without much difficulty, for the new regime, while allowing an extension of democracy, and indeed making the protection of basic liberties its main feature, nevertheless upheld with some vigour the principles of economic *laisser-faire* which were central to Liberal thought. Liberalism was thus able to identify with a Republic which resisted demands made by the Left for economic equality. But Liberalism in France in the Third Republic (1870–1940) found it difficult to formulate a clear definition of the functions of the State, and to reconcile its distrust of the State with the increasing need for State intervention in economic and political life as this became more complex.

This dilemma was starkly posed in the economic depression of the 1930s and reappeared in the worsening economic conditions of the 1970s and 1980s. Valery Giscard d'Estaing, even before he became President of the Republic in 1974, had led a distinct political grouping which supported the dominant Gaullist party, but which attempted to distance itself from both Gaullism and Socialism by basing its approach on classical Liberal tenets. But even though Giscard still claimed in 1981 that he as *'un libéral inguérissable'*, and despite reforms during his Presidency which extended the freedom of individual choice (for example, legalised abortion), modern Giscardism has a conservative, even Orleanist, streak which is barely hidden by a surface fidelity to classical Liberalism.

Republicanism
The problem with Republicanism is that in contemporary French politics it has inevitably come to mean that political viewpoint which does not advocate a monarchy, an imperial regime, a military junta, or any other regime to which the name Republic cannot be given. Yet even though the Republican form of regime has become in modern times so comprehensive and well established, it must not be forgotten that there was no Republic in France between 1940 and 1944, the years of the Vichy regime, and moreover that there was a distinct threat of a military dictatorship in 1961 when sections of the Army attempted a putsch in Algeria, and, it can be argued, of a totalitarian regime in 1958 as one of the options to solve the Algerian problem. A consequence of the all-embracing nature of the Republican regime is that groups and parties of widely divergent political orientation can claim that they alone are the heirs to (and guarantors of) the authentic Republican tradition which their adversaries have distorted and betrayed. Much of the opposition to Gaullism in its dominant phase from 1958 to the early 1970s was in the name of Republican defence.

Conversely, the Socialist victory of 1981 led the Gaullist Jacques Chirac, on assuming the leadership of the Opposition in all but name, to say that they should draw up *'un projet républicain pour l'avenir'*.

Traditionally, Republicanism became synonymous with the fundamentals of modern democracy – abolition of privilege, assertion of popular sovereignty, insistence that executive power should be accountable and human rights unfettered. In this, Republicans were the direct heirs of the French Revolution, with an often emotional commitment to the advance of democracy through political equality. They were anti-monarchist, anti-clerical and (as a corollary of popular sovereignty) strongly nationalist. The lack of coherence of this ideology allowed the Second Republic of 1848 to be captured by Louis-Napoleon and conservative forces, and democratic Republicanism, as an anti-regime force, was repressed and had to operate clandestinely during the Second Empire.

The Third Republic was proclaimed in 1870, but the National Assembly had, until 1876, a Royalist majority, and Republicanism triumphed only because of deep divisions in Royalist ranks and the intransigence of the pretender. The Republic was accepted as the regime with the least divisive consequences rather than as the positive vehicle of the political aspirations of most Frenchmen. As the new parliamentary regime settled down after 1877, the Republicans as such became the satisfied defenders of the status quo against anti-Republican forces such as the Church. The turn of the century saw the establishment of political parties which worked within the Republican framework, attempting through electoral competition to dominate the Parliament on which the legitimacy of executive power was based. Threatened particularly by fascism in the 1930s, temporarily ousted between 1940 and 1944, and somewhat tarnished by the inappropriateness of its format from 1946 to 1958 (the Fourth Republic), Republicanism nevertheless continues to furnish a sufficiently ample frame of reference to establish a consensus about the fundamentals of democracy first concretised in the French Revolution.

Radicalism

Radicalism in France in the 1830s and 1840s was identical with the Republican faith, and a distinct doctrine, if such can be said to exist, emerged with the establishment of the Third Republic. Radicalism represented the strongest and clearest strain of anti-clericalism, making Democracy a kind of religion to be used against the Church: Radicals were among the fiercest proponents of a state elementary education system. Radicalism was anti-liberal in rejecting conflict between individuals, and anti-sociast in rejecting conflict between classes, yet it contained within itself many differing strands:

1   the provincialism and strong anti-clericalism of Emile Combes;
2   the nationalism and Jacobinism of Georges Clemenceau;
3   the technocratic approach of Joseph Caillaux.

If there was a common thread, it was fidelity to the memory of the French Revolution, but to the more moderate demands of 1789 rather than the principles of 1793. And if Radicalism started out being ideologically on the Left, as the Third Republic progressed, it became in parliamentary terms the epitome of the Centre, defending the status quo of the Republic. Radicalism was a doctrine, or at least a state of mind, which appealed to the lower bourgeoisie and professional classes of the provinces, the local worthies (*notables*) who could rally peasants and artisans in the defence of their economic interests against Paris, or landowners, or State agents. It steadfastly occupied the parliamentary middle ground during the Third Republic, and this role persisted to some extent in the Fourth Republic. Radicalism however had become so bound up with Assembly-dominated Republics that it resisted the attempts of one of its number, Pierre Mendès-France, to resurrect in the 1950s the technocratic, scientific approach to politics. In contemporary French politics, Radicalism has little impact, and the existence after 1973 in both the Majority and Opposition of groups claiming the inheritance of Radicalism shows that the catholicity of the doctrine which in previous Republics may have been its main strength is now, in different political circumstances, a distinct disadvantage.

Socialism
Among the ideas which made their appearance during the Restoration and July Monarchy, a great period of ideological incubation, were those of Saint-Simon, who, in opposition to liberal individualism, proposed a complete socialist system. Inspired by moral, even religious notions, this system tackled the social problem of production, and advocated the planned organisation of the economy and the socialisation of the means of production. But this new approach, and the often analogous ideas of thinkers such as Fourier, Louis Blanc, Blanqui and Proudhon, had little impact outside a small bourgeois intellectual élite until the uprising of 1848 and more particularly the Paris Commune of 1871, when the

combination of Socialism and Democracy assumed a popular hue. The rise of Socialism was therefore closely linked with the vicissitudes of Republicanism, and although it made some headway among the working class in the Second Empire, it was in the framework of the Democratic Republic infused with the memory of the French Revolution that Socialism grew, as a political and economic doctrinal response to the Industrial Revolution. Such appeal as it had sprang from the post-1870 democratisation of political institutions and secularisation of the state, but also from circumstances peculiar to France: the advent of male universal suffrage at an early date, and the existence of a large number of smallholding peasants.

The establishment of a homogeneous doctrinal content for Socialism is usually attributed to Karl Marx, and although the Marxist synthesis also contained elements from British political economy and German philosophy, much of Marx's thought was grounded in French experience and was widely disseminated from the last third of the nineteenth century onwards. Socialism as an ideology is concerned with promoting social appropriation of the means of production, comprehensive economic planning to adjust production to demand, and the reduction of income differentials. Socialism as a movement sees itself as an inevitable step in the historical development of society, transcending capitalism with its inherent contradictions and deleterious effects, and allowing the State to wither away as no longer necessary. In theory, the followers of the French revolutionary tradition had a better opportunity to achieve their aims than in the German or English case because of the long gap between the disappearance of a feudal society and the full emergence of a capitalist one. The difficulty they encountered however was the historical importance in France of the strong centralised state which not only predated the process of industrialisation and thus could control it, but also successfully resisted more or less determined assaults on itself between 1830 and 1968. French government repression of the emerging Socialist movement, while never total, was nevertheless harsh, and it is not surprising that both the political and syndicalist wings of the French labour movement subscribed, at least in theory, to revolutionary ideologies. But when a Socialist party finally emerged in 1905, it was a fusion of Marxist and non-Marxist elements, of the ideologically committed and the pragmatic, of revolutionaries and reformists.

Political realities in France after 1871 often obliged even the most intransigent Socialists to accept the reformist case and the

need to achieve their aims gradually by working in a parliamentary framework. For this, a large electoral following was necessary, inevitably containing a large proportion of peasants. Since the latter were either property owners or aspired to this state, the result was that the ideological purity derived from Marxism had to be abandoned or at least camouflaged. Thus Socialism as it continued until the 1960s needed to speak of a future revolution while operating in a reformist present. This gave it some degree of coherence, and made it possible for Socialism to distinguish itself from Radicalism and Communism. But such ideological baggage made difficult the adaptation of Socialism to the changed circumstances of the Fourth and especially the Fifth Republics. Socialism in power in the 1980s has had to modify, even abandon, much more categorically than in the Third Republic, its social and ideological inheritance in favour of doctrinal pragmatism.

Syndicalism
Syndicalism appeared in other European countries, and in the United States, in a variety of guises, but nowhere was it so well developed as in France, both as a movement and as a doctrine. The explanations for this are various, but revert to a single cause, that of the peculiar character of the industrialisation process in France, which was spread over a long period. This gave rise to a movement aiming to protect the many artisans and small-scale industries which a rapid industrialisation would have all but swept away. Syndicalism as a doctrine argued that these small units would be the basis of a future reorganisation of society, where the State would have no role to play.

The failure of the revolutions of 1848 and especially 1871 showed, for syndicalism, the unwiseness of trying to change society from above, by national and political means. The revolutionary proletariat should organise from below, avoiding the temptation of parliamentary politics, until the State could be replaced by a syndically organised society in one final heave – the theory of the general strike, or 'social revolution'. This basic revolutionary approach, and that of anarcho-syndicalism which wanted to have the *syndicat* providing not only work but also culture and economic support in time of need, meant that syndicalism always kept its distance from groups such as Socialists who worked through political institutions to change society. Thus there has never been a move towards 'Labour' or 'Trade Union' candidates in elections, although the fact that Socialists and syndicalists were fighting a

common capitalist adversary led to some crossing of the divide by
individuals.

The syndicalism of small-scale economic units inevitably
suffered when, with economic modernisation in the twentieth
century, the old craft unions gave way to the large mass unions
which now dominate syndical life. But the old-style syndicalism
finds contemporary echoes in the growing importance of the idea
of self-management of social and production units (*autogestion*),
which characterised the far Left disillusioned with the political
approach after the events of May–June 1968, and which was strong
enough to oblige political parties on the Left to try to accommodate
it in the 1970s and 1980s.

Nationalism
The nationalism of the French Revolution began by being defensive
– it was necessary to defend the new regime which was faced with a
dynasty trying to regain power against the national will to establish
human rights and a form of democracy. Even if the sovereignty of
the people was a new concept with but a shallow grounding in fact,
it was real enough for the 'people' to rally round to defend it from
attacks both internal and external. But patriotism which waged
defensive war soon found the justification to wage offensive war
–the emancipation of what were seen as oppressed nationalities
from their tyrannical rulers. Even after 1815, the democratic
opposition to the restored Monarchy was vigorously nationalist; it
thought that Liberty should be imposed by force, and opposed
alliances with autocratic governments.

As the nineteenth century progressed, nationalism became an
increasingly complex concept, and one which underwent analytical
refinement. The rise of stronger nationalisms on the European
continent, for example that of Germany, richer in resources, and
Italy, made French nationalism more inward-looking; a vigilant,
almost paranoic patriotism. The Left increasingly looked towards
internationalism to stop needless wars; the Right towards defence
–of the national territory, of traditional values, and of the status
quo.

It was the Dreyfus case which highlighted the way in which
nationalism, once the preserve of the radical democratic outlook,
had become that of the Right. Dreyfus, a Jewish army officer, was
in 1894 wrongly found guilty of spying for Germany and was
sentenced to deportation for life. By 1898 the case had become
politicised; there were those who saw Dreyfus' condemnation as an
outrage perpetrated by a military establishment seeking a scape-

goat, and others who saw the issue not as the guilt or innocence of one man, but the right of society to be protected from upheaval, even at the cost of condemning an innocent man.

Nationalism pervaded literature and cultural life, building on the shock of the loss of most of Alsace and part of Lorraine in 1871. But in the political sphere, there grew up organisations dedicated to the replacement of the parliamentary democracy of the Third Republic by a regime (for example, a monarchy) which was more surely committed to the defence of what they saw as the nation's interests. The most prestigious of such organisations was the small group around the journal *L'Action française*, advocating a restoration of the monarchy by means of revolution, vehemently anti-semitic, and militantly Catholic. Parliamentary democracy was further threatened between the wars by organised groups often inspired by Italian, then German, fascist models. These were anti-parliamentary, and nationalist in the sense that the nation state was regarded as the highest achievement of human endeavour.

In contemporary French politics the concept of nationalism is usually articulated as that of the independence of France, the achievement of as much freedom of manoeuvre as possible in inter-state relations and the reduction of constraints on this freedom. This notion is central to Gaullist thought and even though the Fifth Republic is no longer dominated by Gaullism, national independence has become as important in inspiring political and diplomatic action as the Presidency has become the keystone of the institutional structure. Direct elections to the European Parliament, first held in 1979, provided the spectacle of four main political groupings vying with each other in their desire to prove to the electorate how determined they were not to allow the European Parliament to increase its powers at the expense of the French National Assembly.

Communism
The history and contemporary importance of Communism in France is very closely linked to that of the Communist Party. Ideas and initiatives called 'communist' appeared in the French Revolution and throughout the nineteenth century, but as a separate ideology, Communism, or at least Marxism–Leninism, in France was boosted by a reaction to a particular event – the success of the 1917 October Revolution in Russia. This was seen by many Socialists as a renewed opportunity for a revolutionary upheaval which the 'integrative' role of Socialist parties in the Third Republic had made unlikely. Any ideological and strategic strengths they possessed had been rendered nugatory by a well-

established state apparatus grounded in capitalism. Communism put renewed emphasis on revolutionary theory, which brought together the revolutionary experience of the proletariat in every country, but which at the same time had to be able to adapt to changing political circumstances. Political action towards the revolutionary goal was channelled through the party, which alone had the resources to apply a 'correct' ideology to the task of interpreting social realities.

The key concept is that of the general crisis of capitalism, which is viewed as an outmoded economic and social regime. In relying on competition and profit, it creates the conditions for its own downfall; these were reinforced by the establishment first of a socialist state in the Soviet Union and then of a whole socialist 'camp' in the 1940s. But the dynamic of capitalism led to capitalism of a monopolistic kind, dominated by large (later multinational) companies and bolstered by the powerful apparatus of the authoritarian State. Communism in its 'pure' form postulated the withering away of the State, which would be unnecessary in a socialist system, but Lenin was unsure, in the absence of concrete examples, about when and how this might happen.

Communism in France came to follow the Stalinist line that, since the State was not about to disappear, the Party should constitute a strong apparatus of bureaucratic control from above. It should thus face its hostile environment while awaiting, and trying to create, a situation which was propitious for removing all oppression and promoting true democracy under the dictatorship of the proletariat. Communism in France has concentrated as much on building a basis of support in local electorates and industrial work units as it has in increasing its parliamentary representation. Although intensely nationalist in its defence of things French against antagonistic forces, Communism has often appeared to be at the mercy of international events. Its anti-fascist stance in the 1930s was compromised by the Nazi–Soviet non-aggression pact which lasted for two years from the summer of 1939. Its participation in French governments just after the war was terminated by its exclusion from power in 1947 at the onset of the Cold War between East and West.

Much Communist ideology has had to be softened or even tactically ditched during the Fifth Republic as the forces of the French Left tried to regroup to counterbalance the dominant influence of, first, Gaullism with Giscardian support, then Gaullism and Giscardism combined. Communist thinkers have had to confront questions about the role of the Party in a Western parliamentary democracy, and its structure in relation to intellectuals. That aspect of Communism which stressed revolutionary vanguard activity began in the 1960s to be concretised in *groupuscules* usually described as 'extreme Left', but Communism can in many respects still be regarded as a counter-community, with its own values and organisation, and as the political voice (the 'tribune') of all disadvantaged people. Moreover especially in its economic analyses, Communism has strong traces of its ideological origins in Marxian, then Leninist and Stalinist, thought.

Gaullism
Gaullism as a political force began on 18 June 1940, when the refusal of General de Gaulle to accept the consequences of French military defeat was turned into a positive appeal to fellow Frenchman, by radio from London, to fight for the reinstatement of the French State temporarily in the hands of German invaders and, soon afterwards, to become a collaborationist regime in Vichy. This act of defiance, and the whole of de Gaulle's wartime policy, was inspired by his own interpretation of French history – *une certaine idée de la France*', as he said in his *Mémoires de Guerre*. This was that France was a country with a glorious past sometimes rendered '*médiocre*' by the faults of its inhabitants, and an exceptional future which could be one of greatness or misfortune depending on whether Frenchmen could overcome their 'propensity to division'. (see Texte 1.1).

The theme of greatness as the distinctive feature of France involves consciousness of the changes in the relative strength of major powers, but even in a modified historical context, France must mobilise itself to achieve an economic, and above all, a moral greatness, treating lesser nations with 'generosity'. The precondition to achieving this greatness was that France, indeed any nation, should be independent, free from entangling alliances and foreign domination. World politics was still, in the Gaullian view, based on relations between independent sovereign states, freely cooperating. The maximisation of resources, economic as well as purely military in the modern world, would give France the power to achieve the greatness which was its destiny.

The 'political effervescence' of Frenchmen which had always vitiated this ideal would be countered in two ways. Firstly, by establishing a strong State framework for national political life which would prevent the dispersal of national resources and allow France to be strong in the international field. The President of this new-style Republic was to have clear and extensive powers to decide how best to give France its rightful place in the world. Secondly, social conflicts were to be reduced by getting opposing interests to see that an effective and humane economic system was possible, and political conflicts by playing down the traditional role of parties representing sectional interests, and bringing Frenchmen together in a *rassemblement* to conduct their political affairs in the national interest.

Several of these characteristics of Gaullism, and the experiences of the Fourth Republic with organised Gaullism, led commentators in the first stages of the Fifth Republic to suggest that there were close affinities between Gaullism and Bonapartism. Comparable features were:

1   Emphasis on the international standing of France, and a recovery of lost prestige.
2   Belief in a moral obligation for France: to free nations from autocratic tyranny (Louis-Napoleon) or from colonial rule (de Gaulle).
3   Desire for a strong centralised state to mediate between opposing groups which pay insufficient attention to the national interest.
4   Belief in the need to obtain, by consulting the people, confirmation of political legitimacy: de Gaulle's incarnation of the Republic from 1940; Louis-Napoleon's incarnation of the Bonapartist legend.
5   Policy of economic modernisation to maximise resources.
6   Mistrust of politicians, and emphasis on efficiency as a determinant of policy.

Gaullism differs from Bonapartism, however, in remaining faithful to the basic traditions of parliamentary democracy, and the distinctive feature of Gaullism in contemporary French politics is the combination of this with clear political authority and the concerns of a strongly nationalist outlook.

Two main approaches have generally been used to show the importance for contemporary French politics of the above, whether they are called doctrines, ideologies or belief systems.

Left and Right

The first approach is to say that the best ordering device is to apply the concepts of 'Left' and 'Right', since this is a frame of reference still real for a great many Frenchmen, who, if pressed, will articulate their own fundamental attitudes, and their view of political organisations, in these terms. Figure 2.1 locates ideologies of contemporary French politics within a Left–Right framework, and gives an indication of when they first made their appearance.

In 1789, the Right was constituted by reference to the desire to give the King an absolute veto over proposed laws: the Left by its

Figure 2.1
Ideologies and political families

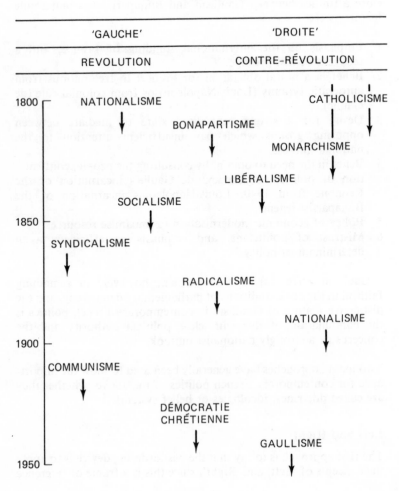

refusal to allow this. In such a situation there was hardly the possibility of a third position. It has been argued by Maurice Duverger[1] that even when, later, moderates on both Left and Right collaborated in Parliament, as was sometimes the case in the Third and Fourth Republics, they never constituted a separate doctrine of the Centre: there was always a Centre Left and a Centre Right. Furthermore, he said that when an electoral system favoured a multiparty system in Parliament by having some form of proportional representation, there was still a basic unity (of doctrine, of vocabulary) between two groups of parties, one on the Right and one on the Left.

However, the validity of the claim that the Left–Right divide is the basic, most readily intelligible, motivating factor in political life – almost an instinctive need to occupy one side or other of hypothetical barricades – is reduced unless one is careful to note that social and economic circumstances change considerably. To be Monarchist–Imperialist or Republican up to the 1870s, to be clerical or anti-clerical in the nineteenth century (and later) is explicable in social and economic terms, but is calling these Right and Left any more than convenient shorthand? And can the Left–Right analysis adequately explain first that nationalism was of the Left until the turn of the century and then of the Right, certainly up to the 1930s, or second that regionalism, implying decentralisation of power, was of the Right until well after the Second World War, but is now of the Left?

Francois Goguel[2] preferred to look at basic political orientations in terms of 'order' and 'movement' – not the same as Left and Right since, for example, the authoritarian Left would be included in the 'order' group, and so would the Radical Party, despite its doctrinal posture. But the most important alternative was the Marxist–Socialist one, which regarded the Left–Right division as mere squabbles within the bourgeoisie, and postulated a duality of proletariat and ruling class, differing in their relationshp to the means of production. Twentieth-century developments have in many ways led to a fusion of this analysis, resting on a correlation of socio–economic status and political identity, and the Left–Right division, which may be less amenable to scientific enquiry but which appears inordinately tenacious. François Mitterrand's view of the changes which brought him and the Socialist Party to power in 1981 was that finally a majority in socio-economic terms had translated itself into a political majority which was a Left majority.

In this view he is of course helped by the conventions of self-ascription; although the appellation 'Left' is a positive one, no group readily accepts being called Right and no political party has included this in its name since the turn of the century. The *Nouvelle Droite* of recent years is not a party, but a group of intellectuals who attempt to give philosophical respectability to élitist and anti-egalitarian ideas. These distortions may be accepted without difficulty, but the usefulness of a Left–Right analysis is also reduced by the existence of political doctrines and parties which deliberately reject it, preferring, like Bonapartism and Gaullism to regard political life, at least in theory, as amenable to a *rassemblement* of wide-ranging application. A final point is that there have been deep divisions over major issues in recent French history which were not founded on a Left–Right dualism:

1 Elements of the Right opposed the policy of appeasement of Germany concretised in the Munich agreements (1938).
2 Elements of the Left (especially the authoritarian Left strand) collaborated with the Vichy regime and the German occupiers (1940–4).
3 Elements of the moderate traditional Right supported self-determination (in effect, independence) for Algeria during 1959–62, while an earlier Left-wing government (1956–7) had opposed it.
4 Elements of the Left supported the methods and policies of de Gaulle in the 1960s, and *gaullisme de gauche* still claims a separate identity in the 1980s.

Political families

The second approach is to say that although the complexity of political life makes analysis in terms of Left and Right less than totally useful, nevertheless it is possible to discern political 'families'. This notion implies that in present-day France, political parties, whatever their labels might be, are in each case heirs to a long tradition of shared memories, attitudes and beliefs which predate individual memories, and that significant aspects of parties (their language, their programme, their view of each other) are best understood as the exercise of collective memory. This approach will agree that duality exists, and, as competition and conflict, is basic to political life. But it will suggest that instead of one single duality, there are several. It is possible to base an explanation of the existence of six political families in contemporary France on three divisions.

1 *Anti-clerical* (column A in Fig. 2.2) or *Clerical* (column X): this is long established, but for its importance in modern times to be appreciated, it is necessary to note that it refers as much, if not more, to the social base of a party electorate as it does to ideological stance regarding the influence of the Church in socialisation agencies such as education and the family.

Figure 2.2
Differentiating features of political families

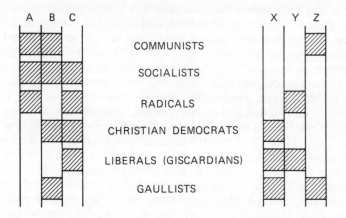

2 *Interventionists* (B) or *Liberals* (Y) regarding national economic activity: this represents a general doctrinal divide expressing an ideal rather than a reality – the degree of economic intervention by all post-war French governments has been high.
3 *Nationalism: not so strong* (C) or *strong* (Z): some political families are not so strongly nationalist in the sense that they emphasise cooperation with other European states or global economic interdependence, though much will depend on what the specific issue is (for example, European Parliament's powers; energy resources).

In terms of 'profile' based on these divisions, the six political families of contemporary French politics can be differentiated as shown in Figure 2.2.

The 'political families' approach emphasises an ideological complexity which a Left–Right analysis, sometimes confusingly, seeks to minimise. This approach also has a certain interpretation of the phenomenon of contemporary French politics known as bipolarisation.

Bipolarisation

This can be said to have become a feature of contemporary French political life in two ways. Firstly, in the method of election of the President of the Republic. The procedure laid down by the Fifth Republic Constitution in 1958 was changed in 1962, and the system obtaining since then is that no matter how many candidates present themselves – there were 12 in 1974, and 10 in 1981 – if no candidate gains 50 per cent plus one of valid votes cast, a second round is fought between the two candidates who received the highest number of votes, allowing for any withdrawals. This has meant that the French people, in choosing their President in elections since 1965, have, unless they abstain, the choice between two candidates, two declared sets of policies, even two views of society. This bipolarisation of public electoral preference took place also in another context – that of legislative elections to the National Assembly. Opinion became bipolarised from the 1970s in the sense that in the second round of parliamentary elections since 1973, electors in almost all constituencies had a choice of only two candidates, committed to supporting either the kind of policies pursued by the previous government or those of the opposition to that government.

This aspect of bipolarisation came about in two ways. Firstly, a 1966 law allowed first-round candidates to stay in the ring for the second round only if they obtained support amounting to 10 per cent of registered voters (later increased to $12\frac{1}{2}$ per cent) instead of 5 per cent of actual votes cast, as before. This had the intended effect of reducing the chances of a second-round third choice with a separate identity. Secondly, the Centre itself was quite happy to align with the Right-wing majority in the 1970s, either by extensive second-round cooperation in 1973, or by incorporation into a larger pro-government grouping in 1978. It remained in that grouping when it went into opposition in 1981.

However, the approach to contemporary French politics which emphasises the persistence of political families based on long-established ideological divides argues that this bipolarisation is very much the result of institutional factors (the method of electing the President of the Republic) and political factors which are not necessarily permanent (the preference of the electorate for a stable majority to give the policies it approves a good chance of being put into operation). This approach will point out that the majority and opposition are not single disciplined groups, but contain component elements corresponding to ideological families. Ignoring minor groups, these are shown in Table 2.1.

Table 2.1
Bipolarisation in the French party system

Opposition 1978–81 Majority 1981–		Majority 1978–81 Opposition 1981–	
Parti Communiste Français (PCF)	Parti Socialiste (PS)	Union pour la Démocratie Française (UDF) comprising	Rassemblement pour la République (RPR)
Communists	*Socialists*	*Radicals Centrists* (ex-Christian Democrats) *Giscardians*	*Gaullists*

Moreover, each of the above four components presented separate lists in the 1979 elections to the European Parliament, and shared the 81 seats allocated to France in that Parliament: and they each put up serious candidates in the 1981 Presidential elections.

This approach, therefore, argues that, strictly, bipolarisation is applicable only in the context of elections to the National Assembly since the 1970s and to Presidential elections since 1965 (though the choice in 1969 was between a Gaullist and a Centrist). It argues that 'political families' are permanent in the sense that they are grounded in ideological stances and reinforced by collective memory, while admitting that the pattern may alter from one half-century to the next. It claims that the Left–Right approach may be an attempt to put a simplified framework for explaining politics on to a complex socio-economic structure. In all this, it remembers particularly the line taken by Giscard d'Estaing when he was President. Giscard argued that the 'Manichean' distinction between Right and Left would give way to what he regarded as the strong desire of France to be *'gouvernée au centre'*. This was based on his perception of an affinity between his own brand of modern Liberalism and a Social Democratic strand which inspired important 'currents' in the Socialist Party. He hoped also to attract some Gaullist elements into this new dominant grouping, which he claimed would be Centrist, by offering participation in power. Giscard's attempt was not successful because the Socialist Party remained firmly attached to a united Left-wing stance (*'ancré à gauche'*). Moreover, any temptation to abandon this for participation in a Giscardian government, disappeared in 1981 when François Mitterrand became President and a new majority was elected to the National Assembly which was made up of Socialists, Communists ánd Left Radicals. Giscard's idea remains unrealised, but serves to remind us that the Left–Right analysis may sometimes have to be set aside.

Bibliographical guidance

Ideological background in general:

P. Braud and F. Burdeau, *Histoire des idées politiques depuis la Révolution* (Montchrestien, 1983)
J. Droz, *Histoire des Doctrines Politiques* (PUF, 1975)
M. Duverger, *La Démocratie sans le peuple* (Seuil, 1971)
J. Touchard, *Histoire des idées politiques*, vol. 2, *Du XVIIIe siècle à nos jours*, 8th ed. (PUF, 1981)

On specific ideologies:

M. Anderson, *Conservative Politics in France* (Allen & Unwin, 1974)
J.-P. Apparu, *La droite aujourd'hui* (Albin Michel, 1979)
F. Bluche, *Le bonapartisme* (PUF, 1981)
E. Cahm and V.C. Fisera, *Socialism and Nationalism in Contemporary Europe (1848–1945)*, vol. 2 (Spokesman Books, 1979)
J. Defrasne, *La gauche en France de 1789 à nos jours*, 2nd ed. (PUF, 1975)
L. Delwasse, 'Vive le roi! Mais lequel?', *Le Monde* (19 April 1981)
G. de Broglie, *L'Orléanisme* (Perrin, 1980)
M. de Saint-Pierre, *Lettre ouverte aux assassins de l'école libre* (A. Michel, 1982)
F.-G. Dreyfus, *De Gaulle et le gaullisme – essai d'interprétation* (PUF, 1982)
R. Girardet, *Le nationalisme français – anthologie 1871–1914* (Seuil, 1983)
Institut Charles de Gaulle: *Approches de la philosophie politique du Général de Gaulle* (Cujas, 1983)
C. Nicolet, *Le Radicalisme* (PUF, 1974)
J.-C. Petitfils, *L'extrême-droite en France* (PUF, 1983)
J.-C. Petitfils, *La Droite en France de 1789 à nos jours* (PUF, 1978)
Pouvoirs, no. 9 (1979) devoted to Le Giscardisme

Pouvoirs, no. 27 (1983) devoted to Le Mendésisme

R. Rémond, *L'anti-cléricalisme en France de 1815 à nos jours* (Fayard, 1976)

S. Rials, *Le légitimisme* (PUF, 1983)

R. Tiersky, *French Communism 1920–1972* (Columbia University Press, 1974), translated as *Le mouvement communiste en France 1920–1972* (Fayard, 1973)

C. Willard, *Communisme et socialisme en France* (A. Colin, 1974)

S. Williams (ed.), *Socialism in France from Jaurès to Mitterrand* (F. Pinter, 1983)

T. Zeldin, *Conflicts in French Society: Anticlericalism, Education and Morals in the Nineteenth Century* (St. Anthony's Publications, 1971)

On the concepts of Left and Right:

J. Bothorel, *La République mondaine* (Grasset, 1979)

O. Duhamel, *La gauche et la V*^{e} *République* (PUF, 1980) especially introduction

A. Harris and A. de Sedouy, *Qui n'est pas de droite?* (Seuil, 1978)

R. Rémond, *Les droites en France*, 4th ed. (Aubier Montaigne, 1982)

G. Rossi-Landi, *Le chassé-croisé – la droite et la gauche de 1789 à nos jours* (J.-C. Lattès, 1978)

B. Toulemonde, *Manuel de science politique*, 2nd ed. (Presses universitaires de Lille, 1982) pp. 51–75

On political 'families':

D.L. Seiler, *Partis et familles politiques* (PUF, 1980)

Illustrative texts and linguistic exercises

Texte 2.1

Mise en situation

François Léotard, né en 1942, fit ses études à l'Ecole Nationale d'Administration et entra dans l'administration comme haut fonctionnaire (administrateur civil, sous-préfet, directeur d'un cabinet préfectoral). Elu maire de Fréjus (1977) et député du Var (en 1978 et 1981), faisant partie de la seconde génération des libéraux giscardiens, il devint secrétaire-général du Parti Républicain en 1982. L'introduction à l'émission radiodiffusée d'Europe I 'Club de la Presse' dont Francois Léotard était l'invité, fit état de son style personnel décontracté et d'un registre plus chaleureux que ce n'est la coûtume de la part de ceux qui ont son pedigree et portent son étiquette. L'Union pour la Démocratie Francaise (UDF), fut créée en 1978 comme amalgame du Parti Républicain (PR), du Centre des Démocrates Sociaux (CDS) et du Parti Radical. Avec les gaullistes du Rassemblement pour la République (RPR) de Jacques Chirac, elle constitua après les élections de 1981 l'Opposition dans l'Assemblée Nationale. François Léotard démissionna de ses fonctions de vice-président de l'UDF après l'adoption par celle-ci en janvier 1984 d'une liste unique avec le RPR aux élections européennes de 1984.

*   *   *

JEAN-LOUIS SERVAN-SCHREIBER (*L'Expansion*):   Monsieur Léotard, vous êtes un nouveau venu pour l'opinion publique et vous assumez une responsabilité dans un parti dont la définition, à l'heure actuelle, n'est pas extraordinairement claire. Peut-être pourriez-vous nous dire *d'emblée*, au début de cette émission, en quoi, aujourd'hui, le PR, dont vous assumez à la fois la direction et peut-être l'inspiration, diffère du CDS ou du parti radical, peut-être même, à la rigueur, du RPR. Tout cela n'est pas très clair dans l'opinion. Il serait utile que vous contribuiez à cet éclaircissement.

M. LEOTARD: Tout à fait volontiers. Le parti républicain se réfère d'abord, comme son nom l'indique, à la République, c'est-à-dire que nous faisons une équation très simple: le libéralisme, c'est la démocratie; la démocratie, c'est la République. Nous voulons être les héritiers d'une tradition qui a maintenant deux siècles en France et qui est celle des citoyens français. Lorsque nous parlons aux Français, nous ne leur parlons pas simplement en tant que travailleurs mais également en tant que citoyens. Pour nous, l'héritage de la République est le véritable héritage du parti républicain. Nous en sommes fiers et nous souhaitons le porter un peu plus loin. A votre question, je voudrais apporter un élément de réponse qui, peut-être, nous permet de regarder vers l'avenir.

J'ai 40 ans, monsieur Servan-Schreiber, par conséquent, ce qui m'intéresse, c'est de savoir ce qui sera proposé à la France dans les vingt ans qui viennent. Et ce qu'on lui proposera, c'est de sortir du socialisme avec des idées nouvelles, avec des mots nouveaux, avec une conduite du pays différente. Je crois que nous sommes capables de le faire à l'intérieur de l'UDF. Je vous rappelle qu'à l'heure l'UDF est la première des formations politiques françaises en terme d'élus locaux et nous souhaitons nous inscrire à l'intérieur de l'UDF comme ceux qui incarnent le courant libéral. Et encore une fois, ce courant libéral est celui qui vient de la démocratie et de la République. Je n'en dirai pas autant en ce qui concerne le socialisme, j'en dirai un mot tout à l'heure si vous le permettez.

JEAN-LOUIS SERVAN-SCHREIBER: Excusez-moi de préciser ma question, mais dans tout ce que vous venez de dire, qui est intéressant, il n'y a rien qu'un dirigeant du CDS ou du parti radical ou même du RPR ne saurait *assumer au mot près*. Encore une fois, où est la différence?

M. LEOTARD: Il y a dans la vie politique française une tradition démocrate chrétienne, c'est celle qu'incarne actuellement le CDS, avec des philosophes que vous connaissez, notamment comme Mounier. Cette tradition est importante et nous souhaitons travailler avec les gens qui s'y réfèrent. Il existe une tradition radicale qui, si on croit également les idées, a été incarnée par Alain, c'est celle du citoyen contre les pouvoirs. Le parti républicain qui est au milieu de ces deux traditions politiques souhaite, lui, reprendre et approfondir la tradition libérale. C'est-à-dire qu'il y a trois familles politiques au sein de l'UDF, qui travaillent ensemble, qui souhaitent encore d'ailleurs travailler davantage ensemble: l'une *se réfère à* la démocratie chrétienne, c'est le CDS; l'autre se réfère au radicalisme, qui est une vieille tradition francaise, et l'autre se réfère au libéralisme dont je vous rappelle qu'elle fut une famille politique antérieure au socialisme.

HENRI TINCQ (*La Croix*): Monsieur Léotard, je voudrais en rester sur votre projet politique et l'avenir de l'opposition. Il y a quelques années, Valéry Giscard d'Estaing souhaitait gouverner la France au centre. Sans insister sur son échec de l'an dernier, je me demande si le centrisme aujourd'hui, n'est pas mort d'une certaine manière. Dans cette phase de crise, tout ce qui ressemble de près ou de loin à une formation libérale ou centriste semble soit rejetée complètement à droite, soit rejetée du pouvoir. On vient d'en avoir des exemples en Espagne et en Allemagne. Dans les sondages aujourd'hui, dans les résultats électoraux partiels, le courant chiraquien continue de dominer le vôtre. Ma question est simple: ne pensez-vous pas, François Léotard, que l'avenir du courant que vous représentez, libéral, centriste, est complètement bouché?

M. LEOTARD: Je vais vous dire le fond de ma pensée très franchement. pour ce qui me concerne, le mot 'centre' ne me plaît pas beaucoup. Je vais vous dire pourquoi. Je suis convaincu qu'on ne répondra pas aux échecs du socialisme actuel en en faisant un peu moins mais en faisant autrement. Si le mot 'centre' signifie faire un peu moins que ce que font les socialistes actuellement, ce n'est pas ce que nous voulons, ce n'est pas ce que je veux. Nous voulons véritablement faire autrement, autre chose. Cet 'autrement' et cet 'autre chose' est tourné vers l'avenir. Je crois effectivement, comme vous, que les réponses de l'avenir *s'inscrivent* dans l'histoire du passé. Les réponses de l'avenir vont demander pour nous hélas – pour le gouvernement actuel c'est plus difficile – *une extraordinaire réflexion*, une extraordinaire imagination. Et la thèse que nous défendons, qui me semble fondamentale, c'est que le socialisme c'est le passé. En effet, cela ne répond pas aux aspirations des Français, comme on le voit, ni au pluralisme, ni au besoin de niveau de vie des Français. C'est le passé parce qu'on applique des vieilles recettes: les nationalisations, la lutte des classes, *la croissance de l'Etat*. Il suffit de voir les images de M. Mitterrand au Panthéon. C'est le passé parce que le socialisme, de lui-même, se réfère au passé. C'est le passé, enfin, – et c'est peut-être plus grave – parce que c'est un retour en arrière; c'est la régression sociale.

Le libéralisme que nous voulons est un libéralisme du futur. Nous ne voulons pas appliquer à la France une médecine du XVIIIe siècle, c'est-à-dire *la saignée*. Ce que l'on est en train de faire actuellement. Nous voulons appliquer les recettes qui soient des recettes du futur. C'est cela qui nous intéresse et nous allons nous y attacher. Je crois que cela demandera du temps mais, je le répète, nous allons nous y attacher.

HENRI TINCQ: Dans la bipolarisation actuelle, puisque vous voulez rejeter le socialisme, ne craignez-vous pas d'être rejeté complètement à droite?

M. LEOTARD: Qu'est-ce que cela signifie? Est-ce être à gauche que de faire baisser le pouvoir d'achat? Est-ce être à gauche que de *bloquer les salaires* et d'augmenter les impôts indirects? Que signifie être à droite ou à gauche? Etait-ce à droite pour M. Giscard d'Estaing que d'avoir augmenté le SMIC deux fois plus vite que les autres salaires? Etait-ce à droite que de s'occuper des familles et des handicapés? Pour ma part, si on me dit que cela c'est être à droite, je veux bien l'être. Cela ne me gêne pas. Si on me dit qu'être à gauche c'est diminuer les salaires et augmenter les impôts indirects, comme on le fait actuellement, je dis qu'il n'y a plus ni gauche ni droite. Notre souci, à nous, encore une fois, c'est d'essayer de *casser ces clivages*, qui mutilent le tissu politique et social français, pour essayer de trouver des réponses nouvelles aux questions qui se posent aux Français. Ces réponses *passent par un constat*: le socialisme, c'est le passé.

SOURCE: François Léotard, invité au Club de la Presse d'Europe I, 7 novembre 1982.

Exploitation du texte

1 Expliquez en quelques mots les expressions en italique.

2 Expliquez les allusions dans les phrases suivantes:

   des philosophes comme Mounier
   incarnée par Alain
   résultats électoraux partiels
   les images de M. Mitterrand au Panthéon
   avoir augmenté le SMIC

3 Selon François Léotard, quelles sont les différences entre l'orientation politique de son propre parti et celle du socialisme?

4 Pour quelles raisons François Léotard prétend-il

   (i)   ne pas aimer le mot 'centre'?
   (ii) rejeter la dualité gauche–droite?

5 Faites une liste des mots qui font l'objet d'une attitude

   (i)   favorable, p. ex. 'tradition'
   (ii) défavorable, p. ex. 'passé'

   de la part de l'interviewé.

Texte 2.2

Mise en situation
Roger-Gérard Schwartzenberg (né en 1943) professeur à l'Université de Paris II et à l'Institut d'Etudes Politiques, fut élu député à l'Assemblée

européenne en 1979 et devint président du Mouvement des Radicaux de Gauche (MRG), groupe politique qui prit ce nom deux ans après la scission du Parti Radical en 1971. Le MRG fut le troisième signataire du 'Programme Commun de Gouvernement' avec le Parti socialiste et le Parti communiste français, et après 1981 fit partie de la Majorité parlementaire soutenant le gouvernement Mauroy et la politique du Président Mitterrand. Roger-Gérard Schwartzenberg est l'auteur, entre autres ouvrages, de 'Sociologie Politique' (1974), de 'L'Etat spectacle' (1977) et de 'La Droite Absolue' (1981) et collaborateur du *Monde* et de divers journaux de gauche. Cet article parut dans *Le Monde* en septembre 1979, entre la défaite de la Gauche dans les élections législatives de 1978 et la préparation de l'élection présidentielle de 1981.

* * *

Jamais l'échec n'a été si évident. Jamais le pouvoir n'a été si impopulaire. Jamais l'attente d'un changement n'a été plus profonde. Mais jamais *l'alternance* n'a paru si lointaine. Mais jamais la gauche n'a autant déçu. A force de gérer la défaite de 1978. A force de *ressasser ses griefs*. A force d'exhiber querelles de clans et d'états-majors.

Les rencontres bilaterales actuelles sont donc, par elles-mêmes, un fait important. Meme si chacun en mesure les limites. Mais ce qui compte surtout, c'est la réflexion programmatique engagée dans chaque parti. Tant il faut dessiner le visage d'une autre gauche. Plus diverse. Plus concrète. Plus nouvelle.

Gauche diverse

Gauche diverse, d'abord. Acceptant son pluralisme. Acceptant la diversité de ses composantes. Pour s'en enrichir et convaincre le plus grand nombre d'électeurs de se reconnaître en elle. Car l'union de la gauche *ne passe pas par l'uniformisation*. Par la banalisation de ses divers partis. Bien au contraire.

Le PC défend sa propre doctrine et ses propres thèses. Avec la dernière énergie. C'est son droit. Et même son mérite. Mais il appartient au reste de la gauche de faire de même. Il lui appartient d'affirmer aussi nettement sa propre culture. Son propre 'modèle'.

En vérité, il a toujours existé deux grands 'modèles' au sein de la gauche. L'un de type étatique et centralisateur. L'autre fondé sur la décentralisation et la redistribution du pouvoir vers la base. Vers les collectivités et les associations.

A la gauche non communiste de défendre et d'approfondir sa conception propre. Sans céder au conformisme ou à la complaisance. Sans converger à l'excès vers les dogmes et les normes d'autrui.

Ce serait le cas si, d'aventure, son nouveau projet comportait finalement plus de centralisme que de décentralisation. Plus d'étatisme que d'autogestion. Plus d'extension des nationalisations que d'influence sur l'économie.

Gauche concrète

Ce serait le cas s'il privilégiait la reconquête du marché intérieur au point de verser dans le protectionnisme. Sinon dans *l'autarcie*.

Ce serait le cas s'il était plus soucieux d'indépendance nationale que d'internationalisme. Ou s'il préférait la 'détente' en Europe à la construction européenne.

Ce serait le cas, enfin, s'il se référait davantage aux valeurs traditionnelles qu'aux libertés nouvelles, dont la revendication est portée par *la contestation légitime des 'marginaux'*.

Du reste, face à la crise économique et aux échecs du pouvoir, les Français attendent de la gauche autre chose qu'un débat scolastique sur les dogmes centenaires du marxisme élémentaire. Ils attendent, sans doute, une gauche moins brillamment théoricienne. Mais plus praticienne. Et plus opérationnelle.

Une gauche les pieds sur terre et le front sur les dossiers. Bref, une 'gauche de gouvernement', de type mendésiste, prête à prendre demain les commandes de l'Etat. *En prise directe sur* les grands problèmes de ce temps que *le pouvoir* traite avec tant d'insuccès ou d'*impéritie*.

Comme la crise de l'énergie. Avec ses périls pour la balance commerciale, l'activité économique et l'emploi. Comme la politique industrielle. Avec l'effort nécessaire vers les productions à haute technologie, créatrices d'emplois, qui représentent l'aventure industrielle du vingt et unième siècle: *l'informatique*, la microélectronique, l'astronautique, l'exploitation des océans, la bioindustrie, les énergies nouvelles.

Bien sûr, cette politique industrielle est à définir dans le cadre d'une planification démocratique. Pour dégager une rationalité et une volonté collectives. Pour empêcher le simple *pilotage à vue*, qui remet la conduite de l'économie nationale à l'arbitrage des grands groupes privés.

Que la majorité se désintéresse du Plan est *dans l'ordre des choses* et conforme à la logique "libérale". Mais la gauche et ses élus auraient pu se montrer plus inventifs et plus offensifs dans le débat parlementaire sur les grandes options du VIIIe Plan – ce document sceptique et *velléitaire* qui donne une forme molle à notre destin collectif.

Gauche nouvelle

Desormais, d'ailleurs, la gauche devrait proposer que ce Plan économique se double d'un 'Plan social'. Pour programmer, avec précision, la réduction des inégalités. Pour organiser, avec force, la solidarité nationale en faveur des chômeurs, des personnes âgées, des handicapés.

Mais la gauche n'a pas seulement à apporter des réponses concrètes à la crise économique. Il lui faut aussi répondre à la crise 'culturelle'. A ce 'malaise dans la civilisation', qui se développe de proche en proche.

C'est vrai: tout un électorat, souvent jeune et attentif aux luttes nouvelles, se reconnaît mal dans la gauche traditionnelle. Car celle-ci leur paraît accepter la société de malaise. Pour ne pas dire la société 'répressive', au sens de la psychanalyse. Celle qui sacrifie les tendances naturelles et les besoins véritables. Celle qui répand la tension, l'aliénation, la contrainte.

Cet électorat critique attend une gauche innovatrice et non conformiste, qui dessine le projet d'une société différente, où vivre autrement. Une gauche nouvelle, qui soit le lieu d'expression des sensibilités nouvelles. Celles des jeunes, des écologistes, des régionalistes. Une gauche qui connaisse Marx et Engels, mais qui n'ignore pas Reich et Goodman, Roszak et Mumford. Bref, une gauche en mouvement, qui développe une 'stratégie de rupture' aussi avec la société répressive.

Six luttes

Cette gauche nouvelle lutterait pour casser le système *politicien*. Pour faire que la vie publique cesse d'être une profession, un spectacle et le territoire de l'argent-roi. Elle proposerait de développer, au plan local et national, les possibilités d'initiative populaire et de référendum. Elle réclamerait qu'on plafonne strictement les dépenses électorales, et que l'Etat assure leur financement. Elle se battrait pour le droit à l'expression des petites formations et des groupes minoritaires.

Cette gauche nouvelle aurait à coeur de limiter l'Etat. De remettre l'Etat à sa place. Pour rendre vie à la *'société civile'*, anesthésiée et écrasée par les grands appareils centraux. L'objectif serait de redistribuer le pouvoir vers le bas. Non de remplacer une technocratie de droite par une technocratie de gauche.

Elle chercherait à freiner *la société de démesure*. La 'grande société anonyme' des mégalopoles et des multinationales, qui écrase l'individu. Elle reprendrait le slogan: 'Small is beautiful'. Pour dessiner une économie à hauteur d'homme, qui favoriserait les implantations industrielles de petite ou moyenne dimension, mettant en oeuvre des technologies douces et plus économes en énergie.

Cette gauche nouvelle s'emploierait à inverser la société d'uniformité, qui rend chacun pareil à chacun. Normalise. Standardise. Elle encouragerait l'épanouissement des différences. La variété des genres de vie et des cultures. Elle reconnaîtrait le droit de chaque région à sa personnalité. Pour faire revivre une France de saveur et de couleur. Une France de la diversité. De la Bretagne à la Corse. De l'Alsace à l'Occitanie.

Cette gauche vivante s'attacherait à empêcher la société de la pollution et du *tout-nucléaire*. La société de l'Amoco-Cadiz et de Super-Phénix. Elle se mobiliserait pour préserver la nature et les grands équilibres biologiques de l'écosysteme.

Enfin, la gauche nouvelle agirait avec instransigeance pour défendre les droits de l'homme. Elle refuserait de se taire ou de balbutier seulement de timides reproches devant les salles de torture d'Argentine et les camps du goulag. Elle refuserait de se taire devant l'extermination par la faim, qui frappe des millions d'êtres humains dans le monde.

SOURCE: Roger-Gerard Schwartzenberg, 'Changer la gauche' *'Le Monde'* (26 septembre, 1979).

Exploitation du texte
1 Expliquez en quelques mots les expressions en italique.

2 Expliquez les allusions dans les phrases suivantes

plus d'étatisme que d'autogestion
une 'gauche de gouvernement', de type mendésiste
Reich et Goodman, Roszak et Mumford
De la Bretagne à la Corse. De l'Alsace à l'Occitanie
La société de l'Amoco-Cadiz et de Super-Phénix

3 Faites une liste des expressions utilisées par l'auteur pour décrire, dans les différents domaines de la vie politique, les aspects positifs de sa propre conception·de la gauche et les aspects négatifs de la gauche 'traditionnelle'.

4 Qu'est-ce qui confère à ce texte son style saccadé?

5 Comment les conjonctions et les répétitions d'expressions contribuent-elles à faire avancer le raisonnement de l'auteur?

Texte 2.3

Mise en situation
Francine Demichel est une jeune universitaire (professeur à l'Universite de Lyon II) et intellectuelle communiste. Elle est auteur ou co-auteur de livres sur Cuba, les dictatures européennes, les institutions et le pouvoir en France, et la psychanalyse en politique. Elle a décrit son livre *La Lutte idéologique dans la France contemporaine* comme 'un acte de combat', disant qu'il est essentiel 'de faire admettre que les "idées politiques" ne sont pas une matière morte, relevant de la seule Histoire. Elles font partie de notre vie.' Elle estime que, malgré le changement apporté à la France en 1981, 'l'idéologie bourgeoise n'a pas cessé pour autant et comme par miracle d'être dominante'.

*   *   *

Nous vivons à l'évidence dans une société conflictuelle, dont les bases mêmes ne peuvent faire l'objet d'une adhésion unanime. Il est clair que dans une telle société, la paix civile exige un compromis de classes sur les règles du jeu, c'est-à-dire sur les modalités du gouvernement. Mais vouloir passer de ce nécessaire compromis au consensus, c'est un abus de langage qui est destiné à confondre deux réalités: le compromis sur les procédures et l'accord sur le fond. On vise par là même à *marginaliser* tous ceux qui entendent mettre en cause le type de société actuellement inhérent à la logique capitaliste. En effet, il s'agit bien de cela: l'opération-consensus' est, dans notre type de société, purement idéologique. Il faut que le pouvoir obtienne une adhésion globale et diffuse non pas tellement à un programme, ou même à des options, mais à un type d'appréhension, passive et résignée, des problèmes actuels. Il s'agit de faire admettre, par le plus grand nombre de personnes possible, un mode de raisonnement selon lequel nous ne sommes pas maîtres de notre destin. Et c'est à partir de là que tout devient possible. Y compris de voter pour des hommes ou une politique que l'on juge médiocres, tout simplement parce qu'ils sont là, au nom de tous, *pour assumer les orages*. Mais cela ne suffit-il pas au pouvoir bourgeois qui n'a, en fin de compte, cure d'une approbation enthousiaste, mais qui recherche simplement une *caution* démocratique, fut-elle procédurale et fondée sur la simple passivité ... ?

Quels sont donc les fondements de ce consensus triste où veut nous conduire l'idéologie dominante? Et comment fonctionne cette idéologie?

Le consensus qui est proposé à l'ensemble du peuple a d'abord un fondement économique: la peur de la 'crise'. Mais il a aussi un fondement politique plus élaboré: la théorie du 'centre'.

A   *Le fondement économique: la peur de la crise*

Le discours de l'idéologie dominante est ici assez simple, voire simpliste: en cas de péril, il faut serrer les rangs, se grouper autour du chef responsable, et qui sait comment on peut franchir l'obstacle. Et pour renforcer ce raisonnement, les comparaisons affluent: dans la tempête, on ne change pas le capitaine, et même, on ne le conteste pas. Tout le monde doit participer, sous ses ordres, au sauvetage du navire. Et comme, par surcroît le péril vient ici de l'extérieur – car il est bien connu que la crise c'est avant tout le prix du pétrole brut, il convient de faire taire les dissensions sociales internes pour faire face à l'agression. Ainsi, le chef de l'Etat, comme jadis Clemenceau, 'fait la guerre'. Mais pour cela, il n'est plus temps d'être 'le premier flic de France', il suffit d'en être le Président élu, pourvu que cette élection ne soit pas une simple procédure, mais témoigne d'un consensus généralisé. La démonstration est *fruste*, et au surplus manque totalement d'originalité. Mais elle n'est pas dépourvue d'efficacité dans la mesure où l'idéologie dominante donne à la notion de 'crise', une dimension psychologique qui en renforce la portée: le sentiment de culpabilité.

La crise, on l'a dit, est produite, d'après le discours bourgeois, par *les seigneurs du pétrole*. Mais elle est présentée aussi, comme résultant de l'incurie et de l'irresponsabilité des victimes elles-mêmes, c'est-à-dire de nous tous en tant que consommateurs d'énergie. La France en effet, et c'est un des arguments majeurs de l'idéologie de droite, vit, depuis des années, au-dessus de ses moyens, *dans l'insouciance du lendemain*, et sans aucune vision globale de l'évolution du monde, et des contraintes qu'implique cette évolution. Or, les années noires arrivent, et nous sommes tous coupables de n'avoir pas voulu le comprendre, et de continuer à *danser sur un volcan*. Et ce péché collectif ne pourra nous être pardonné qu'à la double condition d'accepter – ensemble – les sacrifices nécessaires et de faire confiance à ceux qui ont suffisamment de science et de lucidité pour dominer les secousses de la crise et suffisamment de courage pour dire au peuple la dure vérité ...

B   *Le fondement politique: le thème du centre*

La notion de centre est l'une des plus contestables que véhicule le vocabulaire politique, en tous cas l'une des plus ambiguës. Le terme 'centre' peut en effet être utilisé pour désigner le point où se rencontrent, en certaines circonstances et dans certains cas de figures politiques, la droite et la gauche: ainsi est-il exact de parler de 'conjonction des centres' sous la troisième république. Mais il n'est pas scientifiquement précis de faire du centre une tendance politique autonome, située entre la droite et la gauche. Car le centre, pris en ce sens, n'existe pas, faute d'avoir un contenu spécifique. Ainsi si la notion de centre peut être utilisée pour qualifier une stratégie, elle ne peut l'être pour qualifier une idéologie. C'est pourtant en ce sens que le discours giscardien use de la notion de centre, comme fondement du consensus. Le 'centre' se voit même attribuer une signification sociale et économique, avant d'être transformé en réalité politique.

1 Du point de vue social et économique, l'explication n'est pas sans rappeler certaines analyses pseudo-marxistes sur l'évolution des classes sociales. On explique, en effet, à grand renfort de statistiques, que les transformations de la technologie et des formes de production éliminent à la fois les grandes fortunes et la grande misère. Plus précisément la conversion des entreprises mi-artisanales en grandes unités complexes réduit la place et le pouvoir des simples possédants au profit des managers salariés. Tandis que l'intellectualisation croissante des tâches d'exécution marginalise progressivement les simples manoeuvres au profit des techniciens. Selon cette version modernisée du thème du 'tertiaire', les concepts de bourgeoisie et de prolétariat apparaissent comme complètement dépassés. La société toute entière devient une immense classe moyenne, qui s'uniformise par le centre. Il reste des inégalités, certes, et elles doivent être corrigées, mais elles sont, en toute hypothèse, résiduelles, car l'évolution même de la société tend à les éliminer. Dans ce contexte, la lutte des classes apparaît comme totalement périmée.

2 Du point de vue politique, le centre est présenté comme la seule base possible pour le gouvernement d'une société démocratique. Il correspond d'abord à l'évolution socio-économique décrite. Il a ensuite des vertus politiques spécifiques, car il constitue un amalgame entre une droite éclairée qui a *exorcisé ses vieux démons réactionnaires*, et une gauche raisonnable, *sortie de son infantilisme révolutionnaire*. Le centre est tolérant, et pragmatique, attentif aux réalités notamment économiques. Il sait que tout n'est pas possible et que la fonction de la politique n'est pas de provoquer des bouleversements inconsidérés dans la société, mais de gérer, du mieux possible, les contraintes de l'économie. Ces qualités d'une tendance politique se doublent en outre des qualités individuelles de ceux qui ont le tempérament correspondant à cette tendance. L'homme du centre est concret, soucieux du quotidien, éloigné de tout dogmatisme idéologique.

SOURCE: Françoise Demichel, *La Lutte idéologique dans la France contemporaine* (LGDJ, 1982)

Exploitation du texte

1 Expliquez en quelques mots le sens des expressions en italique.

2 En quoi diffèrent, selon l'auteur, les concepts de 'compromis' et de 'consensus'?

3 Preparez un discours qui traite des mêmes thèmes que l'auteur, mais qui les présente de façon positive (c'est-à-dire en utilisant le minimum de 'ne ... pas', etc.)

4 Quels indices permettent de relever les passages que l'auteur reprend directement du langage que tiendrait un gouvernement de droite? Montrez comment elle retourne à son compte les passages traitant:

   (i) de la crise économique
   (ii) du changement socio–économique
   (iii) du 'centre'

Exercices de comparaison et d'application

1 Malgre l'obédience politique divergente de ces trois personnes (l'interviewé du Texte 2.1 et les auteurs des Textes 2.2 et 2.3), peut-on dire que, de temps à autre, leur argumentation vise les mêmes phénomènes, et révèle des points de vue convergents?

2 Le dualisme gauche-droite a-t-il un sens dans la politique française contemporaine?

3 A partir du vocabulaire de ces trois textes, composez des slogans ou des grafitti susceptibles de
   (i) mobiliser les militants d'un parti ou d'un courant politique
   (ii) réconforter ceux qui ont une opinion plutôt défavorable de la politique et des hommes politiques.

4 Dressez la liste des substantifs se terminant en '–isme'. Augmentez-la au cours de vos lectures personnelles et parallèlement ajoutez-y des adjectifs formés à partir des noms de personnalités politiques.

3
Political Culture – Behaviour, Participation and Style

Political culture can be defined as the pattern of orientations or attitudes which characterises a political system. Political thinkers since Plato have argued that man is not born a political being (a 'citizen'), but that he becomes one. There is, in any society, a distinct, and therefore describable, political culture which gives form and meaning as well as some degree of predictability to the political process, in the same way that culture in general gives coherence and integration to social life.

Political culture as a concept is more clearly political, and more amenable to analysis, than 'public opinion' or 'national character', which can include beliefs about the norms of moral life. The concept is a problematic and far from uncontroversial one, and difficulties arise in trying to separate cognitive aspects (belief about what things actually are) from evaluative or normative ones (belief about what they ought to be).

Since belief systems include conscious learning, formal education as an agent of political culture is important. But this may lead to interaction of the two aspects in that knowledge about the workings of a political system may be diffused in such a way that it includes inculcation of the belief that the system ought to work in that way. In other words, there may be an 'official' political culture of ideology and practices prescribed and promoted by the state, or by an élite of political decision-makers, contrasted with a 'mass' political culture applying to the population at large. And in fact, the concept of a national political culture may be entirely notional, replaced by the idea of an aggregate of political sub-culture based on occupation, social class, religion or regional identity.

Within the wider concept of political culture, with its potential to contribute in particular to the understanding of political change, lies the question of the determinants of political behaviour, and especially electoral behaviour. The assimilation of values and attitudes was familiar to Plato who analysed 'citizenship training', and this is in present times more generally known as 'political socialisation' – the process whereby an individual learns about and develops attitudes to politics. There are several agents of socialisation: in the early years of an individual's life, his or her family plays a major role, but as he or she goes through school, becomes exposed to peer-group influences, and enters professional life, the socialisation process becomes increasingly complex.

Young people and politics in France

Regarding the political attitudes of young people, and their electoral behaviour, two assumptions are frequently made – that their interest in politics is not very great, and that they are more Left-wing than older age groups. This latter is true on specific questions – opposition to nuclear power stations and a nuclear deterrent force, support for nationalisation and egalitarian measures – but less than a third of young people between 18 and 24 were in favour of changing society by revolution in a 1977 opinion poll. The level of interest which young people in a 1975 poll said they had in politics was no less than that of other age groups, but other indices of a sustained degree of interest show them for example to be less inclined

to register as electors (the right to vote was given to 18-year olds in 1974);
to think of politics as a participatory process;

and more inclined

to abstain from voting even if registered;
to reject the notion of 'professional' politicians, especially if they claim to speak for young people.

The apparent 'depoliticisation' of young people was observed in comparing findings made in 1969–70[1] with an identical study of a similar group eight years later.[2] But the conclusions were that politicisation had merely taken a different form and different orientations. In the late 1960s, political language and organised direct actions were emphasised; in the late 1970s mistrust of political organisations had led to a more thoughtful approach, seeking a new basis for collective relationships, and bringing politics and everyday experience closer together. The late 1960s saw attacks on social structures which were considered too fixed, on bureaucracy, on the concept of heirachy, on a rigid State apparatus; later, political activism was as much directed to more individualistic concerns, or more diffuse values such as progress, change (very much the theme of the 1981 elections) and the environment. This latter orientation is both the strength and weakness of the ecological movement, which gets a quarter of its support from 18 to 24-year olds, but which would lose that support if it adopted the characteristics of a political party, since parties and professional politics are regarded with suspicion.

Peasants and politics in France

The peasantry had been in the vanguard of progressive forces in nineteenth-century France, but by the mid-twentieth century had ceased in general to be a force for change. The relative economic weakness of farmers and peasants has provoked the need for the State apparatus to ensure representation of their interests. Yet politics appears to interest the peasantry less than other occupational groups; in a September 1977 poll only 7 per cent said they were interested 'a lot' compared with 14 per cent of workers, and the percentage for other categories was even higher. Economic underprivilege coupled with social and educational disadvantages have meant that, of all groups in French society, peasants tend to participate least in national politics, in the sense of lack of interest in political and social problems, though actual voting turnout varies little across occupations.

In terms of voting preferences, peasants since the Second World War have constituted an increasingly conservative element of the French electorate. In every election, peasants have been less likely to vote for Left parties than the electorate as a whole. The emphasis on economic planning by the Left is not found by peasants to be congenial. But the picture is not always clear-cut, and although Left-wing parties tend to give primary attention to the interests of urban workers and underpivileged, there is a strong rural Left-wing tradition in Provence and in Limousin (the *départements* of Corrèze, Creuse and Haute-Vienne): it is a telling example of the extent to which voting for Left-wing parties in post-war France can be traced to local historic circumstances and traditions. Moreover, any notion of peasant unity is contradicted by the heterogeneous structure of professional organisations in the rural context.

Catholics and politics in France

Of all the experiences of, and influences on, individuals within groups in which they participate, whether family, professional or confessional, none shows a closer link than that between religion and political variables. This is true whatever the characteristics of the individuals, whether objective (sex, age, social class, educational attainment) or subjective (class consciousness, self-ascribed location on a Left–Right continuum). The conclusion seems to be that it is more than a matter of a purely 'external' relationship between religious practice and electoral behaviour; the link goes deeper, to the level of value systems and the manner in which an individual represents to himself the totality of his social experience.

The close correlation between a high level of integration into Catholicism and a propensity to vote for Right-wing candidates and to have corresponding political attitudes has a long tradition, confirmed since 1945. In Presidential elections under the Fifth Republic, this trend continues:

· *1965* (first round): 56 per cent of those with no religion voted for François Mitterrand, the candidate of the Left, but only 7 per cent of Catholics attending mass every Sunday.
· *1974* (second round): 77 per cent of regularly practising Catholics opted for Giscard, 23 per cent for Mitterrand: 86 per cent of atheists supported Mitterrand, 14 per cent Giscard.
· *1981* (first round): 50 per cent of regularly practising Catholics supported Giscard, 12 per cent Mitterrand.

These figures reflect the fundamental reality of a link between Right-wing electoral choice and Catholics who describe themselves as *'très pratiquants'*. Traditionally the latter were statistically important in three areas of France: the west (Brittany and neighbouring *départements*), the east (particularly Alsace), and the south-eastern part of the Massif Central (the *départements* of Lozère, Aveyron, Cantal and Haute-Loire). And it has been argued that any ground the Left has made in recent elections in these areas has been due less to a switch of allegiance than to a decline in the number of staunch Catholics. While in 1948, 38 per cent of French adults were *'très pratiquants'*, only 17 per cent were that in 1977. The steady decline in religious practice (or 'religiosity') means that it no longer creates serious active rifts between political parties as it did as late as the Fourth Republic.

Moreover, the Catholicism–conservatism link is not wholly

unequivocal. Just as the son of a manual worker who is not himself one can emphasise either his affective affinity, or the lack of it, with his family background, so can the message of Catholicism be interpreted by highlighting either its hierarchical or its egalitarian potential. Much has been made in recent electoral studies of the extent to which the political dispersal of Catholics throughout the electoral spectrum, and especially the convergence of evangelical Catholicism and reformist Socialism, has made less clear the coincidence between religion and political attitudes. In 1981, 13 per cent of those who voted Socialist were staunch Catholics, which is very close to the percentage of all adult French people.

Media and political behaviour

The politicisation of contemporary societies is not only a product of increased State activity for a century or more, but is directly linked to the development of means of social communications –press, radio and television – which in France, as elsewhere, have gradually broken down the former compartmentalisation of social and political life. French politics has become much more national in scope, and in large measure this is attributable to the availability of advanced media technology in the 1960s, and the use to which this was put. The 1965 Presidential election was the most telling example of this, when the candidature of Jean Lecanuet was presented using techniques of political marketing developed in the United States.

The media in general (*l'audiovisuel*), but particularly television became more influential on electoral outcomes as strong party allegiance declined and politicians concluded, rightly or wrongly, that they had to win the support of a large body of floating voters. This was particularly so in Presidential elections, where the constituency is the whole country, and the choice in the second round is between two candidates. The preponderance of television among all information sources is shown in the following percentages in Table 3.1, which exceed 100 in total because of multiple answers.

However, what is far from proved is that the effect of political messages in the media is more than short-lived, and the suspicion lingers that media-based political comment crystallises pre-existing attitudes rather than changing them. Certainly, despite charges that radio and television in the Fifth Republic are dominated by the government, the law is careful to provide the opportunity during actual election campaigns for electors of all political persuasions to

Table 3.1

Information services influencing electoral behaviour

	1978(1)	1980(2)
Television	58	46
Newspapers	41	39
Radio	28	37
Conversations	22	–
Magazines	–	16
Opinion Polls	7	19
Meetings, leaflets, posters	13	–

SOURCES: for col. (1) Louis Harris France in *Télérama*, 4–10 March 1978. Question: *Parmi les moyens suivants, quels sont ceux qui, à vous personnellement, vous sont les plus utiles pour vous aider à savoir comment voter?* for col. (2) Indice-Opinion in *Nouvel Observateur*, 9 February 1981 (poll conducted July 1980). Question: *Voici une liste de moyens d'information: pour chacun d'eux pouvez-vous indiquer si, pendant la campagne électorale, vous seriez d'accord ou pas d'accord pour dire que vous vous ferez une opinion grâce à eux?*

hear arguments they can approve, if this is what they want. In 1981, only 7 per cent of viewers said their voting intention in the first round of the Presidential election had been modified by what they had seen on television, and they were mostly young well-educated top managers.[3]

In the domain of political communication, the conclusion drawn from the 1981 Presidential and Legislative elections, as well as from by-elections in January 1982, was that there was perceptible electoral gain to be made in not appearing too 'distant' from television viewers, in not speaking in too logical and technical a manner, but in projecting oneself as down-to-earth, sincere and sympathetic to the reality of everyday life. Mitterrand's use of *emploi, énergie, une France tranquille et solidaire* contrasted with Giscard's frequent use of *effort, paix, monde, une France forte.* The contemporary format of televised politics (interviews, debates, round tables) has produced a greater participatory awareness at grass-roots level, to replace political paternalism. Giscard and his advisers were aware of the power of television and tried to use it for explanatory, ostensibly non-political, purposes, as for example his twice-monthly series of *Une heure avec le Président de la République* in 1979–80, but in the end he failed to overcome his 'technocratic' image; failed to realise, in effect, that political communication implies exchange and interaction.

Radio and television are one aspect of the now widely accepted notion of *le marketing politique*, and one of the ways of creating a favourable political image. Mitterrand's campaign team in 1981 included a group of advertising people who produced the slogan '*la force tranquillle*', generally regarded as successful, and a photograph to accompany it on posters, Giscard's campaign, on the other hand, suffered from a clash of emphasis between the image of an incumbent President, and his desire to be a '*citoyen-candidat*'. Professional advertising people may well be claiming too much by implying that such different success rates affected the final outcome, or by attributing Georges Marchais' poor performance to his disdain for their skills (he said the other candidates' approach was '*une campagne à l'esbroufe*'), but their participation in the process of influencing political behaviour must be taken as a permanent new element in contemporary French politics.

Opinion polls

As a major part of the attempt to discover attitudes on political matters, opinion polls have been used by governments, political parties, presidential and parliamentary candidates, and local administration since 1954, when Pierre Mendès-France as head of the government commissioned the Institut Français d'Opinion Publique (IFOP) to find out the main preoccupations and aspirations of French people. Two years later, Guy Mollet tried to discover what they thought of the Algerian question. Since then, it is claimed they have achieved a degree of refinement which allows a clear reflection of attitudes and voting intentions, and an accurate prediction of election results[4].

Polls for public consumption, for private use (for example in helping a politician decide whether he should stand for election) and for scientific research have become a part of the flavour of contemporary politics in France as in other Western-type democracies. They are instant indicators not merely of popularity but, it seems, of a more fundamental legitimacy – a right to govern. In 1980, after a violent attack on the synagogue in the rue Copernic in Paris, the most effective counter to opposition attempts to provoke the resignation of the Minister of the Interior was for him to say in Parliament; '*J'ai vu avec plaisir que les sondages montraient que la majorité des Français souhaitent que je reste à mon poste.*' An important reason for Michel Rocard's declaration of candidature for the 1981 Presidential elections, which he later withdrew in favour of François Mitterrand, was that polls showed him to be more popular with the electorate at large than the latter –and this continued after Mitterrand had been elected. More importantly, when polls showed in 1982 that the percentage of people dissatisfied with Mitterrand as President was greater than that of those satisfied, some Gaullist members argued that Mitterrand's continuing as President was no longer legitimate, since he no longer had majority support.

Opinion polls have been attacked on the grounds that they inevitably contain a distorting element, either in relation to what they measure – is it the true intentions of voters, their idealised aspirations, or their conformism? – or in relation to how they go about it, in the formulation of questions, the representative nature of the sample, or the way results are presented. But the major question is the extent to which opinion polls as a source of information influence electoral behaviour, and therefore political attitudes and culture. Various possible effects have been discerned:

1 increased support for a poll leader (bandwagon effect);
2 increased support for a candidate who is trailing (underdog effect);
3 abstention because a favoured candidate has, according to polls, little chance of winning (wasted vote effect);
4 abstention because a favoured candidate is virtually certain to win (demobilisation effect);
5 participation in an election because polls (plus other factors) have increased the voters' interest (mobilisation effect);
6 voting so as to show independence and prove polls wrong (perversity effect).

While a claim can be made that one or more of the above operated in elections in European democracies since the 1960s, opinion polls can have an important role in the specifically French context. Their influence on the functioning of the political system is more direct in a situation such as the run-up to a Presidential election, where rules about how parties or groups of parties operate are less clear than in other contexts. In this context, opinion polls may well fulfil the function, ill performed by the parties themselves, of resolving conflicts within parties, or within coalitions of parties, in a way which is then merely confirmed by the first round proper. Even before the first round, the two candidates likely on poll evidence to go through to the second round fourteen days afterwards usually conduct their campaigns in anticipation of this run-off.

Feelings in France about the deleterious effect of the publication of opinion polls on political behaviour and attitudes led to attempts to force this into a legal framework. In 1972 the Senate unanimously approved a draft law by one of its members to ban publication of polls during the official election campaign, but the government of the time refused to submit it to the National Assembly, over whose agenda it has very tight control. In 1977, however, a law was passed forbidding publication of, or comment on, opinion polls during the week up to and including each election round or referendum. This does not affect the publication of estimates of results after the close of all polling stations, and such publication by competing radio and television channels is now a set feature of the evening of elections.

Political participation

The basic level of political participation is that of voting in elections. In France, besides referenda and plebiscites, citizens are called on to choose their representatives at various levels:

1 President of the Republic;
2 *députés* to a parliamentary assembly;
3 members of a regional assembly – Corsica from 1982; overseas departments from 1983; perhaps regions in metropolitan France at some future date;
4 members of a council at the level of the *département (conseil général).*
5 members of a council at the level of the *commune (conseil municipal).*

The development of the suffrage in France is a reflection of the chequered history of political regimes and crises. The system under the Ancien Regime, when it operated, was that representation was a function of belonging to a specified group – aristocracy, clergy, propertied middle class. A different concept of political rights which emerged after the Revolution was that of the *citoyen actif*, who had to be male, over 25, resident in the commune, registered on the list of National Guards, and fulfil a tax-paying qualification. These 'active citizens' chose 'electors', who had to have a higher tax assessment and who directly elected national representatives and local administrators. Virtually universal masculine adult (over 21) suffrage was introduced for elections to the Convention in 1792 and as a feature of the Constitution which this body drew up. But this Constitution never came into effect, and the Directory in 1795 reverted to an indirect system, with political rights restricted to tax-paying citizens. Napoleon abolished the tax-paying qualifications, but elections were a sham in that the indirect element was extended and in any case the assembly thus chosen had minimal power. The Restoration brought renewed emphasis on a suffrage strictly limited to property-owners and top office-holders (*régime censitaire*).

After the Revolution of February 1848, the system of universal masculine adult suffrage through direct elections was reinstated and was applied five times nationally and locally during 1848 and 1849. Although Louis-Napoleon as Emperor distorted its working by ensuring the election of many Government-sponsored candidates, and by reducing the power of the elected assembly to a minimal consultative one, the final victory of universal manhood direct suffrage was achieved. In historical terms it was an early victory, predated only by some states of the United States of America, and the tradition of some Swiss cantons to have an assembly of all adult males. On the other hand, the right to vote was granted to adult women only in 1944, comparatively late in the general context of political emancipation in advanced countries. This was due to the inertia of the Centre-right which dominated the Third Republic, and to fears on the Left that female suffrage would benefit their opponents. Later, lack of certainty about who would benefit from the electoral support of 18- to 20-year olds meant that there was no major problem in giving them the right to vote as one of the consequences of reducing the age of majority in 1974, soon after the election of Giscard d'Estaing as President.

Electoral abstention

The addition of 18- to 20-year olds to those having the right to vote further enlarged the number of those qualified by reason of age, which population growth was also affecting. By 1981, this figure was approaching thirty-nine and a half million, but because the law requires that an elector be registered (*inscrit*) in order to vote, the total of this is smaller: in the 1981 parliamentary elections, it was 36.25 million.

Obviously, not all registered electors vote, and if they do they may, deliberately as a protest, or through ignorance, not vote in the prescribed way, and their votes are void (*blancs et nuls*).

Subtracting the number of these, and the number of valid votes cast (*suffrages exprimés*) from the total of registered voters gives an official figure of those who did not participate in the electoral process at any one time. These percentages in the Fifth Republic, at national level, in the first and second rounds where applicable, are shown in Table 3.2.

Table 3.2

Abstention rates in Fifth Republic elections

		percentage
1958	Referendum (on Constitution)	15.0
	Legislative (1)	22.9
	(2)	23.7
1961	Referendum (on Algeria)	29.3
1962	Referendum (on Algeria)	24.4
	Referendum (on Constitution)	22.7
	Legislative (1)	31.3
	(2)	27.3
1965	Presidential (1)	14.9
	(2)	15.4
1967	Legislative (1)	19.0
	(2)	31.3
1968	Legislative (1)	19.9
	(2)	22.0
1969	Referendum (on Regions, etc.)	19.4
	Presidential (1)	21.8
	(2)	31.0
1972	Referendum (on Europe)	39.5
1973	Legislative (1)	18.7
	(2)	18.1
1974	Presidential (1)	15.1
	(2)	12.1
1978	Legislative (1)	16.6
	(2)	15.3
1979	European	38.8
1981	Presidential (1)	18.9
	(2)	14.1
	Legislative (1)	29.6
	(2)	25.6
1984	European	42.9

The main reasons for electoral abstention may be summarised as follows:

1 The part of political culture which leads to the view, however false objectively, that the domain of politics is characterised by 'bad' things (conflict, contentiousness) and inhabited by people with selfish overweening ambition and a propensity to corruption.
2 The feeling on the part of individual electors that they are powerless, since the link between voting, government policy, and the outcome of issues is perceived as tenuous.
3 The failure of *instruction civique* to achieve its object: the state school system, non-partisan bodies, and to a certain extent organisations such as the Catholic Church and the Communist party, try to foster an ideal of the vote as a duty, as well as a right. But poverty, ignorance and diffidence militate against these efforts.

Classe politique

The varying degree of political participation by individuals leads to the notion that there is a group not only whose participation is such that politics can be regarded as their profession, but also that, occupying the top rungs of organisations and institutions which are central to the political system, they in effect run the country. A pyramidal representation of this increasing degree of involvement might be as shown in Figure 3.1.

The last stage includes all those who wield political influence at a local or national level. At the local level, it implies that an individual is a personality of some standing (a *notable*), who could influence the outcome of local issues. By long tradition he was distinguished by wealth and a high income, by being president of local groups, and by having the kind of job (doctor, veterinary surgeon, lawyer, pharmacist) which gave him a wide network of contacts. The increasing complexity of local administrations and of the local echelons of central government has made the concept of *notable* less clear-cut, and a local bigwig in industry, the press, law or education may well be as influential as a personality who relies on the ballot box for his power base. But the emergence of Alain Poher as a serious Presidential candidate in 1969, and as interim President of the Republic in 1969 and 1974 showed that the *notable* had not entirely disappeared from the centre of the political stage.

Figure 3.1
Involvement in politics

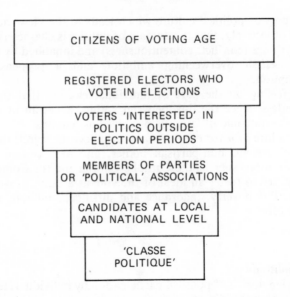

Poher's career as mayor of a small town near Paris, and then as senator, is an example of how the holding of local and national political offices is regarded as normal in France,[5] and it is by no means the rule that the local elective office predates the national one. This *cumul des mandats* has been defended by arguing that local requirements need a strong voice in Paris or Strasbourg, but the practice leads to the perpetuation of an élite composed of professional politicians, and demands for limitations of the permissible number or type of elective office have been growing. In any case, the granting of greater local powers under the Left government's decentralisation policy has somewhat modified the traditional framework in which the *classe politique* operated. There has also been a weakening of the notion, of which Giscard was a prime example, that a major characteristic of representative democracy was for a politician of national standing to be supported by small parliamentary groups who were themselves drawn from and supported by local *notables* aware of national issues but assiduously protecting local interests.

The style of contemporary French politics

Observers of French politics have commonly stressed that certain factors, particularly class and education, were especially signficant in shaping attitudes and behaviour. It is these factors, sometimes referred to as *les pesanteurs sociologiques*, which have been widely studied as indicators, for example, of the potential affiliation of individuals to political parties, or their support for a particular set of policies at election times. Political culture shapes attitudes and styles of behaviour, and has in part determined how effective French political and social institutions have been. The picture of contemporary French politics as a conflictual one is a result of the existence of a multiplicity of cultures rivalling one another for the attention of the individual.

On one level this shows itself in the frequency of electoral combat: to the list of national elections on page 70 must be added cantonal elections to the *conseil général* of the *département* which occur in half the country every three years, and especially elections to the *conseil municipal* of every commune in France which, though they occur at intervals of six years, have become so politicised that they have increasingly assumed the role of a popularity test of national governments. But it is not just the frequency of electoral consultations (often in two rounds) which heightens the element of conflict. Campaigning is semi-permanent in that the Assembly can be dissolved at any time by the President, who can therefore be continually urged by supporters and opponents alike to call elections before their due date (*élections anticipées*). Politicians can keep up the electoral heat by referring to a coming electoral consultation as a '*troisième tour*', after just failing to swing opinion in their favour in a previous two-round election. The campaign for the 1981 Presidential election occupied virtually two years since during this time it was safe to assume that barring accidents Giscard d'Estaing the incumbent President would be a candidate, fighting on his political record.

For this heightened, semi-permanent electoral conflict the *forces vives* of the country are in a state of virtually continual mobilisation. Political parties, economic interest groups (employees' unions and employers' groups) and single-issue associations with a political purpose devote money and effort to putting across their point of view. Traditional political party campaign activities – meetings, rallies, posters – may have declined, but apart from more instant appeal through television and radio, parties are just as likely to vie with each other at a higher level, that of a comprehensive 'blueprint for society' (*projet de société*) serving not just as an election manifesto, but as a well thought out, even philosophical, discourse on political fundamentals. Individual politicians, it seems, feel obliged to speak frequently of '*réflexion*' in political matters, to give the impression of *gravitas*, and yet political conflict in France is such that the merest hint of scandal affecting prominent politicians is exploited. Because of this, it seems more prevalent in France than in similar Western-style democracies. François Mitterrand was a victim in 1959, though he suffered no lasting political harm, but in the 1970s the names of Pompidou, Chaban-Delmas, Chirac, Poniatowski, Marchais, and especially Giscard were all associated, in varying degrees of justification, with political scandal. This and other negative factors in contemporary French politics often lead to the contemptuous view that it is a question of 'politics for its own sake' or 'politicking' (*la politique politicienne*). This kind of attitude may be inspired by the fact that, as in similar countries, politics has become not just more salient, but also more banal. Party managers, with an eye to the media, tend to emphasise stories and personalities at the expense of argument and policies. Despite this, the effectiveness of French political institutions may have been demonstrated not just by their organic evolution since 1958, and not just by the orderly transfer of power (*alternance*) in 1981, but by the strength of political commitment, and the vigour of political discourse which characterise contemporary French politics.

Bibliographical guidance

On political culture and electoral behaviour in general:

J. Capdevielle *et al. France de gauche, vote à droite* (Presses de la FNSP, 1981)
M. Duverger, *Sociologie de la politique* (PUF, 1976)
G. Goguel, *Chroniques électorales*, vol. 2, *La Cinquième République de général de Gaulle*, and vol. 3, *La Cinquième République après de Gaulle* (Presses de la FNSP, 1983)
S. Huet and P. Langenieux-Villard, *La communication politique* (PUF, 1983)
A. Lancelot, *Les attitudes politiques* (PUF, 1974)
A. Lancelot, *Les élections sous la Vᵉ République* (PUF, 1983)
A. Lancelot, *La participation des Français à la politique* (PUF, 1971)

H. LeBras and E. Todd, *L'Invention de la France* (Livre de Poche, 1981)
W.R. Schonfeld, *Obedience and revolt – French behaviour towards authority* (Sage, 1976)
B. Toulemonde, *Manuel de science politique*, 2nd ed. (Presses Universitaires de Lille, 1982) pp. 77–147

Specific groups or aspects of political culture are covered in:

P. Bosc, *Les notables en questions – 30 portaits politiques* (Presses du Languedoc, 1977)
R.A. DeAngelis, *Blue-collar workers and politics – a French paradox* (Croom Helm, 1982) especially ch. 5
G. Groux, *Les cadres* (Maspéro, 1983) part 3
G. Lavau et al. *L'univers politique des classes moyennes* (Presses de la FNSP, 1983)
G. Michelat and M. Simon, *Classe, religion et comportement politique* (Presses de la FNSP, 1977)
J. Mossuz-Lavau and M. Sineau, *Enquête sur les femmes et la politique* (PUF , 1983)
A. Percheron et al. *Les 10–16 ans et la politique* (Presses de la FNSP, 1978)

Opinion polls and media influence on politics are treated in:

R. Cayrol, 'The mass media and the electoral campaign' in H.R. Penniman (ed.) *The French National Assembly Elections of 1978* (American Enterprise Institute, 1980)
D. David et al. *Le marketing politique* (PUF, 1978)
A. Lancelot et al. *Les sondages dans la vie politique française* (Universalia, 1981)
Démocratie cathodique – l'élection présidentielle et la télévision; *Les Cahiers de la Communication*, vol. 1, nos 4–5 (1981)
A. Max, *La république des sondages* (Gallimard, 1981)
J.-L Missika and D. Wolton, *La folle du logis – la télévision dans les sociétés démocratiques* (Gallimard, 1983)
M. Moir, 'L'utilisation des techniques de marketing dans une campagne présidentielle' *Pouvoirs*, no. 14 (1980)
'La télévision, quatrième pouvoir?' *Projet*, sept–oct. 1979
R.-G Schwartzenberg, *L'Etat spectacle* (Flammarion, 1977)
SOFRES, *Opinion publique – enquêtes et commentaires 1984* (SOFRES, 1984) refers to 1983 and now published annually

On "classe politique" and élites, see for example:

P. Birnbaum, *Les sommets de l'etat – essai sur l'élite du pouvoir en France* (Seuil, 1977)
A. Duhamel, *La République giscardienne* (Grasset, 1980) chs 2 and 3.
J. Julliard *Contre la politique professionnelle* (Seuil, 1977)

J. Howorth and P.G. Cerny (eds), *Elites in France* (St. Martin, 1982)
E. Suleiman, *Elites in France – the politics of survival* (Princetown UP, 1978) translated as *Les élites en France – grands corps et grandes écoles* (Seuil, 1979)

On the 'style' of contemporary French politics:

J. Bacelon, *L'affaire de Broglie* (Jean Picollec, 1981)
F. Brigneau, *Mon village à l'heure socialiste* (Table Ronde, 1982)
J. Derogy and J.-M Poutaut, *Enquête sur les mystères de Marseille* (R. Laffont, 1984)
S. Huet, *Tout ce que vous direz pourra être retenu contre vous...* (Jean Picollec, 1981)
J.-P. Moulin, *Qu'est-il arrivé à la France? – un étranger dans l'hexagone* (Seuil, 1982)

Illustrative texts and linguistic exercises

Texte 3.1   Temperaments

Mise en situation
Guy Rossi-Landi (né en 1944), universitaire à Paris, et auteur de plusieurs ouvrages politiques, traite – non sans humour – dans son livre *Le chassé-croisé* d'une France coupée en deux, où droite et gauche s'affrontent et tentent parfois de se rapprocher. Pour Guy Rossi-Landi, la frontière entre elles est mouvante et souvent confuse.

Alors, comment expliquer que droite et gauche restent intactes à travers les âges et les régimes? Qu'elles échangent leurs thèmes, éventuellement leurs leaders, mais non pas leurs votes? François Goguel a montré que la carte du vote pour François Mitterrand, le 19 mai 1974, était presque identique à celle du vote en faveur du premier projet de constitution proposé en mai 1946 par le PC et la SFIO. Mêmes zones de force et de faiblesse.

Mais il y a plus surprenant encore: ainsi, les départements qui on résisté au coup d'Etat du 2 décembre 1851 continuent-ils de voter à gauche. Depuis le livre, paru en 1913, d'André Siegfried, père de la sociologie électorale qu'il nommait plus modestement géographie électorale, 'Tableau de la France de l'Ouest' (et confirmé par des recherches ultérieures comme celles de Paul Bois sur le département de la Sarthe), on sait qu'*au canton près* les mêmes attitudes politiques se sont perpétuées depuis la Révolution. Tel village chouan continue à voter à droite; tel autre resté loyaliste en 1793 ne manque pas de soutenir l'union de la gauche. Mai si le phénomène frappe par sa régularité, on est, en revanche, bien en peine pour l'interpréter. Plusieurs hypothèses ont été formulées.

La facilité des communications peut fournir un indice. Il est vrai qu'à la fin du XIXe siècle la carte politique et la carte des voies ferrées se ressemblent étrangement: là ou le chemin de fer passe, il apporte, en effet, par les journaux et les revues qu'il diffuse, les idées nouvelles. Là ou il ne passe pas, les *colporteurs* continuent à vendre des almanachs moins novateurs. C'est donc dans les régions les plus *enclavées* que se conserve le mieux l'influence des notables, du châtelain, du sous-préfet, du curé. Sans doute. Mais, à l'heure des médias, cette influence, *battue en brèche*, s'est bien amenuisée et pourtant la fidélité demeure.

On a pensé aussi qu'il pouvait y avoir un élément d'explication dans le type d'exploitation agricole des diverses regions. Les pays de petite propriété auraient été les plus égalitaires, les plus à gauche; ceux de grande propriété, les plus à droite; le *faire-valoir direct* serait à gauche; le *fermage* ou le *métayage* à droite (on sait que les domestiques et les concierges sont particulièrement réactionnaires). Mais comment expliquer alors que l'exode rural et l'urbanisation n'aient pas *chamboulé* les comportements politiques?

Il faut se méfier du déterminisme géographique du genre 'Au-dessus de 800 m, on vote à droite' ... François Goguel écrit: 'Dans le Gers, la carte politique et celle de la production d'eau-de-vie d'Armagnac ne sont pas sans rapports. André Siegfried a montré qu'en Vendée les cantons granitiques sont conservateurs alors que les cantons calcaires sont républicains.' Jacques Fauvet renchérit: 'La Risle est une grand frontière politique en France. Bernay qui a les pieds humides vote à droite et Saint-André-de-l'Eure qui les a au sec vote à gauche.' Le coeur sec serait à droite et les pieds secs à gauche.

Mais l'auteur reconnaît qu'il est un peu vain d'opposer *schématiquement* la France du nord et celle du midi, la France de la vigne et celle de l'olivier, la France du blé et celle de la betterave, a France de la grande propriété et celle de la plus petite, la France du *droit coutumier* et celle du droit écrit, la France catholique et la France 'déliée', etc.

Et François Goguel, très honnêtement, a dû nuancer de façon très sensible son hypothèse selon laquelle les *cantons dynamiques* voteraient gaulliste et les cantons statiques seraient de gauche. Il a dû faire intervenir d'autres variables. Pas plus que de déterminisme géographique il n'en est de sociologique. D'ailleurs la différenciation droite–gauche est bien antérieure à toute distinction de classe. En 1974, 27 pour-cent des ouvriers ont voté contre François Mitterrand et 37 pour-cent des cadres supérieurs pour lui.

De tous les critères (âge, sexe, catégorie socio-professionnelle, etc.) qui peuvent agir sur le comportement électoral, celui qui offre le plus fort taux de corrélation avec le suffrage, c'est le comportement religieux. Les spécialistes distinguent les 'messalisants' réguliers (à la messe tous les dimanches), les 'messalisants occasionnels (pour les fêtes carillonnées), les catholiques non pratiquants (n'allant à l'eglise que pour être baptisé, marié ou enterré) et les incroyants. Eh bien, 90 pour-cent des premiers on voté en 1974 pour M. Giscard d'Estaing et 90 pour-cent des derniers pour François Mitterrand. Mais là encore, il ne s'agit que d'une constatation. On remarque qu'il y a un comportement cohérent au nom duquel on vote à droite et on va à la messe, mais on ne peut pas dire qu'on vote Giscard parce qu'on va à la messe ni qu'on va à la messe parce qu'on vote Giscard ...

Peut-être alors, comme le pensait Jacques Maritain, existe-t-il une opposition fondamentale du tempérament humain: on serait de gauche ou de droite comme on naît bilieux ou sanguin. La caractérologie est-elle *l'auxiliare la plus précieuse de la science politique?*

SOURCE: G. Rossi-Landi, *Le Chassé-croisé – la droite et la gauche en France de 1789 à nos jours* (Lattès, 1978) pp. 99–102.

Exploitation du texte

1 Expliquez en quelques mots les expressions en italique.

2 Expliquez les allusions dans les phrases suivantes:

le premier projet de constitution proposé en mai 1946
le coup d'Etat du 2 decembre 1851
un village chouan
l'union de la gauche

3 Trouvez (par example, dans '*Le Monde*') une carte du vote pour François Mitterand en 1974 et faites une analyse des zones de force et de faiblesse. Comment les expliquez-vous? Faites éventuellement une comparaison entre la carte de 1974 et celle de 1981.

4 Ecrivez une dissertation d'environ 1200 à 1500 mots sur le sujet suivant:

'La caractérologie est-elle l'auxiliaire la plus précieuse de la science politique?'

5 Ce texte pourrait-il être la transcription d'une présentation orale? Relevez les traits qui l'apparentent à un 'texte écrit' et ceux qui l'apparentent à un 'texte parlé'.

6 Résumez ce texte en 300 mots environ, en français 'soutenu'.

Texte 3.2   Pour de nouveaux modes de vie

Mise en situation

La déclaration du Conseil permanent de la Conférence épiscopale française fut préparée pendant le printemps et l'été de 1982, et publiée le 22 septembre, après avoir été l'objet d'échanges avec des syndicalistes, des chefs d'entreprise, des hommes politiques et des moralistes. La déclaration fit couler beaucoup d'encre, tant à gauche qu'à droite; celle-ci reprocha aux évêques d'avoir apporté leur soutien au gouvernement socialiste et d'avoir soutenu des positions hasardeuses ou discutables sur des problèmes très techniques. Voici la troisième des quatre sections.

*   *   *

Changer les habitudes

5 – En premier lieu, il est indispensable que tous les citoyens de notre pays acquièrent une idée réaliste de l'état du monde et de la situation de la France. Cette exigence implique que les gouvernements et les oppositions successives n'entretiennent pas l'illusion de solutions faciles et rapides, contribuant ainsi à la *démobilisation des énergies;* que les mass media développent un effort courageux et coordonné pour éduquer réellement. Les rêves sont vains, le désespoir inutile, le sentiment d'impuissance injustifié. Il s'agit de permettre à chacun de comprendre la situation et de s'interroger sur la contribution personnelle qu'il est en mesure d'apporter.

6 – Nous appelons tous ceux qui contribuent à la vie économique, sociale et, pour ce qui nous concerne, les membres des communautés chrétiennes, les mouvements et les regroupements divers, à s'informer *sans exclusive* et à réfléchir aux raisons de la crise. Tenter une telle analyse est une entreprise complexe, même pour des spécialistes. Il est néanmoins urgent de s'y efforcer. Il est également très important de mettre au clair *les ressorts qui sous-tendent* le fonctionnement de la vie économique et sociale et expliquent les durcissements et les *blocages.* Sans cette prise de conscience, il est impossible de concevoir une transformation positive des institutions.

7 – Sans préjuger des résultats de cette analyse ni prétendre en épuiser le champ, nous croyons important d'évoquer quelques traits des mentalités courantes qui ont régné pendant toute la période de croissance continue et que constituent aujourd'hui des obstacles à vaincre.

(i) L'un des moteurs efficaces de la consommation a été, pour chacun, le vif désir d'atteindre le niveau de vie de la catégorie sociale jugée immédiatement supérieure à la sienne.

(ii) Le besoin de consommation ainsi stimulé a fait naître parfois, pour anticiper sa satisfaction, la course aux emprunts entraînant la pratique excessive du *cumul des emplois.*

(iii) La croissance continue a entraîné des pratiques inégalitaires. *Des groupes catégoriels* ont su s'organiser pour obtenir des avantages contractuels ou légaux garantis indéfiniment.

(iv) Le sentiment illusoire qu'il resterait des surplus à partager entre tous a engendré un système de protection sociale tellement complexe qu'il est parfois inaccessible aux plus *démunis.* Etendu à l'indemnisation du chômage, il est facilement altéré par des abus, malgré les valeurs qu'il comporte.

(v) Enfin, le passage, en une génération, du monde rural au monde industriel urbain, l'objectif prioritaire de l'enrichissement individuel, le manque de participation des citoyens à une gestion des affaires jugée trop complexe pour eux, l'amenuisement des *corps intermédiaires*, ont suscité des comportements largement démunis d'idéal, insoucieux des autres et surtout de la *collectivité.* Les premiers symptomes de crise ont cristallisé ces tendances au *repli*, qui rendent spontanément inaptes à la *solidarité.*

8 – Il ne s'agit pas de juger ni de condamner. Nous constatons des faits. La persistance d'un tel état d'esprit rendrait impossible le nécessaire partage à la fois de l'emploi et du revenu. Déjà techniquement difficile, un tel partage serait impossible à réaliser sans transformation des mentalités individuelles et catégorielles.

C'est donc à un examen critique que nous convions les catholiques. Les insuffisances en matière de justice et d'équité, tout aussi importantes hier qu'aujourd'hui, étaient plus ou mois masquées par l'effet d'une croissance rapide. La crise actuelle met en lumière les inégalités et l'insécurité d'un grand nombre. Nous sommes appelés à nous montrer solidaires sans plus tarder. Personne ne peut *se dérober*. La confrontation avec l'Evangile appelle à de nouveaux comportements.

Par le sacrement de réconciliation, objet du prochain Synode, le Christ qui nous réconcilie avec le Père nous appelle à une réconciliation avec nos frères. Par l'Eucharistie, Il nous convie à une partage effectif.

SOURCE: Les évêques de France, *Pour de nouveaux modes de vie*– déclaration du conseil permanent de l'épiscopat français sur la conjoncture économique et sociale, 22 septembre, 1982 (Le Centurion, 1982) pp. 21–5.

Exploitation du texte

1 Expliquez en quelques mots les expressions en italique.

2 Reformulez avec vos propres mots les cinq 'traits des mentalités courantes ... qui constituent des obstacles à vaincre', selon la Déclaration (paragraphe no. 7).

3 Préparez un exposé susceptible de réfuter un de ces cinq 'obstacles'.

4 Comment les mass media pourraient-ils 'éduquer réellement'?

5 Relevez toutes les occurences de 'nous'. Est-ce que ce pronom renvoie toujours au même ensemble de personnes?

6 Reformulez en utilisant le discours indirect libre les paragraphes 5, 6 et 8, comme si vous rendiez compte de la Déclaration pour un journal quotidien.

Texte 3.3   Un nouveau langage politique

Mise en situation

Le Club de l'Horloge, club de réflexion politique de l'opposition giscardienne, organisa à Paris en octobre 1982 une conférence–débat sur le thème 'La bataille des mots, quel langage pour l'opposition?' Cette intervention d'Yvan Blot, son président, posa sept principes qui devraient permettre d'obtenir 'une meilleure efficacité, c'est-à-dire une meilleure écoute de la part des Français', en faisant notamment une analyse critique du vocabulaire de la majorité et de l'opposition. A l'époque, divers professionnels de la communication et en particulier les experts en marketing politique réfléchissaient à une refonte du langage utilisé par les hommes politiques.

*   *   *

1 Une langage autonome

L'opposition sera d'autant plus efficace qu'elle se battra sur son propre terrain. Elle doit donc récuser les catégories de langage de l'adversaire et les antithèses auxquelles elles conduisent (par exemple, l'antithèse droite/gauche). Il s'agit, comme au jeu de go, de savoir 'changer de damier' lorsque c'est nécessaire. A l'heure actuelle, le débat politique serait plus fécond s'il portait sur l'antithèse 'socialistes/républicains'.

Un langage *autonome* signifie aussi qu'il doit être le véhicule d'un projet autonome distinct du projet du pouvoir en place. Il doit donc être fondamentalement plus 'créatif' que 'réactif'.

2 Un langage démystificateur

Le langage de l'opposition doit permettre de décrire la nature véritable du socialisme, ses résultats pour le pays et pour les Français ainsi que l'avenir du socialisme (et donc les perspectives d'espoir pour l'opposition).

(i) Il faut dévoiler la nature réelle du socialisme: les *forces féodales* qui le dirigent, le *fonds de commerce* électoral qui le soutient, son caractère non républicain, la force et les faiblesses du voile que constitue son langage officiel, etc.

(ii) Il faut décrire les résultats du socialisme non seulement en termes d'efficacité économique ou diplomatique, mais aussi au regard des grandes valeurs républicaines: liberté, égalité, fraternité, paix, justice, unité, unité nationale, etc.

(iii) Il faut analyser les perspectives d'avenir du socialisme (évolution de ses bases géographiques, sociologiques et historiques) non seulement en fonction des *péripéties* de l'actualité immédiate, mais essayer de déceler les traits essentiels des évolutions en longue période.

3 Un langage humain et humaniste

Il est nécessaire d'éviter toute déviation technocratique. If faut s'adresser aux intelligences mais aussi parler au coeur. Il faut ne pas trop sacrifier à la logique froide des statistiques et savoir se référer aux grands exemples de l'Histoire de France. Il faut un langage politique qui s'adresse aux hommes et pas seulement un langage technocratique et sans âme. Le langage de l'opposition républicaine est construit autour d'un projet qui met l'homme au centre de ses préoccupations. Il doit traduire cette hiérarchie des valeurs qui place l'homme au-dessus de la société et la nation au-dessus de l'Etat. Il doit être résolument antitotalitaire.

4 *Un langage unitaire*

L'opposition est républicaine à travers ses différentes composantes. Son langage doit donc être unitaire et refléter cette convergence des valeurs philosophiques fondamentales des différentes composantes de l'opposition. Il doit permettre de *minoriser* l'adversaire sur le plan du langage. Plus profondément, le langage de l'opposition doit être unitaire en ce qu'il vise à rassembler les Français. Le fonds de commerce électoral du marxisme est l'exploitation des divisions entre classes. Le langage d'une opposition républicaine doit être un appel permanent à l'unité nationale et à la fraternité au sein de la nation. Il doit se situer prioritairement dans le cadre d'une stratégie haute de rassemblement autour d'un projet.

5 *Un langage populaire*

L'opposition doit s'adresser à l'ensemble des Français et doit apporter un message d'espoir au peuple tout entier. It doit donc répondre aux aspirations réelles de la population et ne pas se laisser influencer par le *snobisme* de certaines élites qui prétendent dominer la culture politique du pays. Un langage populaire dénoncera les féodalites partisanes qui sont liées au *pouvoir actuel* et en appellera à une démocratie authentique fondée sur le recours au suffrage universel et sur le respect des aspirations populaires, par delà les fractions, les prétendues 'élites' qui cherchent à s'approprier la souveraineté nationale.

6 *Un langage actuel*

Le langage de l'opposition doit être attentif aux problèmes actuels qui se posent aux Français. Il doit apporter un espoir fondé sur des solutions appropriées à notre époque et non inspirées par le XIXᵉ siècle lors des débuts de la révolution industrielle. Il doit attacher une particulière importance au besoin croissant d'identité et de liberté qui se manifeste dans la nation, notamment parmi les jeunes. Il doit tenir compte des aspirations montantes vers plus de liberté et plus d'*enracinement*.

7 *Un langage enraciné dans la tradition républicaine*

La mémoire permet à l'homme d'assumer sa liberté. La mémoire, la conscience historique permet à un peuple de lutter contre la servitude. Il faut redonner vie aux valeurs fortes de notre tradition républicaine et rappeler les paroles des grands républicains, Carnot, Lamartine, Clemenceau et bien d'autres, qui critiquèrent le socialisme ou son *avant-garde* en leur temps. Les socialistes et les communistes n'ont pas le monopole de l'Histoire. Le langage de l'opposition, résolument enraciné dans l'Histoire et tourné vers le futur, doit mobiliser les Français pour la défense des grandes valeurs de la République, liberté, égalité, fraternité, sécurité, propriété, résistance à l'oppression, qui sont remises en cause à présent.

SOURCE: Y. Blot (Président du Club de l'Horloge) conférence donée à Paris, 14 octobre, 1982

Exploitation du texte

1 Expliquez en quelques mots le sens des expressions en italique.

2 Faite une liste des caractéristiques négatives imputées au socialisme par l'auteur.

3 Ecrivez une brève biographie politique de Carnot, Lamartine et Clemenceau pour montrer combien ils étaient de 'grands républicains'.

4 Rédigez un bref discours politique inspiré par le nouveau langage de l'opposition que prône l'auteur.

5 Remplacez les occurences de 'falloir' par 'devoir' et vice versa en apportant les modifications syntaxiques nécessaires (ordre des mots, substantif, etc.)

6 Quels sont les problèmes posés par le choix du sujet (pronom ou substantif) du verbe 'devoir' là où il remplace 'falloir'?

7 Faites une liste des mots qui renvoient à l'idée d'"unité' et de ceux que évoquent une idée opposée.

Exercices de comparaison et d'application

1 A partir des propos contenus dans ces trois textes, de quels points de vue la France serait-elle 'coupée en deux'?

2 Préparez un débat en précisant les arguments pour et contre la thèse que la France contemporaine est coupée en deux.

3 Quels seraient les traits caractéristiques de la vie politique et économique en France si les aspirations des auteurs des Textes 3.2 et 3.3 étaient réalisées?

4 Reformulez les sections 4 à 7 du Texte 3.3 en employant la voie de l'appel direct adopté dans le Texte 3.2.

4

The Presidency and Executive Power

The French Fifth Republic was set up in 1958 during a few hectic months which saw in quick succession:

1   the collapse of the Fourth Republic when the possibility of a significant modification of the constitutional rules by which it had operated was accepted (3 June).
2   the drafting of a new Constitution, its approval by the people in a referendum (28 September), and its promulgation (4 October).
3   the election of parliamentary assemblies under the new Constitution: National Assembly (23 and 30 November), Senate (26 April 1959).
4   the election of a President of the Republic – Charles de Gaulle (21 December 1958).

Presidency

When the French Parliament, on 3 June 1958, decided to allow the newly-formed government under General de Gaulle (as *Président du Conseil*, the equivalent of Prime Minister) to set about recasting political ground-rules in a new Constitution, it was following the logic of its having accepted the same government as a solution to a longstanding problem – that of Algeria. Successive governments of the Fourth Republic had been unable to cope with the conflicting demands of European settlers in Algeria who feared the erosion of their privileged position, of Muslim nationalists waging guerilla warfare since 1954, and of the French Army in Algeria which resented the constraints of political control from Paris on its mission of 'pacification'. The crisis of May 1958, when government buildings in Algiers were occupied by European settlers, was the culmination of challenges to the authority of the Fourth Republic.

Most leading politicians realised that any hope of a solution would involve significant changes in the regime, but after two weeks of uncertainty, preferred a de Gaulle solution to other possibilities (military junta, Left dictatorship) because it was the best guarantee of a regime that would be republican in nature. Although there were doubts in Left-wing circles about de Gaulle's commitment to republicanism, he was willing to accept conditions which ensured that the future new Constitution would be a traditional Western parliamentary democratic one, with universal suffrage as the source of legitimacy, the separation of powers, and a Government accountable to Parliament. He also agreed that a consultative committee of leading politicians of the Fourth Republic should be closely associated with the whole process of drafting of the new Constitution, which occupied the summer of 1958.

But despite these limitations on the freedom of the government of de Gaulle, he and his close followers such as Michel Debré, the Minister of Justice (*le Garde des Sceaux*) were able to shape the 1958 Constitution according to their own views of what had been wrong with the Fourth Republic and what needed to be done to set up a modern, efficient republican regime. Debré, attracted by the British parliamentary model, was intent on establishing a *parlementarisme rationalisé* where the Government, in carrying out its programme, was not at the mercy of a Parliament with extensive powers, although it was ultimately accountable to it and could be obliged to resign.

The main inspiration of the 1958 Constitution, however, was the experiences and thoughts of Charles de Gaulle. His experience of 1940 made him conclude that in a crisis the nation needed a strong man to guarantee the continuity of the State. The President of the Republic (Head of State) during the German invasion of 1940 was unable to do this, for temperamental but above all for constitutional reasons.

Moreover, de Gaulle came to conceive of the President in normal times as *'un arbitre au-dessus des contingences politiques'*. This is the description given in the second part of his speech at Bayeux in June 1946 (*Texte* 7.1), where an important paragraph is devoted to the duties and powers of the President of a Republic with significantly different emphasis from the ones envisaged by the government in power at the time. The Constitution drafted and accepted by the people twelve years later was very close to de Gaulle's ideas enunciated at Bayeux, especially regarding the role and powers of the Presidency. The Fifth Republic Constitution laid down that the President:

A   As Head of State
1   Takes care that the Constitution is respected, and makes sure by
    mediating if necessary that the public powers (legislative,
    executive, judiciary) function properly, and that there is
    continuity of the State and maintenance of national
    independence and territorial integrity (Article 5). To help him in
    this task, he (along with others) has the power not only to refer
    a law to a new body, the Constitutional Council (Article 61), a
    third of whose members he appoints (Article 56), but also in a
    national or international crisis threatening the normal activities
    of the State, the power (the duty, even) to take 'the measures
    required by those circumstances' provided these are designed to
    return matters to normal as quickly as possible (Article 16). If
    an international treaty signed by France is referred to the
    Constitutional Council, and this body decides it contains a
    clause contrary to the Constitution, the Constitution itself must
    be revised on that matter before the treaty can be ratified and
    come into operation (Article 54).
2   Has the powers in the field of foreign policy to accredit
    ambassadors (Article 14); negotiate and ratify treaties (Article
    52); chair the most important bodies concerned with defence,
    and command the armed forces (Article 15).
3   Makes sure that the judiciary remains independent, helped by
    the Higher Judiciary Council (*Conseil supérieur de la
    magistrature*) (Article 64) which he largely appoints, and whose
    meetings he chairs (Article 65). He can also pardon convicted
    criminals (Article 17).

B   In an Executive role
1   Appoints the Prime Minister and, on the proposal of the latter,
    other government ministers (Article 8) and chairs meetings of
    the Council of Ministers (Article 9), signing any decrees which
    this body draws up, as well as any ordinances (executive orders
    under powers specially delegated by Parliament); he appoints
    top civil servants and military personnel (Article 13).
2   With regard to Parliament, can dissolve the National Assembly,
    but not if this is less than a year since the elections which
    followed a previous dissolution, or when Article 16 is being
    invoked (Article 12); promulgates laws passed by Parliament,
    or asks it to look at them again (Article 10); has the right to
    have messages sent to Parliament read out before it (Article 18);
    and issues the executive order opening and closing
    extraordinary sessions of Parliament (Article 30).

C   As elected representative of the people
1   Can, if it is proposed by both assemblies or by the Government
    when Parliament is in session, submit to referendum any draft
    law which affects the way public powers are organised (Article
    11).

The majority of the Articles referred to in the above list confer
powers on a Fifth Republic President which are very similar to
those possessed by his predecessors in the Third and Fourth
Republics. There are however in this list powers which were granted
to a Fifth Republic President beyond the traditional ones of the
office. These are Articles:

11   referendum to get draft laws passed;
12   dissolution of Parliament;
16   emergency powers;
18   messages to Parliament;
54   obstacle to effect of international treaties;
56   appointment of three members of the Constitutional Council;
61   referral of a law to the Constitutional Council.

To these must be added the first paragraph of Article 8,
appointment of Prime Minister, because, although this was a
longstanding Presidential power, the previous Constitution had
made it dependent on immediate approval (*investiture*) by the
National Assembly, and de Gaulle did not want this strict
condition, which gave considerable power to the Assembly, to
apply to the new 1958 Constitution. These eight Articles
representing new powers are listed in Article 19, which also makes
it clear that the circumstances of their exercise are different from
those applying to traditional powers. The difference is that in
exercising these new powers, the Fifth Republic President is kept
completely apart from the sphere of political argument and conflict
normal in a Western democracy. Because the countersignature
(*contreseing*) of the Prime Minister or other minister is not needed,
politicians cannot oblige the President to account in Parliament for
his action. The President, who is not in any case personally
responsible to Parliament (Article 68), is not even indirectly open to
attack through one of the government ministers as far as these new
powers are concerned. In this way he is able in complete
independence to carry out his function using the method of
mediation (*arbitrage*) between contending groups, which is central

to his office (Article 5) and which de Gaulle had since his entry into active politics regarded as the guarantee of a strong and durable republic.

The problem was that there were ambiguities and uncertainties in the text of the 1958 Constitution, in two principal, and interconnected, senses. One was that the Prime Minister also had duties and responsibilities, and powers to enable him to carry them out, in the drawing up and implementation of policies to promote the efficient functioning of the political and economic life of the country. This role could well overlap with that of a President of the Republic who interpreted in anything but a passive way the task which Article 5 gives him of making sure that the Constitution is respected, and that public powers function properly. The second was that the method of *arbitrage* between conflictual groups was open to different interpretations. The maximalist interpretation of *arbitrage*, based on the fact that the wording of Article 5 associates it with the guardianship of the national interest, justified active intervention in the field of policy making and implementation, that is, the executive function. The outcome was an adjustment, in the President's favour, of the boundary between his and the Prime Minister's executive roles. Successive Presidents have been responsible for changing the nature of the Fifth Republic. It began as a parliamentary regime with provisions to allow firm governments and the protection of the State and its institutions from the effects of warring factions in normal times and threats from inside or outside the country in times of crisis. But it developed into a regime which has been variously called by politicians and commentators:

une monarchie parlementaire républicaine
un régime présidentiel parlementarisé
une monarchie élective
une monarchie camouflée
une république monarchique

The latter description was suggested by Alain Peyrefitte in the presence of de Gaulle, who replied that it was *'plutôt une monarchie républicaine'*! From the 1970s, it was often called *un régime présidentialiste*, a phrase which up to then would have been understood as referring to Latin American-style dictatorships. The way in which successive Presidents have interpreted their constititutional powers is seen in the following survey.

Charles de Gaulle

Background   Born in 1890 de Gaulle became a professional soldier and fought in the First World War, being wounded and taken prisoner. In the 1920s and 1930s he held various staff appointments and wrote books in an effort to gain acceptance for his innovative views on military tactics and organisation. In 1940 he had just been made a General and entered the government as a junior minister when the French military collapse in the face of German invasion obliged him to choose between acceptance of the new state of affairs or continuation of the struggle. His decision to reject the consequences of military defeat and his efforts to become undisputed leader of the Free French forces in the wartime alliance were the basis of a political struggle to protect French interests and lay the foundations of post-war France. Although leader of the first post-war governments, his failure to prevent the eventual establishment of a party-dominated Fourth Republic led him to spend the years 1946–58 out of political power, writing his *Mémoires de Guerre* and setting up a short-lived Gaullist *rassemblement* as one of the bases of a future regime reflecting his constitutional ideas. The opportunity to establish such a regime came in 1958 as one of the conditions he put on his becoming leader of the last government of the Fourth Republic. He was elected President of the Fifth Republic on 21 December 1958 by an electoral college of 81 764 parliamentarians, members of assemblies of overseas territories, and local elected representatives, easily beating two other unknown candidates and receiving 78.5 per cent of the votes cast.

Presidency   De Gaulle began his Presidency having struggled as leader of the government during the second half of 1958 particularly with the problem of the economy and that of Algeria. De Gaulle's government and that of Michel Debré after de Gaulle became President were able to bring the economy to a relatively healthy state by stern fiscal and monetary measures, helped by strong growth in the four years after January 1959 which coincided with, and was partly caused by, the early measures of the European Economic Community. On Algeria, de Gaulle had to tread more warily, but already in this field he was establishing a dominance in the making of policy. The setting up in the Elysée Palace, the President's official residence, of policy advisory groups on Algerian affairs, on matters concerning African colonies (members of a French *Communauté*, but independent by 1960), and on defence issues, together with the close control of foreign affairs in general through the Quai d'Orsay was a reflection of his personal interests and in keeping with his views on the President's role in the new regime. Though his policy initiatives on Europe (close political cooperation only under French management, outside the Brussels machinery) and on the NATO alliance (France, Britain and USA to form a decision-making core) were not successful, the French people, consulted in referenda, supported his policy of self-determination for Algeria in 1960 and the peace which emerged in 1962 from the difficult implementation of that policy.

During this time, it came to be accepted by the regime's supporters that the President initiated policy in the *'domaine réservé'*[1] of foreign and defence matters, and could take over responsibility if he wished in the area, usually left to the Government, of economic and social policy. Parliament, though divided in composition among the six 'political families' of postwar France, nevertheless refrained while the Algerian war lasted from provoking the political crisis which would have resulted from bringing down the government on a vote of censure. De Gaulle's desire, however, to confirm his own view of Presidential domination in constitutional terms, and to increase the legitimacy of his successors, led to a constitutional conflict between the traditional parties and de Gaulle and his supporters. The matter was resolved in de Gaulle's favour by the French people, consulted in a referendum (October 1962) and legislative elections (November 1962). The referendum allowed a change in the method of electing the President of the Republic, no longer chosen by a large electoral college, but by the people as a whole in a two-round ballot; and the elections gave a majority of seats in the new Parliament to deputies willing to support a Government implementing de Gaulle's policies.

Whereas before this change, de Gaulle had spoken of the President as *'le guide de la France'* and the Presidency as the *'clé de voûte'* of the institutional structure, in January 1964 he went further and said that *'le Président est évidemment seul à détenir et à déléguer l'autorité de l'Etat'*, and in the same press conference claimed that *'il n'existe aucune autre autorité ni ministérielle, ni civile, ni militaire, ni judiciaire, qui ne soit conférée et maintenue par lui'*. This assertion has been interpreted as very close to a denial of the total independence of the judiciary, a long-standing tenet of democratic thought.

France under de Gaulle's Presidency enjoyed comparative economic prosperity, but the nuclear striking force (*force de frappe*), later renamed 'deterrent force' (*force de dissuasion*) was expensive and the fruits of growth were in general badly distributed, leaving gaps in social provision, especially housing and education. Serious civil strife in 1968 – the 'events' of May–June –shook the regime, and de Gaulle resigned in April 1969 when he staked his political future on a reform of regional powers and Senate composition (plus a minor constitutional change) rejected in a referendum by the people, whose approval of Presidential policy had always been regarded by de Gaulle as conferring a special legitimacy.

Georges Pompidou

Background Pompidou was born in 1911 in the *département* of Cantal, in the south-eastern Massif Central, of peasant stock, though his parents had become primary school teachers. Educated in Paris, he taught there during the Second World War and, although not one of the *gaullistes de guerre*, he became head of de Gaulle's personal staff, and then a banker in the Rothschild group. Though he was again head of a section of de Gaulle's staff in the second half of 1958, he was not passionately enough drawn to politics to want to participate in the government or seek a parliamentary seat. But he was always close enough to de Gaulle to be given special missions, and to be one of his three nominees on the newly-established Constitutional Council. On the dismissal of Debré in April 1962, Pompidou was appointed Prime Minister by de Gaulle, and remained in that office until July 1968, when ostensibly for showing up de Gaulle's vacillation in the midst of crisis, he was replaced. De Gaulle's premature retirement from politics in April 1969 left the field open for Pompidou to succeed as President, receiving 57.5 per cent of votes in the second round against Alain Poher.

Presidency Pompidou's victory in the Presidential election of 1969 was more than the personal triumph of a formerly reluctant politician who had nevertheless served a successful apprenticeship as Prime Minister. It was confirmation by the electorate that presidential domination was an accepted characteristic of the regime. Pompidou won on a policy of continuing the Fifth Republic in all its aspects – not just those inherent in the 1958 Constitution but those which had been modified (that is, the new method of electing the President) and particularly those which had been developed, sometimes with doubtful constitutionality, by de Gaulle. The victory of any of the other candidates would have meant a return to the letter of the Constitution, though including the 1962 modification. Pompidou's succession signified that the Presidency had become institutionalised, that is, that the dominant position of the Presidency, based on the inherent powers of the office and those which had developed in the first ten years, was not particularly a function of the man who had been President during that time, but rather a function of the office itself. Pompidou in his book *Le Noeud gordien* referred to this new dimension when, in the context of future Presidents, he spoke of *'cette suprématie qu'ils ne tiendront pas du coefficient personnel'*. Pompidou was shrewd enough to abandon some of de Gaulle's more unrealistic policies, by permitting the devaluation of the franc and enlargement of the EEC, though the 1972 referendum on this issue was far from being the approval of his Presidency which Pompidou sought.

His long period as Prime Minister had given him the taste for control of policy-making in social and economic areas, and although his first Prime Minister, Chaban-Delmas, was encouraged to pursue a mild reforming policy under the slogan *'la nouvelle société'*, this was terminated in 1972 by a President fearful of the effects on what he considered to be a basically conservative society. His definition of the functions of President in a 1969 press conference shows how far he continued and developed de Gaulle's views:

A la fois chef suprême de l'Exécutif, gardien et garant de la Constitution, le President est à ce double titre chargé de donner les impulsions fondamentales, de définer les directions essentielles, et d'assurer et de contrôler le bon fonctionnement des pouvoirs publics; à la fois arbitre et premier responsable national.

The final phase of his Presidency, however, was characterised by a worsening economic situation and increasing divisions among his supporters in Gaullist circles and in the country at large. His death in April 1974 came after a long period of progressive deterioration of health.

Valéry Giscard d'Estaing
Background Giscard d'Estaing was born in 1926 in Koblenz, Germany, where his father was a senior administrator in the French occupation authorities. After a brief military career in 1944–5, he completed his education at the *Ecole Polytechnique* and the newly-opened *Ecole Nationale d'Administration*, and became *Inspecteur des Finances*. Elected to the National Assembly in 1956 as part of a loosely-structured group of Independents or *Modérés*, he

welcomed de Gaulle's return to power in 1958 and was a junior minister in Debré's government before in 1962 becoming Minister of Finance, a post he occupied until he was dismissed in 1966. Although he had supported de Gaulle in the 1962 constitutional battle with the old political parties, and formed his own group of *Républicains Indépendants* which backed the Gaullists, by 1969 his reservations led him to oppose de Gaulle's plans for extension of regional powers and reform of Senate composition, which were rejected by the people in a referendum. Hard-line Gaullists held him in great measure responsible for de Gaulle's subsequent resignation, but he was again Minister of Finance under the two Prime Ministers of President Pompidou. On the latter's death in 1974 Giscard proved to be the Presidential candidate on the Right who could mobilise the widest support, and in the second round with 50.8 per cent of the votes, he narrowly beat François Mitterrand.

Presidency Giscard appointed, as Prime Minister, Jacques Chirac, the Gaullist whose support in the Presidential election had been an important factor in his victory. Giscard had in the late 1960s criticised what he called de Gaulle's *'exercice solitaire du pouvoir'* but his own approach, while in form favouring liberal reforms, was in substance a continuation and an extension of the notion that the President decides government policy and ministers are responsible for carrying it out. He said in 1974, *'mon interprétation est l'interprétation présidentialiste des institutions'*, and this led to a less than amicable resignation by Chirac in 1976. Giscard's problem was the incompatibility between what the journalist and philosopher Raymond Aron called *'une philosophie orléaniste et un comportement bonapartiste'*. The suspicion remained that he became President as part of a well-marked career structure[2], rather than to fulfil a mission, or at least that his optimism, initial reforming zeal and desire to reduce the level of conflict in French politics (*la décrispation*) were either less than totally heartfelt, or politically unrealistic. His optimism often sounded hollow in the worsening economic circumstances of the 1970s; his social reforms, while not insignificant at the beginning of his Presidency, later met growing opposition from his own camp; and his efforts to temper what he called the 'Manichean' nature of French politics foundered on the growing conviction of the Left, based on local election successes, that it could well gain a majority in Parliament and capture the all-important Presidency. Like the Orleanist monarchy with which Giscard's Presidency was sometimes compared, by the end of his period of office he seemed to lack a proved coherent policy and a well-structured political organisation, preferring to rely on his own aura, which however was flawed by personal idiosyncracy and misjudgment. Maurice Duverger said in his book on Presidentialism *Echec au roi;* *'Ce grand bourgeois solitaire vit au temps des notables et non des structures.'* But although he reinforced Presidential primacy in all spheres of policy, effectively burying the concept of *domaine réservé* which in 1974 he said he had in any case never accepted, Giscard also refrained from the more doubtful constitutional deformation of which de Gaulle, and to a certain extent Pompidou, had been guilty. In this way, the Fifth Republic regime was able to achieve a measure of maturity, not least in being accepted by the Left, which no longer proposed major changes in the text or practice of the Constitution. Giscard faithfully conformed to the Constitution in three main areas:

Article 11 (referendum):   Whereas the referendum was used by de Gaulle on four occasions and Pompidou once as a means of procuring direct popular support for themselves in times of uncertainty, Giscard said that it should be used, if at all, to decide a specific point when there was an executive–legislative rift, as provided in the Constitution, and not for plebiscitary ends.

Article 12 (dissolution of Parliament):   De Gaulle used his powers in this matter twice, in 1962 and 1968, but the motive was to go directly to the people to solve a political crisis. Giscard, faced with the strong possibility of a Left victory in the 1978 parliamentary elections, which did not in the end materialise, implied that if it happened he would neither resign, nor readily dissolve the new Assembly in the hope that the electorate would have second thoughts and return a Right-wing majority.

Article 16 (emergency powers):   De Gaulle invoked Article 16 in April 1961 when an attempted *coup d'état* by part of the Army in Algeria threatened the integrity of the territory of the Republic, but he was heavily criticised for keeping it in operation until September 1961, though the revolt was crushed after four days. It was never conceivable that Giscard would use the power except in circumstances of acute emergency.

Giscard was also instrumental in adding a phrase to Article 61 of the Constitution, to allow 60 Deputies or 60 Senators to refer a matter to the Constitutional Council, a power until then limited to the President of the Republic, the Prime Minister, and the

Presidents of the two parliamentary assemblies. The new provision has been frequently invoked since than to protect the rights of the parliamentary minority and through this, the rights of individual citizens.

François Mitterrand

Background Born in 1916 in the *département* of Charente of comfortable provincial stock, Mitterrand had a rather studious childhood, which gave him a life-long love of literature and solitude. He completed his higher education in Paris in the 1930s, without becoming particularly politically-minded. An unenthusiastic conscript from 1938, he was wounded and taken prisoner in 1940 but eventually escaped, found a semi-official post with the Vichy administration, then played a significant part in the Resistance. After the war, he was one of the founders of the *Union démocratique et socialiste de la Résistance* (UDSR), a small Left-wing but non-Marxist party, and was elected to the National Assembly in November 1946. From 1947 to 1957, he occupied a variety of ministerial posts, mostly minor, but rising to be Minister of the Interior (1954–5) and Minister of Justice (1956–7). He was a firm opponent of de Gaulle's return to power in 1958 and of the new Constitution which reduced the power of Parliament. During the 1960s he established a reputation as leader of the non-communist Left by his 'Republican' Presidential challenge to de Gaulle in 1965 and his leadership of a Federation encompassing the UDSR, orthodox socialists, the Radical Party and numerous Left-wing political clubs. Serious divisions among the non-Communist Left however, were not overcome until 1971 when the *Parti Socialiste* was founded with Mitterrand as First Secretary. He almost beat Giscard for the Presidency in 1974, basing his approach on cooperation with the Communist party and although this was too fragile to ensure a Left Parliamentary majority in the 1978 elections, it allowed him to turn the tables on Giscard in 1981, when he was elected President with 51.75 per cent of the votes cast in the second round.

Presidency The election of François Mitterrand to the Presidency at the third attempt, and the result of the June 1981 elections which sent a Left-wing majority to Parliament were regarded by most commentators as proof that the Fifth Republic regime could give France what it seemed before to lack – the facility for a peaceful transfer of power (*alternance*) between starkly opposed groups, rather than merely a shift of the governing coalition's location in the political spectrum. But it would not have been possible if the Left had not eventually come to regard the text and the practice of the Fifth Republic Constitution as something they could accept without feeling the need for significant changes. Already in the 1965 Presidential elections, Mitterrand was one of the first on the Left to see that, shorn of the personalisation of power introduced by de Gaulle, the provisions of the new Constitution could in large measure be the basis for Left-oriented policies. In 1974 and 1981 he accepted, as did the parties of the Left which supported him, the supremacy of the President within the institutional framework. His declaration in July 1981 that *'Le Président de la République peut à tout moment faire prévaloir l'opinion qu'il a de l'intérêt général'* seemed in keeping with the maximalist interpretation of *arbitrage* which characterised all his predecessors, as was his detailed outline of future policy in what he had called *'Cent dix propositions pour la France'*.

But his background of practical humanism, and experiences reinforcing that part of his temperament which tended to solitary reflection, made him stand back rather further than his predecessors from the daily and weekly pattern of executive action. While retaining control of foreign and defence matters, and relations with French-speaking Africa, as well as matters of personal interest such as law reform[3], he nevertheless marked his authority less by imposing his personality or making grandiose gestures, than by limiting himself to establishing what he called in September 1981 *'les grandes directions, les grandes orientations'*. Because of this, the Prime Minister and other members of the Government regained some initiative in policy matters. But because the Government had to be a faithful representation of the whole range of opinion which had elected Mitterrand (that is, the *majorité présidentielle*), this sometimes led to public differences of emphasis which served to make the policy process less opaque than previously, but which the President had to arbitrate. On major constitutional matters, it is possible to say that Mitterrand views Article 11 (referendum) and Article 16 (emergency powers) in the same conformist way as Giscard, but in 1981 he used Article 12 (dissolution of National Assembly) in circumstances where Giscard said he would not –that is to solve the problems posed by the clash of a Presidential majority and a Parliamentary majority. The election of a Left Parliamentary majority solved matters in 1981, but as long as the President is elected for seven years and Parliament for five years, the problem remains.

Presidential elections

The positive result of the referendum of October 1962 led to the passing of a Constitutional law which changed the method of electing the President of the Republic. This new method applied in the 1965 elections, and in all others since that date. Presidential elections occur when an incumbent President's seven-year term of office (*septennat*) ends (1965, 1981) or when there is a vacancy because of the President's resignation (1969) or death (1974), which will be filled by the President of the Senate as temporary President until the ensuing election. A move to have the Prime Minister fulfil this role was part of a cluster of proposals rejected in the 1969 referendum.

Before a Presidential election, numerous individuals begin the process of candidature. No doubt hundreds contemplate the possibility of becoming a candidate, but others take it a stage further and make this contemplation known to the media, which then speak of these persons as *candidats à la candidature*: in anticipation of the 1981 elections, there were 64 such cases. Serious would-be candidates must put down a deposit of 10 000 francs which is lost if they receive less than 5 per cent of the votes cast. They must also obtain the support of sponsors (*parrains*) who must be parliamentarians, members of a *conseil général*, the *conseil de Paris*, an assembly of an overseas territory, or mayors – a total 'pool' of some 38 600 people, of whom 16 443 in 1981 returned completed sponsorship forms to the Constitutional Council. The number required used to be 100, but this led to the possibility of too many no-hope candidates (*candidats fantaisistes*), and a 1976 law increased the requirement to 500. To prevent purely regional candidatures, these 500 have to come from 30 *départements* at least, with not more than 50 from any one. The names of a candidate's sponsors are now published in random order in the *Journal officiel*, and this in 1981 caused political parties to worry about 'undesirable' sponsors appearing on their candidate's list.

In fact, the role of parties in Presidential elections is not always central. By no means all candidatures arise from initiatives by a political party. Presidential hopefuls are aware that if they link themselves too closely to one party, they limit themselves, at least for the first round of the election, to the percentage of support which that party would normally expect, and in the fragmented French party system this is much less than the 50 per cent which would get them elected. Candidates with a serious chance of being one of the two to go through to the second round usually either anticipate having the votes of other parties' electorates besides their own (*un report de voix*), or base their candidature in the first place on a specially mobilised group of people representing a wide range of political opinions and on a slogan not identifiable with a specific party, for example, *candidat républicain*, or *candidat d'union*.

French political parties, unlike their US counterparts, have no formal machinery for designating Presidential candidates. The less than total control which they have over Presidential elections has sometimes led to a rash of extra candidates of Left or Right, encouraged perhaps by opinion polls, who challenge front-runners and turn the first round into a US-style primary. In 1981, there were not only two main contenders from the Right-wing majority (Valéry Giscard d'Estaing and Jacques Chirac) but also Michel Debré and Marie-France Garaud from the same camp. On the Left, Michel Crépeau, and on the extreme Left, Arlette Laguiller and Huguette Bouchardeau also challenged François Mitterrand and Georges Marchais. The same fragmentation occurred in 1965 with the anti-Gaullist Right, in 1969 with the Left, and in 1974 with the Right. On the other hand, the 1981 Presidential election confirmed the trend of the 1978 Parliamentary and 1979 European elections in presenting to the electorate the image of a party system which was readily identifiable, that is, four main political groups reducible in a second round to two larger clusters of Right and Left. Before, the absence of a Communist first-round candidate in 1965 and 1974, and of a 'Liberal' in 1969 had given a distorted picture of the party structure.

The importance of the Presidency within the institutional structure means that a politician who aspires to the office must make careful preparations well in advance, planning for at least the next *septennat* but one. In the following Table the first date is the one when a Presidential career might reasonably have been first

Table 4.1

Presidential candidature – prepared in the long term

Candidate	
*Pompidou	1962 → [1965] → 1969 successful
*Giscard	1962 → [1965] → [1969] → 1974 successful
*Mitterrand	1964 → *1965* → [1969] → *1974* → 1981 successful
*Chirac	1974 → *1981* → ?
Rocard	1968 → *1969* → [1974] → 1981 → ?
Barre	1976 → [1981] → ?

contemplated (if not always publicly), and the last date the achievement of this (real or hypothetical). Dates between these show intervening elections without candidature e.g. [1965] or with candidature e.g. *1965* or where a candidature was withdrawn e.g 1981. An asterisk indicates Presidential aspirants who had to ensure that they had control of a major political party, in the sense that it accepted the idea of their Presidential candidacy, and was mobilised towards their victory. On the other hand, even serious candidatures which have matured over a shorter term, that is, less than a *septennat*, have been unsuccessful, as in the cases in Table 4.2.

Table 4.2

Presidential candidature – prepared in the short term

Candidate	
Poher	1969 → 1969 unsuccessful
Duclos	1969 → 1969 unsuccessful
Chaban-Delmas	1969 → 1974 unsuccessful
Marchais	1978 → 1981 unsuccessful

The case of Left-wing politicians in power since 1981 is complicated by the difficulty of establishing when they may have begun entertaining justifiable hopes of a future candidature, and how the Socialist Party will approach the questions of a post-Mitterrand candidate.

The official electoral campaign occupies the two weeks before the first round, ending two days before the ballot, and is supervised by a *Commission nationale de contrôle*. All candidates are given State aid to pay for the printing of election addresses in a prescribed format and for posters on official boards: in law, no other campaign poster can be displayed during the official campaign, but competitive fly-posting is a hallowed French pastime, and in any case a court decided the law was not being broken if hoardings were rented and posters stuck up before the opening of the official campaign, a possibility which gives an advantage to candidates with solid financial backing as well as a modern flavour to Presidential elections.

After the elections the State gives to candidates who have received at least 5 per cent of the votes cast, the sum of 250 000 francs for campaign expenses (raised from 100 000 francs in 1980). But because of the huge stakes of a Presidential election, actual expenditure is much higher – de Gaulle's campaign in 1965 is said to have cost 10 million francs, and that of Mitterrand in 1981 21.85 millions[4] at national level. The State, however, grants up to two hours free broadcasting time on television, and the same on radio, though this can be less if there is a large number of candidates – the share in 1981 was 70 minutes on each medium.

If no candidate obtains more than 50 per cent of the votes cast on the first round, a second round is held two weeks later, with a short official campaign period ending two days before. Only the two candidates who received most votes in the first round, allowing for withdrawals, can stand in the second round, and a constitutional law in 1976 filled a gap by providing that the whole process of election has to be started again if one of these candidates dies or is legally obliged to withdraw. In 1965 de Gaulle was the incumbent President, and in 1969 and 1974, the interim Presidency of Alain Poher ended as soon as the second-round winner was declared. The 1981 election introduced the question of when a defeated incumbent hands over power, which Giscard did 11 days after his second-round defeat, six days after the official declaration of the result, and three days before he was obliged to do so. This contrasts with the two and a half month period in the United States.

The Presidential entourage

Once installed in office in the Elysée Palace, the President of the Republic appoints his personal political staff, of people whom he knows well and whom he has reason to trust. In 1959, de Gaulle appointed mostly civil servants, especially diplomats, rather than rely on more explicitly political supporters, and he organised them into a general secretariat, to liaise with the Prime Minister and government departments, a personal cabinet to make and maintain wider contacts with the country, and a personal military staff to advise and get things done in military matters. A further branch to look after African and Madagascar affairs was influential under de Gaulle, but did not survive Giscard's accession to the Presidency. The importance of the general secretariat in relation to the cabinet has tended to grow, and the number of its *conseillers techniques* and *chargés de mission* can be large. Very much depends on the personal style of individual Presidents – Pompidou appointed close collaborators called *chargés de mission auprès du Président*, and this system has continued since. Giscard had a small personal staff, but Mitterrand preferred a larger number. The true size of a

Presidential staff is often larger than the official list (just over 40 in 1981).

President Mitterrand broke with the habits of his predecessors by not appointing many civil servants to his staff (about one third) but mostly political activists, with whom he had worked closely as leader of the Socialist Party from 1971, and as Presidential candidate in 1981. The proportion of those of his staff who were trained at the Ecole Nationale d'Administration (*énarques*) was also significantly reduced. The work and influence of the Elysée private staff will depend on the temperament of individual Presidents. The main duty is to know what is happening in Government circles, and to ensure that the President's wishes, whether expressed as policy guidelines or more detailed instructions, are not distorted. In this central position between government and President they are an important element in the exercise of executive power under the President's overall control.

Bibliographical guidance

Apart from significant coverage in the books listed under the General Bibliography for Chapters 4–7, the following deal with the Presidency of the Republic:

S. Cohen, *Les conseillers du Président* (PUF, 1980)
C. Debbasch, *L'Elysée dévoilée* (A. Michel, 1982)
M. Duverger, *Echec au roi* (A. Michel, 1978)
J. Massot, *La Présidence de la République en France* (La Documentation Francaise, 1977)
S. Rials, *La Présidence de la République* (PUF, 1981)

Political memoirs containing descriptions of the Executive in action are:

Y. Guéna, *Le temps des certitudes* (Flammarion, 1982)
F. Giroud, *La comédie au pouvoir* (Fayard, 1977)
M. Jobert, *Mémoires d'avenir* (Grasset, 1974)
E. Pisani, *Le général indivis* (A. Michel, 1973)
R. Poujade, *Le ministère de l'impossible* (Calmann-Levy, 1975)

On de Gaulle's Presidency:

C. de Gaulle, *Mémoires d'espoir*, 2 vols (Plon, 1970–1)
O. Guichard, *Mon général* (Grasset, 1981)

J. Lacouture, *Citations du Président de Gaulle* (Seuil, 1968)
B. Ledwidge, *De Gaulle* (Weidenfeld and Nicolson, 1982)
A. Passeron, *De Gaulle parle* (Fayard, 1976)
P. Viansson-Ponté *Histoire de la République Gaullienne* 2 vols (Fayard, 1970–1)
P.M. Williams and M. Harrison, *Politics and Society in de Gaulle's Republic* (Longman, 1971)

On Pompidou's Presidency:

C. Debbasch, *La France de Pompidou* (PUF, 1974)
F. Decaumont, *La Présidence de Georges Pompidou* (Economica, 1979)
G. Martinet, *Le système Pompidou* (Seuil, 1973)
G. Pompidou, *Le noeud gordien* (Plon, 1974)
G. Pompidou, *Pour rétablir une vérité* (Flammarion, 1982)
S. Rials, *Les idées constitutionnelles du Président Georges Pompidou* (PUF, 1977)

On Giscard's political career and Presidency:

J. Bothorel, *Le Pharaon* (Grasset, 1983)
C. Debbasch, *L'Elysée dévoilé* (A. Michel, 1982)
A. Duhamel, *Le république giscardienne* (Grasset, 1980)
T. Ferenczi, *Le prince au miroir* (A. Michel, 1981)
J.R. Frears, *France in the Giscard Presidency* (Allen & Unwin, 1981)
V. Giscard d'Estaing, *Démocratie francaise* (Fayard, 1976)
C. Hargrave, *L'autre Giscard* (Jeune Afrique, 1981)
A. Nourry, *Le combat singulier* (Denoel, 1980)
J.-C. Petitfils, *La démocratie giscardienne* (PUF, 1981)
'Table ronde sur le bilan constitutionnel du septennat in *Revue politique et parlementaire*, March 1981
O. Todd, *La marelle de Giscard 1926–1974* (R. Laffont, 1977)

On Mitterrand's political career and his conception of the Presidency:

T. Desjardins, *François Mitterrand, un socialiste gaullien* (Hachette, 1978)
A. Duhamel, *La république de Monsieur Mitterrand* (Grasset, 1982)
D. MacShane, *François Mitterrand – a Political Odyssey* (Quartet Books, 1982)
C. Manceron and B. Pingaud, *François Mitterrand – l'homme, les idées, le programme* (Flammarion, 1981)
F. Mitterrand, *Politique 2* (Fayard 1981) and other works by Mitterrand containing his political writings and answers to interviewers' questions
C. Moulin, *Mitterrand intime* (A. Michel, 1982)
M. Szafran and S. Katz, *Les familles du Président* (Grasset, 1982)

Among the many reactions by commentators to the political situation in France since 1981, the following are recommended:

La France socialiste – un premier bilan (Hachette, 1983), a collection
H. Amouroux, *Ce que vivent les roses* (R. Laffont, 1983)
Caton (pseudonym), *De la reconquête* (Fayard, 1983; paperback Hachette,
   1983)
Caton (pseudonym), *De la renaissance* (Fayard, 1983)
J. Charbonnel, *Comment peut-on être opposant?* (R. Laffont, 1983)
S. Denis, *La lecon d'automne – jeux et enjeux de François Mitterrand* (A.
   Michel, 1983)
J.-P. Dolle, *Monsieur le Président, il faut que je vous dise ...* (Lieu
   Commun, 1983)
J.-F Kahn, *Si on essayait autre chose* (Seuil, 1983)
A. Peyrefitte, *Quand la rose se fanera* (Plon, 1983)
Pouvoirs, no. 20 (1982), number devoted to 'La gauche au pouvoir'
O. Todd, *Une légère gueule de bois* (Grasset, 1983)
V. Wright (ed.), *Continuity and change in France* (Allen & Unwin, 1984)

Illustrative texts and linguistic exercises

Texte 4.1   Qu'est-il arrivé à la France?

Mise en situation

Jean-Pierre Moulin, écrivain–journaliste suisse, après une vingtaine
d'années passées à Paris, où il représentait la télévision suisse romande,
essaya dans son oeuvre *Qu'est-il arrivé à la France?* de sonder 'l'étrange
mystère français'. Pour lui, les campagnes électorales sont des moments
privilégiés où, dans le psychodrame de la course au pouvoir, la France se
dévoile.   *   *   *

1981

Mercredi 21 janvier: Roger Garaudy   Roger Garaudy se paie une page
entière dans *Le Monde* pour annoncer sa candidature.
   Etrange parcours que le sien. Il fut bon catholique puis, d'un paradis à
l'autre, bon communiste, très attaché à Staline. Exclu du comité central du
PC pour avoir osé noter publiquement quelques variations dans la
composition sociologique de la nation française, il découvre, après les
Pères Marx et Staline, notre Mère Nature. Il écrit des livres bien faits qui se
vendent bien. Ce sont des déclarations d'amour à la Vie. Il nous rappelle
–on ne le fera jamais assez – que 50 millions d'êtres humains crèvent de
faim chaque année et que nous avons tous, sous nos fesses individuelles,
nous autres habitants de la planète, 500 kg de TNT prêts à exploser.
   En conclusion de son *Appel aux vivants*, Roger Garaudy nous indique, *à
tout hasard*, le numéro de son compte de chèque postal.
Samedi 24 janvier: François Mitterrand La tribune du Congrès
socialiste à Créteil. Je n'ai d'yeux que pour François Mitterrand, au centre,
et pour Michel Rocard, relégué en bout de table.
   Mitterrand. Pâleur accentuée. Ses yeux qu'il jette de temps en temps, à

droite puis à gauche, comme pour surveiller l'avancée d'un ennemi potentiel. Prêt à faire front. *A dégainer.* En douceur. Rocard, vêtu de bleu sombre également pâle, l'air inquiet, presque abattu. Malheureux, semble-t-il, d'être *dévisagé*; pathétique quand, à l'interruption de la séance, la tribune se vide et qu'il reste quelques instants seul, comme orphelin. Il attend le départ des autres pour ramasser ses papiers et sa serviette. Regarde la salle. La voit-il telle qu'elle est en cet instant, bruissante, joyeuse, pleine d'exubérance et d'heureuse camaraderie? Tout à l'heure ils frappaient dans leur mains, en cadence, d'un même mouvement, les camarades socialistes. A la manière des communistes, aussi disciplinés, unanimes.

Mitterrand, candidat du parti socialiste! Loin, ce jour d'octobre, à Conflans-Sainte-Honorine. Loin la belle déclaration que Michel Rocard avait préparée pour les Français. François Mitterrand vient d'être désigné. Un vote indiscutable. On ne s'est même pas donné la peine de comptabiliser les rocardiens. Qu'en reste-t-il des rocardiens? Je n'entends plus que les exclamations, une rumeur jubilante. Tout commence ou plutôt recommence ici même. Ici, vient d'être tracée la ligne de départ de la folle épreuve qui doit aboutir, le 10 mai prochain, à l'élection d'un président pour la République française. Ce sera Giscard ou Mitterrand. J'ai l'impression d'être exactement à l'endroit où il faut pour observer le déroulement de la course et assister à un nouvel éveil de l'Histoire de ce pays. Perdu dans *l'enceinte* où les délégués crient plus fort que les haut-parleurs qui *débitent*, Dieu sait pourquoi, du folklore sud-americain, j'en oublie l'Hexagone pourtant directement concerné; j'en oublie les *grands ensembles* de Créteil qui m'ont impressionné quand je les ai traversés tout à l'heure, émergeant du brouillard d'hiver, avec les petites filles sur leur tricycle; les papas qui rentrent du supermarché, cabas de fin de semaine remplis; les jeunes filles en veste de cuir, trottant dans les allées bordées d'arbustes plantés au cordeau en pensant au rock de ce soir ...

Elle a changé, la France pendant le septennat de Giscard. Les enfants de 1974 sont devenus des adolescents à mobylette et les adolescents d'alors ont eu leur carte d'électeur à 18 ans. Ils sont chômeurs ou brillants étudiants.

A l'intérieur de la salle du Congrès, Mitterrand serre la main de Rocard avec un bon sourire fraternel, le temps viendra Michel, tu étais trop pressé, je suis peut-être un vieux mâle, mais un vieux mâle encore dominant.

Le Congrès n'en finit pas d'applaudir, tous mêlés dans l'euphorie, dans l'idée que la victoire est possible, les mitterrandistes *de vieille souche* ou tardivement ralliés, les amis de Mauroy en costume trois pièces, les lecteurs du Nouvel Obs, les vignerons du Sud-Ouest, les profs d'Aix-en-Provence, les cultivateurs catholiques de Bretagne, les derniers cheveux longs, nostalgiques de mai '68, les fonctionnaires qui dirigent la Caisse de Sécurité sociale de leur ville où les pères étaient ouvriers ou instituteurs, les membres du CERES figés dans l'idée narcissique qu'ils sont la conscience de la vraie gauche, celle de la lutte des classes, des nationalisations, de l'An II réunis ...

Mitterrand président! Pour la troisième fois il va tenter l'essai. Un disque est diffusé, *potentiomètre* poussé à mort. Il accompagnera la campagne du candidat. La rythmique en est un peu disco, déjà démodée mais qu'importe: au PS on aime que passé, présent et avenir s'enlacent. L'objectif à atteindre est le bonheur des hommes, et le bonheur chacun le sait, est intemporel, *eschatologique* ...

Je ne résiste pas à consigner dans mon Journal quelques vers de ce cantique laïque:

> Pour vivre autrement
> Pour un monde sans chômeurs
> Qu'est-ce qu'on attend?
> Votons Mitterrand!
> *Au refrain*:
> Mit-ter-rand ... Pré-si-dent ... (*bis*)

Mardi 3 février: Jacques Chirac Coluche: une rampe et des projecteurs. Marie-France Garaud: le salon arts-déco du Lutetia. Mitterrand: la tribune du Congrès socialiste à Créteil. Chaque candidat soigne le décor dans lequel il vient interpréter la première scène de sa candidature. Les privilégiés qui disposent d'une mairie ou d'un palais officiel ont un net avantage sur les *sans-grades*.

Pour Jacques Chirac, ce fut l'hôtel de ville de Paris. Bouffées de rappels historiques. Il parle. Dieu qu'il aime parler. Mais pourquoi se plaque-t-il les cheveux comme le faisaient les jeunes durs des années 40? Il est beau. Beau comme les séducteurs des cartes postales de jadis. Il n'est pas antipathique mais il pourrait le devenir. Il suffirait qu'il durcisse un peu le ton, qu'il crispe quelque chose dans son visage *avenant*, plein de séduction électorale classique: vous êtes si bien, vous, oui vous à qui je m'adresse et moi aussi je suis bien. On va s'entendre, vous savez! Et puis il y a la France ...

'La France est riche d'histoire et de culture. Elle a les moyens de la grandeur et du progrès et pourtant elle s'affaiblit.'

C'est ainsi qu'il faut parler aux Français (du moins le croit-il). Le passé: grandiose! Cela va sans dire. Mais le présent, quel malheur! Le présent est gris, fade et désolante la décadence de la France.

Le vocabulaire chiraquien est en place. Des idées générales, des *formules redondantes*. L'enflure ne fait pas peur au candidat du RPR. Ni le simplisme symétrique de la pensée. La France sans Chirac? Economie qui vacille, lassitude de l'âme nationale, doute, perte de l'idéal, repli sur soi. Avec Chirac? Ambition, volonté, effort, espoir rendu aux familles françaises, autorité républicaine et sécurité du citoyen rétablies.

Sondage-flash servi tout chaud quelques heures après l'annonce de la candidature Chirac: 47 pour-cent des Français pensent que c'est une bonne chose. 33 pour-cent d'un avis contraire.

Un autre sondage. Selon Public SA, une boîte qui a de l'humour, un Français sur dix souhaite être président de la République. Il y aurait de ce fait dans l'Hexagone trois millions huit cent mille candidats potentiels. Je commence à comprendre pourquoi une élection présidentielle en France, c'est beaucoup plus qu'une simple consultation des citoyens: la libération de forces inconscientes, bouillonnantes, qui, sans le *bienfaisant happening*, risqueraient de faire exploser cette nation brûlante de passion politicienne. Jamais plus je ne permettrai à un étranger, fût-ce un de mes compatriotes helvétiques pour qui j'ai de l'indulgence et dont je partage certains effrois à l'egard des *débordements* francais, de critiquer comme il le fait le nombre élevé de candidatures à une 'presidentielle française'.

SOURCE: Jean-Pierre Moulin, *Qu'est-il arrivé à la France? – un étranger dans l'Hexagone* (Seuil, 1982) pp. 160–5.

Exploitation du texte

1 Expliquez en quelques mots le sens des expressions en italique.

2 Ecrivez un brève biographie politique de:

Michel Rocard
François Mitterrand
Marie-France Garaud
Jacques Chirac

3 Donnez plusieurs détails des événements suivants pour en dégager la signification politique:

l'exclusion de Roger Garaudy du comité central du Parti communiste (1970)
la déclaration de candidature de Michel Rocard à Conflans-Sainte-Honorine (octobre, 1980)
la candidature de Coluche à l'élection présidentielle de 1981.

4 Quels sont les effets stylistiques conjugués de l'absence quasi-totale de conjonctions et de la prédominance de phrases courtes?

5 Rédigez une manchette et un résumé (d'une vingtaine de lignes environ) du texte en tant que journaliste écrivant pour un ou plusieurs des quotidiens suivants: *Le Monde, L'Humanité, Le Figaro, France-Soir.*

Texte 4.2   L'Election à la Magistrature Suprême

Mise en situation
Maurice Druon, membre de l'Académie francaise et auteur de romans contemporains, historiques et mythologiques, fut Ministre des Affaires Culturelles en 1973–4. Son livre *Réformer la démocratie*, paru en 1982, fit une analyse des défaillances d'une France où 'toute idée de grandeur ou simplement de survie' semble avoir disparu. Les propositions avancées par l'auteur visent à restaurer ou à instaurer dans l'Etat une éthique de la *res publica* sans laquelle l'avenir de la nation serait compromis.

*   *

L'élection par un collège de notables a été pratiquée en France une fois, au début de la Ve République, et elle a *décemment* fonctionné. Mais n'importe quel procédé eût pu servir aussi bien; le pays sortait d'un désarroi tragique, le drame d'Algérie était à son paroxysme, et il y avait de Gaulle pratiquement désigné par le consensus général de la nation. Nul doute que le système ne se fut à l'usage corrompu et perverti; et il ne faut pas beaucoup d'imagination pour supposer ce que les partis et les manipulateurs électoraux en eussent fait.

L'élection du chef de l'Etat au suffrage universel, introduite dans la constitution française en '62, par voie de référendum, prétendait remédier aux défauts des autres modes de désignation.

On comprend bien les considérations qui inspirèrent de Gaulle. Ce procédé tend à établir un lien direct et secret entre le citoyen et le magistrat suprême. Il est un substitut du sacre. Le peuple vraiment souverain désigne son prince. Dans l'ancienne France, les douze pairs, qui symboliquement soutenaient du doigt la couronne lors du sacre, représentaient l'assemblée des barons et 'hauts hommes' qui choisissaient le roi, du temps de la monarchie élective. Dans la nouvelle France, ce serait la majorité des citoyens qui soutiendrait le siège présidentiel. *Vox populi, vox dei.*

En fait, le système ne s'est pas révélé meilleur que les autres; peut-être même pourrait-il devenir plus nocif encore. En effet, à défaut d'un personnage historique, revêtu d'une légitimité préalable, comme l'était de Gaulle, l'élection au suffrage universel est la voie ouverte *aux démagogues ou aux aventuriers.* *

De Gaulle avait compté sans la capacité des partis, ces hydres dont aucun Héraklès ne coupera jamais toutes les têtes, à se modeler sur n'importe quel système pour l'étouffer.

Il avait compté sans la télévision et les sondages d'opinion, moyens de manipuler les masses qui n'avaient pas encore, en son temps, l'ampleur et les effets formidables qu'ils ont acquis depuis. Il avait compté sans le 'marketing politique', ce terme qui déshonore la langue pour désigner des méthodes qui déshonorent la République. Il avait compté sans l'argent. Si visionnaire qu'il fût, il ne pouvait pas imaginer absolument ce qui était totalement contraire à sa propre nature.

Désormais, une campagne présidentielle, en France, pour avoir quelque chance de succès, pour être 'crédible', réclame des sommes d'argent aussi colossales que celles engagées dans les élections américaines. D'autre part, elle suscite une intervention des partis bien plus directe, bien plus intense que dans une élection par les Assemblées; elle conduit ces partis à devenir avant tout des *appareils électoraux.* Elle amène au pouvoir des hommes qui ont peut-être toutes les qualités qu'il faut pour être portés à la tête d'une

---

*On a dit souvent que la constitution de 58 était taillée aux mesures de De Gaulle, et pour lui seul. Le reproche était faux, ainsi que la suite des choses l'a montré. En revanche, c'est la disposition de '62 qui ne valait vraiment que pour un homme de son exceptionnelle stature.

Cette disposition, dès l'origine, pouvait inspirer de sérieuses inquiétudes sur les dangers qu'elle recelait, non pour l'immédiat, mais pour l'avenir.

formation politique et faire impression à la télévision, mais non celles forcément que requiert le gouvernement d'une grande action. Elle peut amener demain des *chefs de clans* ou de ligues.

La majorité parlementaire, dans la logique de ce système, doit coïncider avec la majorité présidentielle, puisque le président élu devient la source véritable du pouvoir; et cela peut aggraver catastrophiquement les erreurs de choix. En fait, l'élection du chef de l'Etat au suffrage universel peut être un parfait moyen légal de remettre le gouvernement de la République à ceux-là mêmes qui ont pour dessein de la détruire et d'installer à sa place un *despotisme*, fût-ce avec l'aide, pourquoi pas, de l'étranger.

Mais d'où vient, alors, que tous les systèmes expérimentés soient mauvais? De la nature humaine? C'est trop vite dit. N'est-ce pas plutôt dans la nature de la démocratie qu'il faut chercher le vice qui en altère l'exercice?

Le péché cardinal de la démocratie, c'est le fait que l'on soit forcé de se porter candidat, de se présenter soi-même à la fonction élective, et tout spécialement lorsqu'il s'agit de la *magistrature suprême*. C'est la candidature qui pourrit la République.

Car être candidat suppose que l'on se conduise en solliciteur. Cette obligation répugne aux âmes fières, les plus dignes précisément de la fonction.

L'acte de candidature, avec tout ce qu'il implique, a pour premier effet d'éloigner ou dissuader de la compétition des hommes parfaitement aptes à la grandeur de la tâche, parfaitement inaptes à s'abaisser.

Etre candidat à la première charge de l'Etat, c'est aussi faire acte public d'immodestie: 'Je suis le meilleur ...' tout en quémandant aux autres qu'ils vous reconaissent ce mérite; *situation paradoxale* qui met le postulant en position de demandeur, donc d'inférieur, alors que la charge postulée doit lui conférer supériorité sur ceux qui la lui confient.

L'acte de candidature a pour deuxième effet que les électeurs regardent d'avance l'élu come leur débiteur, puisqu'il avait tellement envie de recueillir leur vote. On se plaît à dire que le suffrage est un sacre; mais la candidature *désacralise*.

Les lois, certes, font interdiction de porter atteinte à la personne du chef de l'Etat parce qu'à travers lui c'est à la majesté de la République que l'on *attente*. Mais ce personnage, que tout doit entourer de respect dès son élection proclamée, était, jusqu'à la veille du scrutin, dénigré, *vilipendé* et souvent insulté par ses adversaires; on cherchait à le décrier, et le déshonorer si possible en fouillant dans son passé et celui de sa famille, en répandant sur lui vérités nocives ou *calomnies* déliberées. Celles-ci ne seront pas oubliées, ni dans le pays, ni à l'étranger. Et le voilà élu quand même!

Troisième effet de la candidature: elle amène à une fonction qui requiert le maximum de prestige un personnage contesté, et, aux yeux de certains, discrédité.

Le magistrat suprême doit avoir les mains libres. Or la candidature l'entrave de tous côtés. Car il a fallu au candidat l'appui d'un parti ou de plusieurs. Il est lié de ce côté-là. Il lui a fallu de l'argent, beaucoup d'argent, pour mener campagne; or l'argent ne coule pas toujours de source pure; et ceux qui le lui ont fourni ne l'ont pas fait pour rien. Il leur est lié.

Il a fallu au candidat s'entourer d'agents électoraux et de spécialistes divers, y compris pour les *basses oeuvres* dirigées contre ses adversaires, sans pouvoir se montrer trop exigeant sur les procédés ou les antécédents de ses partisans. Il lui a fallu accepter des *bénévolats* encombrants. Les services rendus, il aura à les payer, de facon ou d'autre, sauf à se faire d'immédiats ennemis de ceux qui l'auront soutenu. Il est lié de toutes parts, quatrième effet de la candidature.

Le candidat à la présidence doit promettre, promettre, promettre à tout le monde, même s'il sait pertinemment qu'il ne pourra pas tenir ses promesses ou que, s'il veut les honorer, elles seront funestes à l'intérêt public. Mais il lui faut flatter la foule et ses catégories ... Jamais candidat, sauf en période de drames et quand le peuple tremble, se fit-il élire sur un programme de rigueur? Mais, une fois élu, ou bien il ne tiendra pas ses promesses et il perdra la confiance de ses supporters; ou bien il les tiendra, et alors c'est le pays qui en pâtira.

Le vainqueur de l'élection est le Président de tous les citoyens, bien sûr; c'est ce qu'on dit, c'est ce qu'il dit. Mais il n'est tout de même l'élu que de cinquante et quelques des électeurs sur cent, et le vrai candidat de trente ou quarante seulement dans le meilleur des cas, les votes complémentaires ne l'ayant pris que pour *pis-aller*. La joie qu'il *affiche*, à la proclamation des résultats, alors que des responsabilités terribles lui tombent sur les épaules, et l'explosion de triomphe de ses partisans ont quelque chose d'inquiétant et d'indécent. On paraît oublier que les perdants aussi font partie de la nation. Prétendre après cela s'élever au-dessus des partis est un leurre. Le pays reste partagé entre vainqueurs et vaincus. Parmi tous les citoyens minoritaires. beaucoup, dans le fond de leur coeur, ne reconnaîtront jamais l'élu de l'autre bord. Il restera, et d'abord pour ses rivaux malheureux, l'insupportable gagnant, dont on espérera les fautes, dont on contestera les succès, dont on attendra ou provoquera la chute. Voilà le cinquième effet, non le moins grave.

Tout cela est la conséquence de la candidature.

Or, il n'est pas certain que ce mal soit incurable. Il existe un système d'élection que les démocraties modernes n'ont jamais expérimenté et qui pourtant a fait ses preuves, un système où l'on n'est pas, où l'on ne doit pas être candidat, où il n'y a pas à faire campagne, où l'on ne s'humilie pas, où l'on ne montre ni ambition ni orgueil, mais où l'on est choisi par des pairs, par des hommes qui tous ont des titres à juger de l'ensemble de qualifications et de vertus requises par la charge, et qui désignent par vote secret celui qu'ils estiment le plus apte à l'assumer. Ce système, c'est celui du *conclave*.

SOURCE: Maurice Druon, *Réformer la démocratie* (Plon, 1982)
pp. 35–42.

Exploitation texte

1 Expliquez en quelques mots les expressions en italique.

2 Résumez brièvement les arguments de l'auteur en faveur de sa thèse: 'la candidature .. pourrit la démocratie'.

3 Faites un bref résumé historique des événements qui on conduit à la modification du mode d'élection du Président de la République en octobre 1962.

4 Pour quelles raisons pourrait-on dire que le terme 'marketing politique' déshonore la langue?

5 Relevez et expliquez toutes les occurrences du subjonctif dans ce texte.

6 Ce texte contient bon nombre de mots émotifs, voire hyperboliques. Faites-en la liste, en les regroupant selon qu'ils sont mélioratifs ou péjoratifs. Quelles attitudes en ressortent de la part de l'auteur?

Exercices de comparaison et d'application

1 Imaginez que vous êtes un des dix pour-cent de Français qui souhaite être Président de la République. Formulez le texte de ce que vous feriez paraître sur une page entière du *Monde* qui vous a été payée.

2 Composez un nouvel Article 7 de la Constitution de la République Française précisant les modalités de l'élection du Président de la République par conclave.

3 Quels seraient les arguments pour et contre l'élection du Président de la République par conclave?

4 En employant le style du texte 4.1, rédigez un article décrivant l'élection par conclave d'un Président de la République et l'annonce du résultat aux foules attendant devant le Ministère de l'Intérieur.

5 En utilisant un langage fortement émotif, faites soit l'éloge soit la critique du phénomène de la présidentialisation du régime de la Cinquième République.

5
Government and Administration

In applying themselves to the problem of establishing the duties and powers of the Government, the body exercising Executive power, the framers of the Fifth Republic Constitution had to bear in mind;

1 their own desire to reduce the ease with which Parliament could overthrow the Government by an adverse vote;
2 the need to make compatible the Government's role in running the country with the new powers given to the President.
3 the tradition, emerging during the course of the nineteenth century, and finally established in the 1870s, of having a Head of Government to coordinate Government activity. The 1958 Constitution called him a *Premier ministre* instead of the previous *Président du Conseil des Ministres*.

The Prime Minister

The Prime Minister's functions are outlined in Article 21, and his responsibility for directing Government activity is made clear in paragraph 1. Many of his duties are carried out in conjunction with the President of the Republic. In military matters, a subtle balance is maintained, in order to ensure that the armed forces are subject to civilian control, between the Prime Minister who is responsible for national defence (Article 21-1), the Government which has at its disposal the armed forces (Article 20-2), and the President who is commander-in-chief, and who chairs the most important defence committees (Article 15). The Prime Minister however chairs these bodies in the President's absence (Article 21-3), and can be given responsibility (Article 21-1) for the appointment of military personnel, which is normally in the President's power (Article 13).

The same is true regarding the appointment of civil servants, and in the general field of administration the principle of the complementarity of Presidential and Prime Ministerial functions is followed. The President promulgates laws passed by Parliament

(Article 10), but the Prime Minister makes sure they are put into effect (Article 21-1). The power to make executive orders (*le pouvoir réglementaire*) to implement policy decisions is also shared. The President issues ordinances as well as decrees drawn up in the Council of Ministers, the weekly meeting of all Ministers (Article 13), and these are countersigned by the Prime Minister.

The latter also has *le pouvoir réglementaire* (Article 21-1), in that he issues decrees not important enough to be the subject of discussion in the Council of Ministers. The Prime Minister chairs the Council of Ministers in the President's absence, but this role must be explicitly delegated to him and the agenda must be agreed in advance (Article 21-4). He has the power, along with the President of the Republic, the Presidents of both Parliamentary

Table 5.1
Prime Ministerial involvement in Presidential powers

Art. 8-2	*Prime Minister*	*proposes* names of Government ministers	before the President appoints them
Art. 11	Government (under *Prime Minister*) or joint motion of both Assemblies	*proposes* a referendum	which the President can put to the people
Art. 12	*Prime Minister* and Presidents of both Assemblies	*are consulted*	by the President before dissolving National Assembly
Art. 16	*Prime Minister* and Presidents of both Assemblies *and* Constitutional Council	*are consulted*	by the President before he takes the necessary measures
Art. 29	*Prime Minister* or a majority of members of National Assembly	*asks for* an extraordinary session of Parliament	which is opened and closed by Presidential decree
Art. 89	*Prime Minister*	*proposes* a revision of the Constitution	which the President can put to referendum, or to Parliament in Congress

Assemblies and, since 1974, 60 deputies or 60 senators, of referring
a matter to the Constitutional Council, which pronounces on its
constitutionality.

A further area in which the functions of President and Prime
Minister intertwine is where the latter is associated with the exercise
of important Presidential powers (see Table 5.1).

However, both the power of proposal and the element of prior
consultation provided for in the 1958 Constitution have never been
fully respected since 1958 (though extraordinary sessions of
Parliament are normal to complete government business). They are
one example of the way in which the supremacy of President and
the concomitant subordination of the Prime Minister have become
a feature of the Fifth Republic regime. The Gaullian concept of the
President's function, and his maximalist interpretation of the
notion of *arbitrage*, were extended or consolidated by his
successors and this led quickly to the abandonment of the idea,
made explicit in Article 20, that under the direction of the Prime
Minister, *'le Gouvernement détermine et conduit la politique de la
Nation'*. A survey of the careers of Fifth Republic Prime Ministers
shows the way in which the function evolved.

Michel Debré: January 1959–April 1962
Debré was appointed Prime Minister by de Gaulle because, while
very close to him politically and a central figure in the drafting of
the new Constitution, he had had sufficient Parliamentary
experience as a Senator to be acceptable to the National Assembly
newly elected in November 1958. Temperamentally, moreover, he
was deferential enough not to let his own views that Algeria should
remain French prevent him from continuing to support and apply
the other main policies of de Gaulle, even when the latter moved to
a position of self-determination (implying independence) for
Algeria.

He accepted de Gaulle's choice of Ministers, mainly from outside
politics, and de Gaulle's interpretation of Article 9 of the
Constitution, whereby the President not only chaired the Council
of Ministers but imposed his policy initiatives on it, thus robbing it
of collegial responsibility. These developments, and the setting up
in the Elysée of policy advisory groups in key foreign and defence
areas all served to deprive Article 20 of meaning and to reduce the
role of the Prime Minister in relation to the President, though
Debré was always a hard-working director of Government day-to-
day business.

After the acceptance by the electorate in a referendum of the terms of a peace treaty with the provisional Algerian government, Debré was thinking in terms of a dissolution and a new Parliament for the return to 'normal' times. De Gaulle however preferred an alternative solution, that of a new Prime Minister and Government, and accepted Debré's resignation. Whether he had asked for a signed, undated letter of resignation on appointing him in 1959 is a matter of dispute between political memoir writers, but de Gaulle implied in his letter of acceptance on Debré's resignation that it had been agreed that the latter would go as soon as he was required to do so.

Georges Pompidou: April 1962–July 1968

Pompidou had never been elected to political office, and when he became Prime Minister, his appointment was taken as – and is usually accepted as being intended to be – a calculated affront to Parliament, which for de Gaulle signified party politics. De Gaulle said of him in his *Mémoires d'Espoir* that *'il incline vers les attitudes prudentes et les démarches réservées'*. Such a man was needed, not only to continue the role of a Prime Minister subordinate to the President, but also to help guide France in a period when Gaullist political ambitions and Frenchmen's increased welfare demands called for delicate management of the economy. His first appearances in Parliament were far from successful, but very quickly he imposed his will on his Government team and on the Gaullist party: the popularity of 'legislative' Gaullism increased as that of de Gaulle as President gradually fell. Pompidou became much better known to his fellow-countrymen than his predecessor, through provincial tours and media appearances – aspects of the increasing 'nationalisation' of French politics in the 1960s. By the gradual introduction of his protégés into party and Government, he established 'Pompidolism' as that particular manifestation of Gaullism which would survive de Gaulle's departure from politics.

But in terms of policy initiative, the end of the Algerian war in 1962 meant a further increase in Presidential influence. Key ministers and top civil servants often formed small committees on important policy areas, chaired by de Gaulle. The pyramidal structure of policy making, far different from the more collegial process of previous Republics, was completed at the base by interministerial committees and working parties which, even if chaired by the Prime Minister, would normally include a representative of the Elysée. The two aspects of the Prime Ministerial functions – cooperation but subordination – were fully accepted by Pompidou. He said in a National Assembly debate in 1964: '*Je ne saurais continuer à porter mes responsabilités si je n'étais pas pleinement d'accord avec lui (le chef de l'Etat) sur tous les aspects de la politique.*' Pompidou's assessment of political situations, more realistic than that of de Gaulle, allowed him to help the latter to recover from the ignominy of not being re-elected President on the first round in 1965, by advising him on how best to prepare for victory in the second-round run-off. This may have contributed to the increasing coolness between the two men. A Gaullist writer later said de Gaulle had asked Pompidou soon afterwards for a signed, undated letter of resignation. When Pompidou's calmness in the disturbances of May–June 1968 allegedly highlighted de Gaulle's vacillation, he was replaced as Prime Minister. In his second book of memoirs, *Pour rétablir une vérité* (1982), he said of his dismissal: '*Il était en effet souhaitable qu'un Premier ministre devenu incombrant s'effaçât au profit d'un autre qui ramènerait la fonction à sa dimension constitutionnelle.*'

Maurice Couve de Murville: July 1968–June 1969
De Gaulle had serious thoughts of replacing Pompidou with Couve de Murville in Spring 1967, but he decided against someone who had an aura of defeat after failing to secure a seat in the Parliamentary elections of 1967. Couve was the temperamental opposite of Pompidou, who had established an image of a rather flamboyant *bon viveur*. He was a long standing follower of de Gaulle, and his post-war career as a diplomat fitted his reserved personality. His total faith in de Gaulle's policies and methods were shown during the ten years from June 1958 when he was Minister of Foreign Affairs.

With Couve as Prime Minister and Debré as Foreign Minister, as well as a massive supportive majority in the newly-elected National Assembly, de Gaulle was able to pursue the main thrust of his foreign and economic policy, and to try to ease some of the socio-political tensions whch may have provoked the events of May–June 1968. In this task, Couve de Murville was a conscientious organiser; as a foreign affairs expert he had little interest in modulating the domestic policies of de Gaulle, who worked through Edgar Faure (to reform higher education) and Jean-Marcel Jeanneney (to try to introduce 'participation'), both former Radical Party politicians, and recent recruits to Gaullism.

But the projected basic reform of social relationships ended up as a referendum on regional reform and on changing the composition of the Senate. On de Gaulle's resignation and Pompidou's subsequent election as President, Couve followed the old Republican tradition by which a Prime Minister resigns when a new Presidential term of office begins.

Jacques Chaban-Delmas: June 1969–July 1972

The simultaneous change of both elements of what had come to be referred to as the *couple indissociable* of President and Prime Minister raised questions of how far constitutional conventions concerning their relationship would survive. Pompidou had been elected President on a programme of fidelity to the regime of the Fifth Republic, but was not opposed on principle to allowing the Prime Minister some latitude. This seemed to fit in with the view of Chaban-Delmas in January 1970 that *'il ne faut pas qu'il y ait subordination rigoureuse, rigide'*. Chaban-Delmas, an experienced politician, was able to take the initiative – at least as far as announcing it – on a wide-ranging policy of mild social reform, which reflected his desire as a liberal Gaullist to get the *'société bloquée'* of the 1960s moving again.

But the reality of Prime Ministerial subordination soon became apparent in increased intervention in Government affairs by Pompidou's own personal staff, reflecting his own increasingly explicit conservative outlook. He could moreover count on a majority of the dominant Gaullist party suspicious of Chaban-Delmas' liberal views. The dubious success of the 1972 referendum led Pompidou to think of changes in his Governmental team, and in this context, Chaban-Delmas was asked to resign, which he did on the basis of his own 1972 declaration that: *'Un Premier Ministre digne de ce nom ne saurait un instant rester en place contre le sentiment du Président de la République.'*

Pierre Messmer: July 1972–May 1974

Messmer served with the Free French forces during the Second World War and as a colonial administrator, before a long career (1960–9) as Army Minister. De Gaulle as a President with strong military interests and Pompidou as Prime Minister coordinating ministerial activities were glad of his self-effacing efficiency, and these traits were the reason for his appointment as Prime Minister in 1972. He did not express strong political views, and posed no objection to reshuffles of his team which enabled Pompidou to bring his own men into the Government. Messmer was the faithful right-hand man of President Pompidou in times of increasing political and economic difficulty. When Pompidou died in 1974, Messmer's resignation, like that of Couve in 1969, was a natural consequence of Giscard's election.

Jacques Chirac: May 1974–August 1976

As in 1969, the election of a new President and the appointment of a new Prime Minister raised questions about the influence of the *'équation personnelle'* (as de Gaulle had called it) on relations between the two. Faced with disarray within the Gaullist camp, leading to a scramble for the candidature in 1974, Chirac led a group of 43 Gaullist deputies to support Giscard's bid for the Presidency. The careers of both Chirac and Giscard were in the ascendancy under Pompidou and both were committed to liberal reforms.

In spite of some hints to the contrary during his campaign, Giscard as President maintained, even reinforced, conventions concerning the Prime Minister's subordinate position: Giscard's approach was later called *'omniprésence'* by Chirac. Given the latter's long term political ambitions to become President by moulding the Gaullist party to this end, Giscard's determination to control all areas of policy was hard to tolerate, but he accepted that Giscard would in the logic of the regime overrule him. What complicated matters however was, firstly, Chirac's temperament (he was called *'dynamique'* by his friends and *'agité'* by his detractors), secondly the fact that disagreements were often made public, and more importantly the composition of the Government. Giscard found it necessary, in distributing ministerial portfolios, to reflect the full range of support which had elected him by a thin majority. The presence in the Government of leading figures of several political parties, as well as non-parliamentarians, made the Government a very mixed one, and ministers in need of mediation in conflicts with colleagues tended to bypass Chirac to go directly to the President or his staff.

In March 1976, Chirac was made 'coordinator of the Majority', but this grouping was becoming less and less homogeneous. His call for a dissolution of Parliament and *élections anticipées* to beat the Left was that of a party leader, and was always rejected by Giscard whose office made him look towards the longer term (*la durée*). All this led to frustration on the part of Chirac, because leadership of the Gaullist party[1] and Prime Ministership had become incompatable in the political circumstances of 1976. He took the initiative in resigning, thus avoiding the ignominy of dismissal by a President with whose whole approach he had come to disagree. He said in his letter of resignation: *'Je ne dispose pas des moyens que j'estime aujourd'hui nécessaires pour assurer efficacement mes fonctions de Premier Ministre, et, dans ces conditions, j'ai décidé d'y mettre fin.'* It can be argued that, strictly in terms of Prime

Ministerial function, these means had long ceased to be available to holders of the office who had any degree of independent political will.

Raymond Barre: August 1976–May 1981

Barre became Prime Minister in 1976 when the delicate relationships within the Majority in Parliament called for a non-party appointment. Giscard's pretext was that, given the need to tackle economic problems, Barre was the 'best economist in France'. He had been a government adviser during de Gaulle's Presidency, Vice-President of the EEC Commission, and only briefly a Minister under Chirac. The idea was that he would bring technical expertise to the Government's implementation of policy (he was also Minister of Finance), and leave coalition management to senior Ministers from the parties composing it. This method proved unsuccessful, and Barre was called on, like Chirac in 1976, to do the more explicitly political job of coordinating the Majority coalition.

Barre continued to work closely with Giscard whose habit was to issue 'directives' which either outlined government policy for a period of about six months, or gave instructions on a specific matter (see *texte 5.3*). These directives were made public but were addressed to the Prime Minister with orders to put them into effect. The last general directive of Giscard's term of office, on 13 November 1980, listing 29 major areas of action, purported to be a distillation of 300 suggestions sent by governmental colleagues to the Prime Minister, who had passed on a list of 90 to the President. But this apparent reversion to determination of policy by the Government (Article 20) and Presidential mediation in the higher interest (Article 5) was an exception, in view of the imminent Presidential election, to a formula for directives which merely confirmed the subsidiary role of the Prime Minister. On resigning in May 1981, Barre was warmly thanked by Giscard for his work as the Fifth Republic's second longest serving Prime Minister. He had also been, as a result of the policy of economic austerity to which his name was attached, the most unpopular.

Pierre Mauroy: May 1981–July 1984

Mauroy was a teacher and party activist in Lille before rising gradually to national prominence in the Socialist Party of the 1970s. He was appointed Prime Minister by Mitterrand mainly in order to bring closer together the various factions within the party. After 1981, he benefited from Mitterrand's wish not to interfere excessively with the working of government. The President said he could *'agir tout à fait à sa guise pour les problèmes de la vie quotidienne.'* It was Mauroy who made frequent provincial tours to explain how the Government was putting into effect the programme on which Mitterrand, and the Socialist parliamentary majority, had been elected. Alain Savary, the Minister of Education, echoed this new-found relative freedom in policy implementation when he said, concerning private education: *'Le gouvernement précisera au cours de la phase de négociations, le contenu de ce qui est défini par les objectifs exprimés par le Président de la République.'* The appointment of Mauroy, a *notable*, member of Parliament and party politician almost in the style of the Fourth Republic, was a departure from the tradition of the Fifth Republic Prime Minister as the principal servant of the State (*le plus grand commis de l'Etat*).

The appointment of Prime Ministers in the Fifth Republic has tended to show a pattern under successive Presidents. The appointment of the first Prime Minister in each case was dictated not just by how well he was known to, and trusted by, the President, but also by wider objective political considerations, particularly the structure of the majority supporting the incoming President. This was true of Chaban-Delmas (need to keep the newly-pledged support of some Centrists), Chirac (need to satisfy the Gaullist party, the 'majority of the Majority'), Mauroy (need to keep the unitary dynamic of a party where factions had independence of expression) and to a certain extent Debré, whose appointment would not antagonise the large numbers of deputies who, like him, were in favour of Algérie Française. In the case of subsequent Prime Ministers, the appointment was much more a matter of free choice by the President, and much less one of constraints arising from Parliamentary considerations. These however can affect the extent to which a President can afterwards impose his policies on a Government accountable to Parliament, as when Gaullist support for Giscard was weak on some issues, or if a Socialist President has to rely on Communist support in Parliament.

On the other hand, the ending of Prime Ministerial office in the middle of a Presidential term has not been a result of parliamentary disapproval. Chaban-Delmas was dismissed six weeks after being given a vote of confidence; Debré was dismissed when there was not yet a coherent party-based majority in Parliament; Pompidou's government was the object of a vote of censure in October 1962, but he stayed in office. The conclusion is that the Prime Minister and his government, accountable to Parliament under the Constitution, are also accountable to the President, whose power of appointment under Article 8 has been extended by usage to a power of dismissal as well. Commentators have suggested the metaphor of the Prime Minister as a fuse which blows when tension within the governing system became too great, to be replaced by another. Under President Mitterrand, the institutional paradigm of Fifth Republic practice survives: in July 1981, he said: *'Entre un Président de la Républiqe et un Premier Ministre, il est entendu ... que c'est le Premier Ministre qui doit s'écarter le jour où c'est nécessaire.'* The consolation is that a former Prime Minister can normally entertain serious thoughts of a Presidential candidature.

The Prime Minister remains, moreover, a powerful number two in the executive hierarchy. He may sometimes be bypassed by a President who, especially on budgetary matters, deals directly with the Finance Minister, but his information network is comprehensive and his coordinating role in the vast sphere of government activity is vital. For this he has at his disposal in (or attached to) the Hôtel Matignon, his official residence:

1   A personal cabinet of political advisers whose background tends to reflect his own, and which has become bigger with the progress of the Fifth Republic – there were over 50 official names after June 1981.
2   The general secretariat of the Government, staffed by 'non-political' civil servants. The Secretary General appointed in 1982 was only the sixth since the war. This body services all policy meetings including the *Conseil des Ministres*, and administers the Government's role in the legislative process; of necessity it works closely with the general secretariat of the Presidency.
3   Functional agencies which for administrative or overtly political reasons are not part of a Ministry: their number varies with political circumstances.

The Government

Members of the Government are appointed by the President on the basis of names suggested, according to Article 8 of the Constitution, by the Prime Minister; in reality, the will of the President prevails, and this was particularly so in the case of Chirac's team in May 1974. There is a hierarchy within the

Government, depending on the title a member carries; in descending order, this is:

Ministre d'Etat: A title which is sometimes used whenever a leader of a political group has a particular importance which needs to be recognised, whether or not he also has departmental responsibilities. De Gaulle as Prime Minister used the device, as did Giscard for a time; from 1981 to 1983, Mitterrand, to underline their representative value in the Government, gave the title to leaders of main Socialist Party factions, to an ex-Gaullist, to a woman (May–June 1981) and to a Communist (from June).

Ministre: This is the normal title of a person responsible for a major Government department.

Ministre délégué: A title given to a Minister who has significant responsibilities, but for a sector of government which is part of a larger grouping – traditionally the Prime Minister's area of responsibility, but from 1981 within other large ministries as well. An innovation of the Mauroy III government was the appointment of two 'autonomous' *Ministres délégués*.

Secrétaire d'Etat: These have areas of responsibility not important enough to warrant the title of Minister, and can be attached to the Prime Minister or to a large Ministry. During the Giscard Presidency, there was a brief experiment with the status of *secrétaire d'Etat autonome*, with independent departmental responsibility. This also applied to the official spokesman in the Mauroy III government.

The career structure leading to membership of the Government was normally established in previous Republics within a political party, but de Gaulle preferred his wartime followers, and career civil servants. The 1970s saw a widening of the recruitment base, but with the emphasis still on expertise. The Left-wing victory in 1981 represented some measure of return to a recruitment on the basis of party, but about a quarter were also civil servants.

The exact composition of a government, in terms of boundaries between ministerial responsibilities, and the number of members of the Government who attend every Council of Ministers and not just those involving their area of responsibility, depends on how far the President thinks it important for achieving policy objectives. The Governments of Pierre Mauroy in 1981 and 1983 are given in Table 5.2.

Table 5.2

Two examples of government structure and hierarchy

Gouvernement Mauroy II (juin 1981)	Gouvernement Mauroy III (mars 1983)
Premier Ministre[2]	Premier Ministre[2]
Droits de la Femme[3]	Droits de la Femme[3]
Relations avec le Parlement[3]	Relations avec le Parlement[3]
Fonction Publique et Réformes Administratives[3]	Fonction Publique et Réformes Administratives[6]
	Environnement et qualité de la vie[6]
Extension du Secteur Public[6]	Plan et aménagement du territoire[6]
	Techniques de la communication[6]
Rapatriés[6]	Porte-parole du gouvernement[5]
Intérieur et Décentralisation[1]	Intérieur et Décentralisation[2]
Départements d'Outre Mer et TOM[6]	Départements d'Outre Mer et TOM[6]
	Sécurité publique[6]
Justice[2]	Justice[2]
Relations Extérieures[2]	Relations Extérieures[2]
Affaires Européennes[3]	Affaires Européennes[3]
Coopération et Développement[3]	Coopération et Développement[3]
Défense[2]	Défense[2]
Défense[6]	Défense[6]
	Anciens Combattants[6]
Commerce Extérieur[1]	Commerce Extérieur et Tourisme[2]
	Tourisme[6]
Economie et Finances[2]	Economie, Finances et Budget[2]
Budget[3]	Budget[6]
Plan et Aménagement du Territoire[1]	Consommation[6]
Recherche et Technologie[1]	
Industrie[2]	Industrie et Recherche[2]
Energie[3]	
PTT[2]	PTT[6]
Urbanisme et Logement[2]	Urbanisme et Logement[2]
Transports[1]	Transports[2]
Mer[2]	Mer[6]
Agriculture[2]	Agriculture[2]
Agriculture[6]	Agriculture et forêts[6]
Commerce et Artisanat[2]	Commerce et Artisanat[2]
Consommation[2]	
Travail[2]	

Table 5.2 cont

Gouvernement Mauroy II (juin 1981)	Gouvernement Mauroy III (mars 1983)
Formation Professionnelle[2]	Formation Professionnelle[2]
Solidarité Nationale[2]	Affaires Sociales et Solidarité Nationale[2]
Famille[6]	Emploi[3]
Personnes Âgées[6]	Personnes Âgées[6]
Immigrés[6]	Famille, Population et Travailleurs Immigrés[6]
Santé[2]	Santé[6]
Environnement[2]	Rapatriés[6]
Temps Libre[2]	Temps Libre, Jeunesse et Sports[4]
Jeunesse et Sports[3]	
Tourisme[6]	
Anciens Combattants[2]	
Education Nationale[2]	Education Nationale[2]
Communication[2]	Education Nationale[6]
Culture[2]	Culture[4]

NOTES:
[1] Ministre d'Etat
[2] Ministre
[3] Ministre Délégué auprès d'un Ministre
[4] Ministre Délégué 'Autonome'
[5] Secrétaire d'Etat 'Autonome'
[6] Secrétaire d'Etat auprès d'un Ministre

Changes in the composition of a Government can occur without a change of Prime Minister, or indeed without his prior knowledge (Chirac, January 1976). But when this reshuffle (*remaniement ministériel*) follows the resignation and reappointment of the Prime Minister, the convention is to call it a new ministry, and to indicate a series of them by Roman numerals: the government formed in May 1981 was Mauroy I, in June 1981 Mauroy II and in March 1983 Mauroy III. Thus there were four Pompidou ministries, three Messmer ministries, and three Barre ministries. Prime Ministerial resignations, apart from when a new President takes office, are usually after elections when the President may justifiably want to build on his success by giving fresh impetus and a different political complexion to his ministerial team. But a President can try to make an impact on public opinion in this way outside election time, by obtaining the resignation of the whole Government as a pretext for a reshuffle (February 1974; March 1977): exceptionally, a mammoth reshuffle may not involve the resignation of the Prime Minister (31 May 1968). A Government which has resigned other than to facilitate a reshuffle may well stay in office to deal with day-to-day matters – this happened for seven weeks from October 1962, and nine days in May 1981.

In organising their work, Government members have the assistance of a personal political staff. In Autumn 1981, the 44 members of Mauroy's Government had 360 officially designated persons in their *cabinets ministériels*, a higher average than in the previous ministry of Raymond Barre: the existence of unofficial advisers, however, falsifies the statistical picture. But a breakdown of the background of ministerial staff traditionally reveals a large proportion of civil servants, usually graduates of specialised higher education institutions (*grandes écoles*) and particularly of the Ecole Nationale d'Administration (94 in Autumn 1981, 103 under Barre). However, an increase in the number of teachers (13 under Barre, 50 under Mauroy) reflects the professional base of the Socialist Party, as well as serving as a reminder that *cabinets ministériels* are largely political appointments, and their members tend to follow their chief in and out of office. A circular in May 1981 tried to limit personal staffs to eight for a Minister, five for other Ministers in a department, and two for Secretaries of State.

Ministerial cabinets vary in the extent to which they influence decision making in a Government department, while performing the basic function of advising, protecting, and negotiating for, their Minister. The Elysée tries to keep watch on the appointment and functioning of a Minister's staff, but the range and complexity of the process of making and implementing policy means that the Elysée machine is not large or specialised enough to control all aspects, and this allows Ministerial advisers an important role.

Policy-making

The policies which a Government intends to apply in areas where it has the power to influence citizens' lives are formulated and made public in a variety of ways. Giscard as President issued general or specific policy directives which were made public. Mitterrand based his approach on the *Cent dix propositions pour la France* of his Presidential campaign; his overall control of the direction of Government policy was less dramatic or public than Giscard's, but it was nevertheless strong.

Government policy may sometimes be presented to the country as a package, as in the *Programme de Provins* in 1973 or Barre's *Programme de Blois* in 1978. Governments often deliver statements of policy in Parliament which they can make into a matter of confidence, to be voted on by deputies.

The input into the policy-making process is usually an interministerial matter. It is hardly conceivable for there to be policy initiatives by a single Ministry which are passed up for approval to the weekly Council of Ministers, and then put into effect by the same Ministry: financial and wider political implications provoke competing claims and these are mediated in interministerial meetings. These may be *ad hoc* series of meetings on a particular issue, but the important areas are covered by permanent *comités interministériels* which take place under Prime Ministerial responsibility. Examples are the *Comité interministériel pour la coopération économique européenne*, and the *Comité interministériel de l'administration territoriale*. Sometimes, interdepartmental cooperation may require more than a *comité* as when the *Mission interministérielle de la mer* was set up in 1978. It was but one example of an attempt to coordinate policy touching an area of concern to several ministries, without establishing a separate Ministry, though this was later done by the new Left-wing government which established a *Ministère de la Mer* in 1981–3.

After some initial confusion, de Gaulle preferred to call '*conseil*' any policy meeting under his direction at the Elysée, since the word implied that members were there not to make a collective or collegial decision, but to help him arrive at a personal one. The practice has grown up since the early 1960s of having at the Elysée not only the Wednesday *Conseil des Ministres*, which all government ministers, and sometimes secretaries of state, attend, but also meetings (between 20 and 30 in a typical year) whose membership and frequency are not formally fixed, to which the name *conseil restreint* is given. An example was when the six-month prices and incomes freeze in 1982 led to the setting up of a weekly *conseil restreint* to oversee economic and social policy, which was attended by the Prime Minister and eight senior government ministers under the chairmanship of the President. It has been calculated that in the first seven months of the Left-wing governments appointed in 1981, Mauroy and his close collaborators chaired or attended 797 policy meetings at the various levels described.

The central importance of the Prime Minister's role in policy making is shown by the fact that 90 per cent of *arbitrages* (decisions involving the choice between competing options) are made within the Matignon machinery. But if a point needs to be decided by the President, the practice has been to do this before the Wednesday *Conseil des Ministres*. Mitterrand did this during working breakfasts with his own secretary-general, his Prime Minister, and the First Secretary of the Socialist Party. The *Conseil des Ministres* itself is chaired by the President under the Fifth Republic Constitution (Article 9); the same was true of the Fourth Republic, but all important decisions had been made before by the Government. Fifth Republic Presidents have made the chairmanship of the *Conseil des Ministres* the means of imposing their political will on the executive process, in a way which is easily understood, and accepted, by public opinion: decisions contained in the communqué issued after the Wednesday meetings are disseminated by the media. This serves to reinforce the image of the President as responsible for the lives of his fellow citizens. The *Conseil des Ministres* approves draft ordinances (see below) as well as draft laws before they go to Parliament, serves as a forum for the President or Government members to report on an international meeting or visit, and decides on developments which may indicate impending crisis, such as the state of siege (Article 36) and whether a policy or a 'text' should be put to Parliament as a matter of confidence (Article 49).

Policy implementation

Policy decisions which fall within the area where legislation is required need to be put before Parliament as draft laws. But this area is well delineated and rather restricted (see pp. 175–6). Matters not falling within the Constitutional definition of legislation are classed as executive orders (Article 37: ... *ont un caractère réglementaire*'). This provision of the 1958 Constitution, and the fact that Parliament can establish only the basic principles of some matters within the sphere of legislation, both give the Executive a great deal of power. To implement its policy decisions or to apply the provisions of a law, it has at its disposal the following types of executive instruments:

1 Ordinances (*ordonnances*) signed by the President, particularly those where Parliament delegates to the Government, for a fixed period, responsibility in an area normally covered by legislation (Article 38). This is not new to the Fifth Republic, and applied on 15 occasions between 1959 and 1982.
2 Decrees (*décrets*): these can be
    (i) signed by the President, after discussion in the *Conseil des Ministres*, and countersigned by the Prime Minister unless they concern matters listed in Article 19;

(ii) as above, but not discussed by the *Conseil des Ministres*;
This was yet another example of de Gaulle's less than constitutional behaviour, but a case in 1962 made them legal
by virtue of the Prime Minister's countersignature: there
has been an annual average of about sixty since 1959;

(iii) 'general' decrees putting into effect the provisions of law;
these are being more and more replaced for this purpose
by:

(iv) decrees issued by the Conseil d'Etat, where the provisions
of a law require this;

(v) simple decrees, issued in the exercise of his independent
executive function by the Prime Minister (Article 21,
paragraph 1) and countersigned, if appropriate, by a
departmental minister (Article 22). This is the most
frequent kind of executive act.

3 Orders (*arrêtés*) normally issued by ministers within the area of
responsibility of their own department, and also by mayors and
Prefects (now *Commissaires de la République*).

4 Instructions and circulars, which take care of the finer details of
policy implementation.

Although policy decisions which require legislation (because they
concern areas listed in Article 34) have to be submitted to
Parliament for approval, the Government has considerable
political, material and legal means at its disposal to facilitate this
process: political, in that since 1962 there has been a majority in
Parliament whose support of government policy is more or less
predictable (see page 171); material, in the resources of the general
secretariat of the Government, and of the ministry responsible for
relations with Parliament; legal, in Constitutional provisions which
produced a Parliamentary system which was 'rationalised', and
which gave considerable advantages to the Government in getting
any necessary legislative approval of its policies. The advantages it
has are that:

1 The Government controls the agenda of each Assembly, which
must give priority to Government draft laws (*projets de loi*) or
those submitted by parliamentarians (*propositions de loi*) which
the Government adopts (Article 48).

2 The circumstances where a draft law or amendment submitted
by parliamentarians is declared out of order (*irrecevable*) are
wide ranging (Articles 40 and 41).

3 Parliament has to discuss the draft law in the form in which the

Government presents it (Article 42), and not as rewritten by one of its own committees, which happened before 1959.

4 The Government can ask for a vote on a text, or part of a text, in which have been incorporated only those amendments acceptable to the Government (Article 44–3).

The name '*vote bloqué*' has been given to the procedure, which ensures that a draft law broadly preserves its original form. It was used 158 times in the period 1959–81.

5 The Government can prevent obstruction by the Senate of a draft law (Article 45), and by either Chamber of laws concerning the budget (Article 47).

6 The conditions for a vote of censure by Parliament, which obliges the Government to tender its resignation, are stringent. This applies whether the vote is 'spontaneous' (Article 49–2) or provoked by the Government's making the approval of a text a matter of confidence (Article 49–3).

7 Governments have at times taken advantage of uncertainty in the meaning of Article 49–1, to decide against giving Parliament the chance to vote on the Government's policy programme or declaration of general policy, in the first few weeks after a new Government is formed.

In the formulation and implementation of government policy, the role played by the *Conseil d'Etat* is important. This body has functions in the field of judicial review of administrative decisions, but it also acts in a consultative and advisory capacity to the Government in preparing legislation and getting it through Parliament. All draft laws must be submitted to it for comment (Article 39), even though nothing it says has the force of law. If Parliament gives the Government power to govern by ordinances (Article 38), these must be examined by the *Conseil d'Etat*. If, in the exercise of its legislative function, Parliament purports to make a law (more likely a part of law) about something which in fact falls outside the scope of legislation, and therefore is subject to the Government's executive authority, the Government has the power to issue a decree to alter the text, but the *Conseil d'Etat* must be consulted (Article 37–2).

The help given by the *Conseil d'Etat* is in the application of drafting skills to the texts it examines, such as avoiding ambiguities or ensuring consistency. But since it advises the Government in every sense, its reaction to something submitted to it for examination may be not only on strictly legal grounds, but may be based on considerations of the appropriateness or otherwise of the text. It is this which gives a political hue to the function of the *Conseil d'Etat*.

Administration

The conventional image in Western democracies was that a neutral, completely separate group of administrative personnel remained in existence to ensure continuity, however frequently their political masters changed by the normal operation of the electoral process. Their autonomy in France had much to do with the existence of *grands corps* which Napoleon I made the basis of his new administrative structure, having adapted some which already existed under the *ancien régime*. The most prestigious were the *Conseil d'Etat*, the *Cour des comptes* and the *Inspection générale des finances*, and these retain their primacy in contemporary France. The *Corps préfectoral* and the *Corps diplomatique* are often grouped with them and all are regarded as *Les grands corps de l'Etat*, distinct from other, more technical corps. The concept of an administrative corps has been likened to that of military command systems, with their own values and traditions.

Such a hierarchical bureaucracy became the perfect instrument for an increasingly interventionist state in the twentieth century, which in 1946 and 1959 rewarded its administrative personnel with a legal status protecting rights which had accrued over the years. But the increasing complexity of government meant that there was a less clear dividing line between a decision which belongs to the political sphere, and its application which belongs to the sphere of administration. In the Fourth Republic (1946–58), the Administration achieved a dominant position not only because of the efficiency of its hierarchical organisation, but also because in a time of transient Governments, it held a near-monopoly of information, particularly in the economic sphere, and this was important when the emphasis was on post-war reconstruction.

The Fifth Republic created a situation where the two functions –political and administrative – overlap more and more. In establishing the principle of *incompatibilité* which makes it constitutionally impossible to be at the same time a member of Parliament and a member of the Government, the possibility was opened of a radical revision of the previous model. Before 1958, the simplified model located the political function in the Government, and the management function in the Administration. Post-1958 Constitutional provisions, as well as a different concept of the state, allowed the development of a scheme of things which located the political function in Parliament, and the management function in the Government. The Government, freed from the worst of the institutional constraints which pre-1958 regimes imposed on it, became the means for restructuring the State, reuniting the nation, and (often a poor third in practice, but nevertheless part of Gaullist doctrine) reforming society. In this task, experts became indispensable to policymakers, and 'technocrat' came to be the umbrella word to describe those who contributed expertise to the making of policy decisions.

The very stability and political continuity of the Fifth Republic, which the *alternance* of 1981 merely served to confirm, made the Administration less independent. Ambitious individuals could train as administrators, often in the prestigious Ecole Nationale d'Administration and, having risen to near the top in the civil service, join a ministerial cabinet and justifiably think of a Government post. Previously the career path (*filière*) would have been typically by means of a political party through Parliament. Even the latter institution has been increasingly populated by civil servants, with 53 per cent of the 1981 National Assembly, compared with 41 per cent in 1978 and 31 per cent in 1973. Such statistics must however be regarded in the light of the fact that teachers (30 per cent of the 1981 Assembly) are, as State employees, part of the Administration. Moreover, in the wider context, it must be borne in mind that a group of civil servants which numbers over two and a half million can never be treated as a homogeneous category, since it includes not just the central administration and its numerous field services in the provinces, but also employees of local authorities.

It is at the top, however, that the phenomenon of *fonctionnarisation de la politique* has been the object of most attention by commentators. Top civil servants are active participants in policy-making bodies at the interministerial level; they suspend their status to become members of ministerial cabinets, of the Prime Minister's political staff, and of the Elysée staff, and then go back into the Administration; they can constitute a large proportion of Government ministers – it was as high as 32 per cent in Debré's Ministry, though there were none at all between July 1968 and April 1973. In analysing the consequences of the presidentialisation of the regime, Pierre Birnbaum went so far as to postulate a general osmosis between political power and administrative power.[2] President Mitterrand's view was that an attempt should be made to reinstate the principle of the primacy of politics over administration, which is a hallowed Republican tradition, by using the President's extensive powers of patronage to appoint top civil, military and personal staff on criteria which reduced the proportion of civil servants. In doing so, however, he put himself in the dilemma of becoming open to accusations of

operating a 'spoil system' of political appointments, while only
marginally reducing the extent to which politics and administration
have come to overlap.

Bibliographical guidance

On the Prime Ministerial role and the Government's function in general:

M. Alliot-Marie, *La décision politique* (PUF, 1983)
P. and J.-D. Antoni, *Les ministres de la Ve République* (PUF, 1976)
J. Billy, *Les technocrates*, 3rd ed., (PUF, 1975)
P.G. Cerny and M.A. Schain, *Socialism, the State and Public Policy in
France* (F. Pinter, 1984)
A. Claisse, *Le Premier ministre de la Ve République* (L.G.D.J., 1972)
M. Dagnaud and D. Mehl, *L'élite rose – qui gouverne?* (Ramsay, 1982)
M. Long, *Les services du Premier ministre* (Presses universitaires d'Aix-
Marseille, 1981)
J. Massot, *Le chef du gouvernement en France* (La Documentation
Française, 1977)
R. Poujade, *Le ministère de l'impossible* (Calmann-Lévy, 1975)
R. Rémond, *et al., Quarante ans de cabinets ministériels* (Presses de la
FNSP, 1983)
S. Rials: *Le Premier ministre* (PUF, 1981)
G. Tuillier, *Les cabinets ministériels* (PUF, 1982)

On individual Prime Ministers. As well as the appropriate chapters of
books covering the terms of office of Presidents of the Republic, the
following are recommended:

P. Alexandre, *Le duel de Gaulle–Pompidou* (Grasset, 1970)
J. Chaban-Delmas, *L'Ardeur* (Stock, 1975)
M. Debré, *Au service de la nation* (Stock, 1963)
H. Deligny, *Chirac, ou la fringale du pouvoir* (Moreau, 1977)
T. Desjardins, *Un inconnu nommé Chirac* (La Table ronde, 1983)
P. Mauroy, *C'est ici le chemin* (Flammarion, 1982)
C. Ney, *La double méprise* (Grasset, 1980) – on Chirac and Giscard
A. Nourry, *Le combat singulier* (Denoel, 1980) – on Chirac and Giscard
P. Rouanet, *Pompidou* (Grasset, 1969)

On the Administration:

M. Bassi, *La république des petits papiers* (Grasset, 1975)
J.-L. Bodiguel and J.L. Quermonne, *La haute fonction publique sous la
Ve République* (PUF, 1983)
F. de Baecque, *L'administration centrale de la France* (A. Colin, 1973)

F. de Baecque and J.-L. Quermonne, *Administration et Politique sous la Cinquième République* (Presses de la FNSP, 1981)

P. Escoube, *Les grands corps de l'Etat* (PUF, 1976)

C. Grémion, *Profession: décideurs – pouvoir des hauts fonctionnaires et réforme de l'Etat* (Gauthier-Villars, 1979)

E. Joly, *La République des rapports – une enquête féroce sur l'administration* (A. Moreau, 1981)

M. Piquemal, *Les agents de l'état* (PUF, 1977)

P.Sheriff, 'The State Administration' in M. Vaughan *et al.* (eds) *Social Change in France* (Martin Robertson, 1980)

G. Tuillier, *Regards sur la haute administration en France* (Economica, 1979)

C. Wiener, 'Pouvoir politique et administration – le temps de la discorde' in *Pouvoirs*, no. 4 (1978)

Illustrative texts and linguistic exercises

Texte 5.1   Un Conseil des Ministres

Mise en situation

Françoise Giroud (née en 1916) fit sa carrière dans le journalisme et devint le bras droit de Jean-Jacques Servan-Schreiber à la revue *L'Express*, avant d'en assumer la direction. Nommée en 1974 Secrétaire d'état à la Condition féminine dans le gouvernement Chirac, elle était protagoniste d'un rapprochement des giscardiens avec les radicaux de gauche et les socialistes. Après avoir perdu son portefeuille ministériel, elle retourna au journalisme. Son livre *La comédie du pouvoir* est un témoignage de ses expériences comme membre du gouvernement pendant la Présidence de Giscard.

*   *   *

La salle où se tient, tous les mercredis matins, le Conseil des ministres, est l'un des lieux privilégiés où se joue la comédie de pouvoir.

Quand on entre à l'Elysée, par le perron central, elle est située à droite, au rez-de-chaussée. Pour y accéder, on traverse un salon. De chaque côté de la porte, des gardes se tiennent, saluant, sabre au clair, l'entrée de chaque excellence.

On s'y fait.

Dans la longue et haute pièce rectangulaire, donnant sur le jardin, on grelotte, lorsque le vent souffle par les fentes généreuses des deux portes-fenêtres qui composent l'un des pans étroits du rectangle. Le plus éloigné de l'entrée.

Entre elles, une peinture murale représentant la colonne Vendôme.

En face, l'autre pan étroit est un panneau de glace. Devant le panneau, une console Empire supporte une pendule et deux chandeliers. Au-dessus,

Napoléon veille, jeune, en costume rouge, la main sur l'estomac. L'un des pans larges, celui que l'on voit en entrant, est composé de trois portes fenêtres aveuglées. Les volets de bois intérieurs sont rabattus sur les vitres.

En face, le deuxième pan large est fait de trois portes à double battant, séparées par des toiles dont l'intérêt ne m'a jamais paru évident, surmontant deux bibliothèques plates. Sur l'une d'elles, un plateau, quelques verres, une carafe de jus de fruit. Les ministres entrent par une porte. Celle du centre est fermée. Le président de la République et le Premier Ministre arrivent par la troisième. Devant l'une des fenêtres, un petit bureau où officient le Secrétaire général de l'Elysée et le Secrétaire général du Gouvernement.

Cinq lustres à pendeloques de cristal, majestueux, achèvent ce décor ennuyeux, qui cerne une table en forme d'ovale allongé recouverte d'un tapis couleur tabac. Au centre, une petite pendule. De chaque côté, une coupe de fleurs fraîches. Autour de la table, des chaises en tapisserie. Le Président et le Premier Ministre, qui se font face, disposent d'un fauteuil.

Des cartons indiquent à chaque ministre la place qui lui est dévolue. Il trouve également, à chaque place, le dossier dit des 'Mesures individuelles' qui seront prises ce jour-là, du papier blanc, grand et petit format, et des enveloppes à en-tête de la présidence de la République.

A l'intérieur d'un *ordre protocolaire* rigoureux, les places varient pour des raisons qui me sont restées mystérieuses. Il y a les bonnes places – loin des vents coulis et sur le rang opposé à celui où se trouve le Président. Et les moins bonnes, du moins à mon goût. Tout dépend de l'activité personnelle que l'on entend déployer dans cette *auguste enceinte*.

Pour y faire du courrier, mieux vaut, évidemment, se trouver hors de la vue de Président, encore qu'il témoigne à l'égard des plus acharnés dans cette occupation, une *mansuétude*, démentie par le regard, qu'on ne manifesterait pas dans un quelconque conseil d'administration.

Donc, entre 9 h 20 et 9 h 30, tout le monde arrive, serviette à la main, contenant, en particulier, *l'ordre du jour* de la réunion, qui a été fixé le lundi après-midi par le Président et *les projets de loi* qui seront examinés.

Pendant quelques minutes, on se salue, on bavarde, on échange des impressions ou des informations. Le tutoiement est courant, l'emploi du prénom de rigueur.

Enfin l'huissier annonce: 'Monsieur le président de la République …', chacun gagne sa place devant laquelle il reste debout, et le Président paraît, suivi du Premier Ministre avec lequel il s'entretient invariablement avant le Conseil.

Il fait le tour de la table, serrant chaque main, disant parfois un mot à l'un ou à l'autre, rejoint son fauteuil et ouvre la séance en indiquant, éventuellement, qui est absent pour cause de voyage et quels secrétaires d'Etat sont, ce jour-là, présents.

Puis il donne la parole, toujours dans l'ordre de préséance à celui qui, le premier, exposera pourquoi il propose la dissolution de tel Conseil municipal, la nomination ou la mise à la retraite de tel haut-fonctionnaire, l'agrément de tel ambassadeur, de tel officier supérieur. Les grades élevés, dans l'ordre de la Légion d'honneur (commandeur et grand-croix) sont également soumis à l'approbation du Conseil, ou du moins à son *simulacre*.

Car aucune des mesures ainsi 'proposées' n'arrive devant le Conseil sans avoir été soumise et approuvée par l'Elysée, Matignon et le cas échéant, le ministre dont le département est également concerné.

Et, à ma connaissance, aucune proposition au Conseil n'a jamais été refoulée par celui-ci, s'il arrive, en revanche, que le Président, lui, fasse obstacle.

Néanmoins, après chaque intervention, le Président demande: 'Pas d'observation?' Et, levant la main, celui qui tient à accompagner d'un commentaire approbatif telle ou telle 'mesure individuelle' peut prendre la parole. Je n'ai jamais vu qu'un commentaire soit restrictif, sauf de la part du Président lui-même qui manie volontiers l'ironie.

Puis vient, lorsqu'il y a lieu, l'examen des projets de loi inscrits à l'ordre du jour.

Il n'y a pas de loi qui soit négligeable, si certaines ont plus d'ampleur que d'autres dans leur contenu et leurs conséquences. Mais leur exposé, préparé par les services, rédigé en style administratif et toujours selon les règles de la dissertation plutôt que du discours, distille un ennui dont le degré varie avec la voix, l'élocution et les intonations de celui que parle. Ou plutôt qui lit.

Plus la *technicité* s'y mêle, plus il est difficile de trouver dans cette prose feutrée les aspérités auxquelles l'intérêt peut s'accrocher.

Les textes, de surcroît, ont été distribués dans les jours qui précèdent, de sorte que chacun a pu en prendre connaissance. Alors, pourquoi cette lecture à haute voix? Parce que, submergé par ses propres dossiers personne n'a eu le temps de consulter les papiers que le secrétariat général du Gouvernement a diffusé avec la mention 'secret'?

Par curiosité naturelle, et par manie d'apprendre, je me suis astreinte à écouter attentivement les raisons pour lesquelles il convenait de modifier le régime d'indemnisation des sapeurs-pompiers non professionnels ou le régime fiscal de certains investissements dans le territoire de la Nouvelle-Caledonie.

Mais un jour où j'avais atteint le seuil d'intolérance, et ou il semblait que Jacques Chirac, au comble de son agitation naturelle allait, de ses grandes mains et de ses grands pieds, soulever la table tel un squale furieux, j'ai *griffonné un mot* à l'intention d'Alice Saunier-Seïté qui assistait, pour la première fois, au Conseil.

– Chère Alice, vous doutiez-vous qu'un Conseil des ministres peut être aussi ennuyeux?'

Elle m'a répondu en retour:

– Chère Françoise, oui, car j'ai toujours constaté l'insondable puérilité du sexe masculin.

Puérile, en effet, cette façon de s'écouter parler, de *se gargariser de mot*, de jouer à être celui qui tient, suspendu à ses lèvres, le chef de l'Etat, son Premier Ministre, et le Gouvernement de la France.

Suspendus ... En fait, décrochés, en quelques minutes.

SOURCE: F. Giroud, *La Comédie au pouvoir* (Fayard, 1977) pp. 25–9.

Exploitation du texte

1 Expliquez en quelques mots le sens des expressions en italique.

2 Faites une analyse textuelle générale, en vous appuyant éventuellement sur l'approche suggérée dans l'Annexe A (p. 23).

3 A partir de votre analyse générale, faites une étude plus détaillée de l'usage de l'ironie et d'autres marques de désapprobation.

4 Rédigez le texte sous la forme d'une saynète (indications de scène, dialogue, etc.)

5 Transformez le texte, ou une de ses parties, en une description enthousiasmée d'une réunion du Conseil des Ministres.

Texte 5.2   Mitterrand a-t-il tenu ses promesses?

Mise en situation

Le Nouvel Observateur fit sa mue en 1964 en abandonnant le titre de *France-Observateur* et en adoptant les techniques modernes de présentation et de diffusion. Il connut un net accroissement de son tirage dans les années '60 et '70, et se démarqua de la neutralité croissante d'autres hebdomadaires. Il se veut le lieu de rencontre de tous ceux 'qui ont pour patrie commune la gauche'.

*   *   *

Neuf mois après sa victoire du 10 mai 1981, quels sont les engagements du candidat socialiste que le président élu a honorés? Walter Lewino dresse le tableau de ce qui a été réalisé, de ce qui est en voie de l'être, de ce qui est pour l'instant mis en réserve et de ce qui est pratiquement abandonné. Et c'est à nos lecteurs qu'il appartiendra de qualifier 'globalement' ce bilan.

Le 24 janvier 1981, le congrès extraordinaire de Parti socialiste, réuni à Créteil, en même temps qu'il officialisait la candidature de François Mitterrand à l'élection présidentielle, publiait ses '110 Propositions pour la France'. De celles-ci, qui se soucia alors? Qui, dans les médias, risqua une analyse? Le jeu politique nous avait appris depuis longtemps que les programmes ne durent que l'espace d'une campagne électorale. Souvenez-vous du programme de Provins en janvier 1973; quelqu'un *s'était-il donné le ridicule* de reprocher aux gaullistes de ne pas l'avoir appliqué? Chiffon de papier ... Seuls Pierre Mendès-France et, peut-être, Antoine Pinay, une fois au pouvoir, avaient tenu parole, mais sur des points précis, limités.

Au cours de la campagne présidentielle, chaque fois que ses adversaires l'attaquaient sur le programme socialiste, François Mitterrand rétorquait *inlassablement*: tout mon programme mais rien que mon programme. On commença alors à faire la différence entre les 380 mesures du programme socialiste (1980) et les '110 Propositions' de Créteil (1981), *avalisées* par François Mitterrand.

Neuf mois après le 10 mai, le temps d'une gestation, il nous a semblé utile de *dresser le premier bilan* de ce qu'il faut bien appeler le programme

Mitterrand. Où en est-il aujourd'hui de ses promesses? Comment s'est effectué le difficile passage de la théorie à la pratique? Le rêve humaniste a-t-il résisté aux contraintes du pouvoir? Le tableau que nous publions dans les deux pages suivantes entend modestement y répondre. *Par souci de clarté*, nous n'avons retenu qu'un cinquantaine des 110 propositions, les plus typiques et relevant uniquement des affaires intérieures. Nous nous sommes efforcés de ne rien omettre de ce qui a été réellement fait ou de ce qui, *à l'évidence*, a été abondonné.

Personne jusqu'ici n'a tant fait, et si fidèlement à sa parole, en si peu de temps. Il faut remonter à 1869, au programme républicain de Belleville proposé par Gambetta (liberté de la presse et de réunion, école laïque et obligatoire, séparation de l'Eglise et de l'Etat ...) dont la réalisation prit près d'un demi-siècle, pour trouver une telle concordance entre projet écrit et passage à l'acte. Mitterrand jouant sur l'état de grâce a voulu aller au plus vite, au plus court. Cela n'a pas été sans risque. On aperçoit de-ci de-là quelques petites *entorses*; des projets ont *dérapé*, d'autres sont en réserve; des propositions un peu hâtives n'ont pas résisté aux exigences budgétaires, aux contrantes économiques; d'autres encore attendent des jours meilleurs. Mais il y a là une manière de miracle.

Les nationalisations, faites ou tout comme; et la régionalisation; et le statut de la Corse; et la cinquième semaine de congés payés; la recherche réellement stimulée; le prix du livre de nouveau contrôlé; la peine de mort supprimée et la vignette moto ...

Bien sûr, des décisions prises, des lois votées ne l'ont pas toujours été dans l'esprit espéré. L'impôt sur les grandes fortunes a perdu de sa vigueur originelle. La loi sur la révision des loyers, coincée entre intérêts des *locataires* et incitation à la construction, *fait la part belle* aux compromis. L'augmentation du SMIC ne dépasse pas les 7 pour-cent en valeur absolue. Une simple loi ne saurait effacer le racisme latent qui frappe les travailleurs immigrés. Certaines propositions ont été partie réalisées, partie mises en réserve, parti abandonnées. Ainsi, la proposition 54 sur la régionalisation prévoyait dans le même paragraphe un statut particulier pour la Corse (fait) et la création d'un département basque (oublié). Le 52 regroupait l'abrogation de la Cour de Sûreté et celle de la loi anticasseurs (faites), en même temps que celle de la loi Peyrefitte (toujours à l'étude mais en bonne voie).

Floue et souvent arbitraire est la frontière qui sépare ce qui est en réserve de ce qui est en bonne voie. Des projets qui semblent très avancés pourront *capoter*; d'autres, dont on parle peu, voir brusquement le jour. Certains dépendent de l'Elysée (durée du mandat présidentiel: Mitterrand a tout avantage à laisser l'opposition dans l'expectative – pourront-ils, lui et Giscard, se représenter?); d'autres sont bloqueés par des considérations budgétaires (livret de caisse d'épargne indexé, classe de vingt-cinq élèves au maximum) ou de crise économique (réduction du service militaire à six mois: cent mille chômeurs supplémentaires); d'autres, enfin, relèvent de projets globaux en cours d'élaboration (crédit de formation pour les travailleurs, grands travaux publics ...).

Reste ce qui a été abandonné. Provisoirement abandonné ou trahi? Là encore, la frontière est délicate à tracer. Au premier rang, la proposition 38, qui traite du programme nucléaire. A-t-il été réellement 'limité aux centrales en cours de construction'? Trahison, crient les écolos. De toute façon, était-il sérieux et responsable de prévoir à ce propos un référendum que la constitution ne permet pas? Les socialistes songeraient-ils à un référendum à valeur consultative, une sorte de sondage à l'échelle nationale? Gageons qu'ils ne s'y risqueront pas.

Il y avait d'autres naïvetés dans les '110 Propositions'. Témoin, le droit de véto des *comités d'entreprise* en cas de licenciement qui aurait acculé les syndicats au douloureux dilemme: trahir ses *mandants* ou mettre l'enterprise en faillite. Témoin, ces trois cent mille places de crèche prioritaires, alors qu'il n'y a pas de travail à offrir aux mères qui seraient ainsi libérées. Témoin, le droit de vote aux élections muncipales pour les travailleurs immigrés, au risque de *faire basculer* vers la droite toute une partie de l'électorat moyen. Témoin, l'obligation qui serait faite à tous les députés et ministres de déclarer leur revenus.

Alors, bilan positif, bilan négatif? Chacun d'abord, l'histoire ensuite jugera. N'empêche que François Mitterrand aura donné une dimension nouvelle au combat politique. Il fut le premier à rester fidèle globalement à ses promesses, même si, comme il le reconnaît en privé, il a été contraint à quelques oublis. L'ère du *chèque en blanc* est terminée.

SOURCE: Article paru dans *Le Nouvel Observateur*, 13 février 1982.

Exploitation du texte

1 Expliquez en quelques mots le sens des expressions en italique, sauf l'entête.

2 Faites une analyse textuelle générale, en vous appuyant éventuellement sur l'approche suggérée dans l'Annexe A (p. 23).

3 Expliquez les allusions dans les cas suivants:

les promesses d'Antoine Pinay (1952)
les promesses de Pierre Mendès-France (1954)
le Programme Socialiste de 1980
le Programme de Belleville (1869)
le Programme de Provins (1973)

4 Donnez plusieurs détails de la mise en oeuvre (totale ou partielle) d'une des politiques suivantes après 1981:

la statut de la Corse
la cinquième semaine de congés payés
la suppression de la peine de mort
l'impôt sur les grandes fortunes
l'amélioration du sort des travailleurs immigrés

5 Donnez les arguments en faveur:

d'un livret de caisse d'épargne indexé
d'un maximum de 25 élèves par classe
de la réduction du service militaire à six mois
de l'obligation pour tous les députés et ministres de déclarer leurs
revenus

6 Expliquez le 'douloureux dilemme' des syndicats ouvriers si on leur avait
octroyé le droit de véto en cas de licenciement.

Texte 5.3   Deux exemples de lettres directives

Mise en situation

Dès son accession à la Présidence de la République, Valery Giscard
d'Estaing manifesta sa volonté d'accentuer encore le rôle du chef de l'Etat
en inaugurant une pratique 'présidentialiste'. Il en résulta une extension
sensible des différents moyens d'intervention présidentielle, y compris celui
des lettres directives au Gouvernement, dont l'usage ne fut pas totalement
original, mais dont la nouveauté résida à partir de 1974 dans leur
publication quasi-systématique.

*   *   *

A   Une lettre directive spéciale

Paris, le 19 octobre 1976

Mon cher Premier ministre

Il faut faire entrer à nouveau la nature dans la ville, et en particulier à
Paris, insuffisamment pourvu à cet egard.

L'aménagement des terrains des anciens abattoirs de la Villette est une
occasion à saisir pour offrir aux habitants de la capitale un grand parc pour
la promenade, la détente et le repos.

L'Etat étant propriétaire de ces terrains, je vous demande de mettre à la
disposition de la Ville de Paris une superficie d'environ 23 hectares réservés
à un tel parc et de lui présenter des propositions sur les modalités
d'aménagement.

Il m'apparaît souhaitable, d'autre part, de lancer rapidement une *tranche
de travaux* pour qu'un premier *espace vert* proche des quartiers habités,
puisse être ouvert aux Parisiens vers la fin de l'année 1977. Vous
examinerez, en accord avec la Ville de Paris, les *modalités* de mise en
oeuvre de ce projet, pour lequel ces crédits de l'Etat ont été réservés dès
cette année.

Veuillez agréer, mon cher Premier ministre, l'expression de ma très
cordiale considération.

Valéry Giscard d'Estaing

B   Une lettre directive générale

Paris, le 12 octobre 1978

Mon cher Premier ministre,

Après les élections législatives de cette année, j'avais assigné trois objectifs prioritaires à l'action du gouvernement: la poursuite du développement économique, le réduction des injustices qui subsistent dans la société française et la promotion de l'initiative et de la responsibilité, notamment en ce qui concerne les collectivités locales.

Les travaux du Séminaire qui a réuni les membres du gouvernment à Rambouillet les 1 et 2 septembre 1978 ont permis d'évaluer l'efficacité des actions entreprises et de mesurer les difficultés que notre pays doit encore surmonter. A la suite des échanges de vues que nous avons eus depuis cette réunion, l'évolution de la *conjoncture interne* et internationale me conduit à préciser ces objectifs.

En premier lieu, le *redressement économique* de notre pays doit être poursuivi, ce qui implique notamment que la compétitivité internationale des entreprises françaises soit nettement améliorée, et que le rythme annuel de la hausse des prix intérieurs soit *très sensiblement* diminué. Cette action prioritaire doit être menée dans le constant respect de l'objectif de réduction des inégalités sociales et des injustices.

Seule l'adaptation de notre économie à la nouvelle compétition internationale nous permettra de connaître un développement créateur d'emplois nombreux, durables et productifs. Pendant la période d'ajustement que nous traversons, la lutte contre le chômage et le soulagement des difficultés de nos compatriotes sans travail devront être une préoccupation permanente du gouvernement. A cet égard, le second pacte pour l'emploi doit être mis en oeuvre avec la plus grande efficacité et les négociations en cours entre les *partenaires sociaux* doivent être vivement encouragées. En outre, les ressources mises à la disposition du Fonds spécial d'adaptation industrielle doivent être engagées rapidement afin de permettre aux entreprises qui en bénéficieront de *reprendre l'embauche*, en recherchant par priorité des investissements à réaliser en Lorraine et dans le Nord, pour répondre à la capacité industrielle traditionnelle de ces deux régions.

Les soutiens qui permettent aux petites et moyennes entreprises de s'organiser pour surmonter les difficultés économiques auxquelles elles ont à faire face devront être renforcés dans les plus brefs délais. Enfin les problèmes de la conjoncture économique, d'une part, et de la conjoncture sociale, d'autre part, feront l'objet d'un examen trimestriel en Conseil des Ministres.

Assurer la sécurité, la tranquillité et la salubrité publiques est une fonction essentielle et éminente du Gouvernement à laquelle je souhaite qu'il soit porté une attention renforcée.

La multiplication des *atteintes délictuelles* ou criminelles à l'intégrité des personnes et à leurs biens, par le climat qu'elle engendre comme par les réactions quelle suscite, est de nature à *compromettre la sérénité de la vie* que la France a su préserver jusqu'ici. Le développement de la criminalité, et notamment la criminalité qui atteint les personnes, doit être enrayé dans le plus brefs délais. Je vous demande de conduire les actions appropriées, et notamment les actions de prévention, pour assurer la sécurité des habitants de notre pays et d'informer périodiquement le Conseil des Ministres de leurs résultats.

Dans le préparation des investissements publics comme dans l'orientation de notre effort d'éducation et de recherche, et même à l'occasion des actes de gestion courante, le gouvernement doit avoir pour constant objectif de préparer l'avenir de la France. L'obsession du futur doit devenir l'un des éléments de toutes les décisions prises par le gouvernement pour faire face aux problèmes présents. Sans un tel *changement d'optique*, la France ne pourra jouer dans le monde le rôle que nous ambitionnons pour elle, et les Français ne connaîtront pas *l'épanouissement* et le progrès qu'ils sont en droit d'espérer.

Ces orientations devront être mises en oeuvre d'une facon méthodique et *concertée*, sous votre autorité, par chaque membre du Gouvernement et par les administrations qui lui sont subordonnées. Elles inspirent le *calendrier*, ci-joint, des travaux du Conseil des Ministres pour les six prochains mois que j'ai arrêté à la suite de nos récents entretiens.

Je vous prie de croire, Mon cher Premier Ministre, à l'assurance de ma très cordiale considération.

Valéry Giscard d'Estaing

Exploitation du texte

1 Expliquez en quelques mots les expressions en italique.

2 Faites une analyse textuelle générale, en vous appuyant éventuellement sur l'approche suggérée dans l'Annexe A (p. 23).

3 A partir de votre analyse générale, faites une étude plus détaillée des moyens linguistiques employés par l'auteur pour établir le ton impérieux voulu.

4 Rédigez une des lettres que le Premier Ministre aurait pu écrire pour donner suite aux demandes du Président de la République dans sa Lettre A.

5 Reformulez la Lettre A ou une partie de la Lettre B comme si le Président de la République, au lieu d'imposer sa volonté, cherchait à établir un consensus avec le Gouvernement qui, conformément à l'Article 20 de la Constitution de 1958, détermine et conduit la politique de la Nation.

Exercises de comparaison et d'application

1 Ecrivez un dissertation d'environ 1000 à 1200 mots sur le sujet suivant, en vous servant de détails donnés dans les trois textes: 'La mise en oeuvre de la politique en France – moyens et contraintes.'

2 Quels sont les avantages et les inconvénients d'une réduction à 12–15 du nombre des Ministres dans un gouvernement sous la Cinquième République? (Voir par exemple les propositions de Maurice Druon dans le quatrième chapitre de *Réformer la Démocratie* et les commentaires de presse après le remaniement ministériel de mars 1983).

3 En vous référant au schéma du Tableau 5.1, faites une liste d'un gouvernement antérieur à 1981 (détails dans *Le Monde*, par exemple) afin de montrer comment les diverses activités gouvernementales peuvent être réparties entre les différents Ministères ou Secrétariats d'Etat.

4 Dans quelle mesure est-il souhaitable de limiter l'interpénétration de l'Administration et l'Exécutif dans la France contemporaine? Comment cette limitation pourrait-elle être effectuée?

6
Political Parties and Interest Groups

Political parties in the modern sense emerged in France, as in most other Western democracies, at the end of the nineteenth century, from a conjunction of universal suffrage, of loose parliamentary groups, and of local committees formed to support candidates. The traditional approach to the analysis of parties was that they served, or ideally ought to serve, as 'transmission belts' on which political ideas and programmes were conveyed from the citizens to the legislature and the executive. Later, this analysis was extended to interest groups, which supposedly differed only in that they urged policies in specified areas.

Parties and interest groups came to be regarded as 'intermediaries' between the governors and the governed; the will of the citizens was transmitted to their elected representatives who changed it into positive law to be applied by the executive for the citizens' lasting benefit. Even when systems analysis later refined their function to include such concepts as political recruitment and communication, and interest articulation and aggregation, parties and groups were regarded as organisations for channelling political demands.

Economic interest groups in France, however, and particularly employees' unions, were less amenable to this kind of approach because they traditionally distanced themselves from the parliamentary process, either in terms of declared aims (for example, the restructuring of society) or in terms of the way they went about achieving less radical aims such as higher real wages or better work conditions. New analytical approaches have been developed to modify the 'intermediaries' concept. One of these has been the notion of a 'liberal' corporatism which emphasises that policy outcomes are the result of a process of negotiation rather than control. Another approach is to speak of parties, groups, and the recently expanding phenomenon of 'associations' as countervailing forces (*contre-pouvoirs*) which serve to limit the power of the State, even if this is not necessarily their avowed aim.

Political parties: identity

Political parties in the Western sense are usually defined as groups of citizens, more or less organised, who try through elections to gain, or share in, political power in order to apply a programme inspired by a doctrine. In having a comprehensive doctrinal foundation, a broadly based organisation, and the wish to maximise their electoral appeal, parties are distinguished from interest groups, from groups of parliamentarians, and from political clubs.

The latter first flourished during the time of the French Revolution, establishing a tradition whereby small groups of people met to discuss the problems of society and to propose solutions. Political clubs kept alive throughout the nineteenth century the strand of republican humanism associated with the 1789 Revolution, but it was during the 1960s that they performed the function of renewing political discourse, particularly on the Left, at a time when political parties were adapting with difficulty to the new Fifth Republic regime. A group of Left-wing clubs, the *Convention des Institutions Républicaines* (CIR), was an important element in the attempt to federate the non-Communist Left in 1965–8; it was the means by which François Mitterrand came to lead the new *Parti Socialiste* (PS) from 1971, which was an indispensable element in his election to the Presidency. A group operating within the Socialist party from 1965, the *Centre d'Etudes, de Recherche et d'Education Socialistes* (CERES) was analogous to the clubs in its aims and methods, and in the 1970s and 1980s came to play a key role in its continued advocacy of Communist–Socialist cooperation. Political clubs do not put up candidates at elections, and tend to be located in Paris, but in the 1980s their role at all points of the political spectrum, in doctrinal renewal and political education is seen as an important adjunct to the activities of parties, with which they are often associated. After 1981, political clubs, for example *Le Club de L'Horloge* and the *Comités d'Action Républicaine*, were established to help the Right to be constructive in opposition and prepare for the next manifestation of *alternance.*[1]

Groups of parliamentarians can be distinguished from political parties in that they lack a coherent or geographically broad organisation, although they can sometimes exist because the party which elected them has been dissolved – for example, Gaullists in the Fourth Republic Parliament from 1953 to 1958 – and the modern Giscardian *Parti Républicain* (PR) grew out of a loosely-structured parliamentary group of *Républicains Indépendants* (RI) who only gradually from 1962 managed to establish a nation-wide party organisation. Under the rules of the post-1958 National Assembly, deputies have certain privileges – for example, membership of a Standing Committee – only if they are members of an officially constituted political group of at least 30 members. This sometimes leads deputies elected under different party labels and with minimal political affinities to join together under an umbrella title in Parliament, and incidentally adds to the plethora of group and party titles which is an aspect – and for the student a sometimes puzzling one – of the identity of parties.

The problem is, firstly, that parties change their own names, especially when they feel a need to emphasise in the minds of the public that they have a new image. The Socialist party was called *Section Française de l'Internationale Ouvrière* (SFIO) from 1905 to 1969, and the *Parti Socialiste* (PS) from 1971. Figure 6.1 shows its development in the Fifth Republic, with accretions and separations. During the 1969–71 hiatus it was referred to as *'le nouveau parti socialiste'* which was a description rather than a title. The Gaullist party, set up in 1947 but dissolved in 1953, assumed the following titles in the Fifth Republic:

1958 – *Union pour la Nouvelle République* (UNR)
1967 – *Union des Démocrates pour la Cinquième République* (UDV^e)
1968 – *Union des Démocrates pour la République* (UDR)
1976 – *Rassemblement pour la République* (RPR)

Secondly, parties and groups frequently cooperate just for election periods under umbrella titles established only weeks before. Examples have been in the elections of:

1981 – *Union pour la Nouvelle Majorité* (UNM) comprising the RPR and the Giscardian UDF
1981 – *Alternative 1981*, comprising the *Parti Socialiste Unifié* (PSU), most groups of *Amis de la Terre*, the *Mouvement pour une alternative non-violente*, some CFDT activists, and some of the Maoist *Parti communiste révolutionnaire*
1973 – *Union de la Gauche Socialiste et Démocrate* (UGSD) comprising the Socialist Party and the Left Radicals (MRG)
1973 – *Union des Républicains de Progrès* (URP) comprising UDR, RI, and some Centrists.

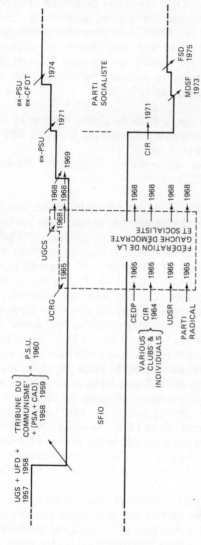

Figure 6.1
Evolution of the SFIO and Parti Socialiste 1957–81

NOTES: CAD *Centre d'Action Démocratique* (Mendésiste); CEDEP: *Centre National d'Etudes et de Promotion* (Pierre Mauroy); CFDT: *Confédération Française Démocratique du Travail;* CIR *Convention des Institutions Républicaines* (François Mitterrand); FSD: *Fédération des Socialistes Démocrates* (Eric Hintermann); MDSF: *Mouvement Démocrate Socialiste de France* (Max Lejeune); PSA: *Parti Socialiste Autonome* (Mendésiste); PSU: *Parti Socialiste Unifié;* SFIO: *Section Française de l'Internationale Ouvrière*; UCRG: *Union des Clubs pour le Renouveau de la Gauche* (Alain Savary); UDSR: *Union Démocratique et Socialiste de la Résistance*; UFD: *Union des Forces Démocratiques* (Mendésiste); UGCS: *Union des Groupes et Clubs Socialistes* (Jean Poperen); UGS: *Union de la Gauche Socialiste* (Claude Bourdet)

Such *ad hoc* umbrella titles sometimes however survive the elections for which they were invented; this gave the Gaullist party its 1967 name, but the best example was the *Union pour la Démocratie Française* (UDF), originally established to coordinate the 1978 electoral activities of parties supporting Giscard; it survived to become in the 1980s the rather shaky vehicle for the continuing attempt by Giscard and Barre to achieve some presidential underpinning. Thirdly, parties may federate under an umbrella title outside election periods, but with future electoral advantage clearly a factor; examples are:

1965–8 – *Fédération de la Gauche Démocratique et Socialiste* (FGDS) comprising Socialists, Radicals and various clubs (see Fig. 6.1)

1971–3 – *Mouvement Réformateur* comprising Radicals and Opposition Centrists.

Parties are further identified in the Fifth Republic, and certainly since 1962, by reference to whether they are part of a parliamentary majority supporting the Government, or part of the Opposition. Because some Centrist groups were trying to maintain a distinct identity, a bipolarisation of Majority and Opposition was not established until 1973–4 (see pp. 46–8). Figure 6.2 shows, with reference to parties represented in the National Assembly, the way in which these were grouped into a Majority and an Opposition up to 1981. The thickness of columns indicates first-round electoral support, since this is when electoral choice is widest. Changes of name are also shown. Another index of party identity is in terms of Left and Right. At the beginning of the Fifth Republic, the Gaullist Party (UNR), reflecting the political ideas of de Gaulle, attracted broad-based support; Right-wing opinions, especially on Algeria, were voiced mainly by sections of the large groups of *Indépendants*. By the end of the 1970s, however, the Gaullist RPR was perceived by voters to be slightly to the Right of the Giscardian UDF[2], which included the Centrist *Centre des Démocrates Sociaux* (CDS) and the Radical Party whose full name is *Parti Radical et Radical-Socialiste*.

The problem of separate identity is exacerbated by the existence at any one time of minor parties, not just on the extreme Right and extreme Left, but also in that part of the political spectrum usually called the Centre Left, where fragmentation is characaterised by a clustering of support round the political figure who founded the party. Examples are:

Centre Républicain (founded 1956) – André Morice
Mouvement Démocrate Socialiste de France (1973) – Max Lejeune
Mouvement des Démocrates (1974) – Michel Jobert
Démocratie Chrétienne Française (1978) – Alfred Coste-Floret
Parti Socialiste Démocrate (1978) – Eric Hintermann
Parti Démocrate Français (1982) – Guy Gennesseaux

Figure 6.2
Majorité and Opposition 1958–81

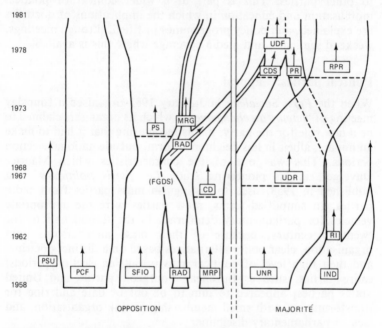

NOTES: CD   *Centre Démocrate*; CDS: *Centre des Démocrates Sociaux*; FGDS: *Fédération de la Gauche Démocrate et Socialiste*; Ind.:   *Indépendants*; MRG: *Mouvement des Radicaux de Gauche*; MRP: *Mouvement Républicain Populaire*; PCF: *Parti Communiste Français*; PR: *Parti Républicain*; PS   *Parti Socialiste*; PSU: *Parti Socialiste Unifié*; Rad.:   *Parti Radical*; RI: *Républicains Indépendants*; RPR: *Rassemblement pour la République*; SFIO: *Section Française de l'Internationale Ouvrière*; UDF: *Union pour la Démocratie Française*; UDR: *Union des Démocrates pour la République*; UNR: *Union pour la Nouvelle République*

A 1982 count identified some seventy-five political parties, clubs and movements across the whole spectrum of contemporary French politics, but of course they also cease to exist, either voluntarily or on being dissolved by the authorities – this happened in 44 cases between 1958 and 1982, 16 on the extreme Right, 13 on the extreme Left, and 15 separatist or 'liberation' movements.

The existence of small parties with no realistic hope of gaining a seat in Parliament suggests that this element of the definition of a political party has to be refined to say that a party contests elections because of the opportunity they give to it through State aid as well as increased public interest, to mark a distinctive identity in relation to other parties. This is part of a wider context of political mobilisation and education in which the implications of doctrines are explained, and policy programmes justified, through meetings, weekend seminars, and media coverage where this is available.

Politcal parties: appeal

When the *Parti Socialiste* in January 1983 organised a four-day meeting of *'acteurs du changement'*, which its organisers claimed to be a new role for the party, it was recognising that it had to make an impact, albeit in less heightened form, outside national election periods. This was one of the characteristics which Maurice Duverger, in his pioneering study *Les partis politiques*, first published in 1953, used to distinguish mass parties from cadre parties. In simplified terms, mass parties were the appropriate vehicles for parliamentary democracy in the second half of the twentieth century, because of their mass membership, tight organisation, clear policy alternatives based on a distinct doctrine, and their high level of political activity outside election periods; cadre parties, such as European bourgeois parties and United States parties, appeared to him to be out of date and ripe for transformation, with small memberships, weak organisation, and lack of parliamentary discipline.

The Fifth Republic, however, brought modifications to this analysis because there emerged in the 1960s a Gaullist party which was not only dominant within the party system, but which clearly kept that position because it had the greatest electoral appeal, even when the Gaullian charisma was waning. It was a party of electors because, having no outmoded ideological baggage, it could be a catch-all party (the French translated this as *un parti attrape-tout*). In capitalising on the wide appeal of Gaullist thought and Gaullist policies, however, it was not so much aggregating opinions and demands as reducing them to their lowest and vaguest denominators. In general, this was true of all major parties in France, and there was in the 1960s a clear reduction in the extent to which actual party programmes were inspired by the ideologies outlined in Chapter 2, though these remain a potent source of slogans and concepts used to mobilise support, justify allegiance, and attack adversaries. Moreover, the phenomenon of regional electoral bastions – for example, the Radical Party in the South-West, the MRP then the Gaullists in Alsace-Lorraine and Brittany, the PCF in the eastern suburbs of Paris and in Limousin, the SFIO in the *départements* of Nord, Pas-de-Calais and Bouches-du-Rhône – is much less marked since the late 1960s. But despite a more even geographical spread of national voting patterns, a vote for a party does not necessarily have the same meaning everywhere. It may be coloured according to the dominant social category, or the power of opposing political forces.

The appeal of parties in terms of sex, age, occupation, income and 'religiosity' is gauged by opinion polls on voting patterns in the first round of parliamentary elections. These establish what percentage of groups within each of the above categories voted for which party, and allow parties to claim, as the Gaullists could in the 1960s and the Socialists in the 1980s, that they are more 'representative' because the sociological profile of their own electorate virtually coincides with that of the country as a whole. The 'profile' of party electorates in the first round of the 1981 parliamentary elections is shown in Table 6.1.

The size of party membership has always been difficult to assess in France, since membership levels have of necessity to be self-ascribed. Parties tend to inflate numbers to prove their own popularity, and in those parties – the heirs to the 'mass' parties of Duverger – which emphasise the possession of a membership card, these are sometimes issued locally to boost representation in higher decision-making bodies at the level of *departement* or national conference, without having the contribution payment record to make them valid. The *Parti Socialiste* claimed over 160 000 members at its moment of victory in May 1981, but accuracy concerning party membership is really possible only in relation to increasing or decreasing trends over, say, five-year periods.

Parties are always anxious to appeal to young people; they try to influence their political education from an early age, and they mobilise their energies at election times. All major parties in France have their youth movements and separate student groups, but the contribution of these can be offset by difficulties in ensuring doctrinal orthodoxy, or by problems arising from disagreement about their purpose – youth movements are sometimes not sure whether they are a force for dynamic independent thought, or breeding grounds for future party leaders.

Table 6.1

'Profile' of party electorates in the first round of the 1981 parliamentary elections

	Total	Parti communiste	Extrême-gauche PSU	Parti Socialiste / Radicaux de gauche / Divers gauche	Écologistes	UDF	RPR	Divers UNM	Divers droite / Extrême-droite
Total	100%	16	1	39	1	19	21	1	2
Sexe									
Homme	100%	17	2	39	1	20	20	–	1
Femme	100%	15	1	38	2	18	22	1	3
Age									
18 à 24 ans	100%	18	2	44	2	14	17	–	3
25 à 34 ans	100%	17	2	46	3	16	15	1	1
35 à 49 ans	100%	17	2	37	1	18	23	1	2
50 à 64 ans	100%	18	1	42	1	19	16	1	5
65 ans et plus	100%	10	1	27	–	27	30	–	5
Catégorie socioprofessionnelle du chef de famille									
Agriculteur, salarié agricole	100%	6	2	32	–	28	32	–	–
Petit commerçant, artisan	100%	10	–	35	–	19	31	–	5
Cadre supérieur, profession libérale, industriel, gros commerçant	100%	7	2	38	3	19	28	3	1
Cadre moyen, employé	100%	16	2	45	2	18	14	1	2
Ouvrier	100%	24	1	44	1	15	14	1	–
Inactif, retraité	100%	16	1	29	–	23	26	1	4

SOURCE: enquête post-électorale SOFRES – *Nouvel Observateur*, 4 juillet, 1981

Political parties in the system

In the Fourth Republic, political parties were central to the system in the sense that the regime was created by their agreement in 1944–6, and foundered because of their disagreement in the mid-1950s. The Fifth Republic regime, on the other hand, was established against a background of opposition to parties. The 1958 Constitution clearly defines the role and purpose of political parties. Article 4 provides that parties and groups play a part in the articulation of the people's will, the implication being that they are not the only means through which this is done – referenda are another method. They have rights to exist and operate like any other association within the 1901 law regulating such groups – there are differences when it comes to elections (for example, access to media) though the question of state financial aid to pursue general political aims is not yet resolved. But they have obligations to respect the principles of national sovereignty and democracy.

This new constitutional framework was the product of the views of Debré and especially of de Gaulle, whose antagonism continued during his Presidency: *'Je voulais briser les partis'* was his comment after the successful 1962 referendum on changing the method of Presidential election; during the 1965 election, he said: *'Le régime des partis, c'est la pagaille.'* Giscard continued in the same vein by saying in 1977 that parties were *'porteurs de division'.*

Parties were also obliged to operate within a new electoral system introduced in 1958 (page 167), and one of the aims of having single-member constituencies was to concentrate voters' attention on the candidate as an individual representative and not on his or her party label. The 1958 legislative election was very much a candidates' election, with nearly a quarter of first-round votes going to *Indépendants* (called *'Modérés'*) most of whom belonged to the loosely-structured *Centre National des Indépendants et Paysans* (CNIP). But the parties soon re-established their influence in this and in other aspects of the political system.

With the presidentialisation of the regime, a parliamentary majority group supporting Gaullist governments became a settled characteristic of the system from 1962 until the election of a non-Gaullist, though Right-wing, President in 1974. This majority group comprised the Gaullist party, Giscard's *Républicains Indépendants* who maintained a separate identity, and from 1969 the Centrists of the *Centre Démocratie et Progrès* (CDP). In this context of the emerging distinction between a Majority and an Opposition, parties regained much of the influence which the framers of the 1958 Constitution tried to take from them. With the systemic need for the widest possible parliamentary majority to support Presidential policies implemented by the Government, parties were in a strong position to demand Government posts, and policies to their liking, as the price of their support. Prime Ministers – even 'technocrats' like Couve and Barre – welcomed the added authority gained from appearing to be the head of a major party in the Majority, though it must be said that only Chirac, in 1974–5, was an actual party leader, and Pompidou refused to let Chaban-Delmas become leader of the Gaullist party.

The establishment of the Majority system in the 1960s, and the emergence of a dominant Right-wing party round which that Majority was built, obliged the Left to attempt to consolidate its own forces. This was a lengthy process, made up of the two aspects – firstly, the federation of the non-Communist Left, and secondly, the close cooperation of the latter with the Communist Party. The stumbling block, however, was that the Left came only slowly to accept the Fifth Republic system. François Mitterrand was one of the first to see in the 1960s that the regime as it had developed in practice could be a vehicle for Left-wing policies, but the call for a return to a more literal reading of the 1958 Constitution was the common thread of the Left's disunited stance in the 1969 Presidential elections.

Mitterrand's attempt to gather the non-Communist Left in a *Fédération de la Gauche Démocrate et Socialiste* collapsed in 1968 (see Fig. 6.1), but he was already convinced that winning the Presidency and a parliamentary majority for the Left was only possible on the basis of a close cooperation with the Communist Party in an *Union de la Gauche*. In pursuing this strategy, he was able to build on the arrangement, started in a modest way in 1962, whereby the SFIO (and the wider FGDS in 1967 and 1968) and the PCF gave joint backing in the second round of legislative elections to whichever of their candidates led in the first round. This is called '*le désistement réciproque*', and sometimes by the parties themselves '*la discipline républicaine*'; electoral cooperation was capped in 1972 by the signature of a *Programme Commun de Gouvernement* intended to be applied once the Left formed a Government.

With the final absorption into the Majority in 1974 of the MRP's Centrist heirs, and the small mainstream Radical Party, the party system was set to take on the shape of a '*quadrille bipolaire*' which was completed by the establishment of the UDF in 1978. In this framework, relations between partners within both Left and Right 'coalitions' assume a high degree of saliency. It can be argued that parties have regained a central place within the system, analogous to the one they had before 1958, because inter-party relations determine:

1 the composition of the Government and its ability to survive (this was especially true of RPR–UDF relations 1976–81);
2 the existence of a credible alternative to make *alternance* a reality (unsuccessful 1978; successful 1981).

The two Right-wing partners continued to emphasise their separate identities after their 1981 defeat; moreover, their attempts to present a single first-round candidate sometimes founder on local rivalries – there were around seventy UDF–RPR 'primaries' in both 1978 and 1981.

The *Union de la Gauche* in the sense of a common determination to apply an agreed policy programme in Government broke down in 1977. This was mainly because the PCF, despite increased ideological flexibility – abandoning the idea of the dictatorship of the proletariat, accepting *alternance*, becoming for a time 'Eurocommunist' – was not willing to accommodate a shift in the centre of gravity (*rééquilibrage*) in favour of the Socialists. There were PCF members in post-1981 Governments, but the term *Union de la Gauche* was not applied to what progressively became '*participation sans soutien*'. The term was used however in 1983 by the PCF leader Georges Marchais to describe electoral cooperation in the municipal elections.

The *Parti Socialiste* itself was able to widen its membership and electoral appeal throughout the 1970s and reintegrated some of the elements which in the years immediately after 1958, when the SFIO supported de Gaulle's return, had gone to form the *Parti Socialiste Unifié* (see Fig. 6.1). Although the PS has a structure which allows factions (*courants*) to be represented on policy-making committees, it nevertheless followed the pattern of 'presidentialisation' of French parties – party leaders and their close associates gained a clear preponderance of influence, and all successful Presidential candidates have had the strong support of their party as the core of their majority. And yet party involvement in executive power is limited, as it is in Presidential elections (pp. 97–8): when people spoke of an 'Etat–UDR' in the 1960s or suggested there might be an 'Etat–PS' in the 1980s, they were saying little more than that there was a dominant party. Parties may well have recovered some of the ground which they lost in the constitutional provisions of 1958, but the Fifth Republic system would never admit the pre-1958 practice of regarding Government members as party delegates accountable to party leadership. A political party may well be indispensable to a Presidential candidate in coming to power, but it will always be subordinate in the system to the Presidency as the pivot of the institutional structure of the State.

Interest groups and trade unions

Interest groups can fulfil the function of providing an alternative vehicle for the articulation of political demands; with the declining specificity of goals pursued by political parties, which have loosened their ideological attachment in order to gain wider appeal, interest groups can prevent the alienation of sections of opinion from the political system as a whole, by focussing on a single issue area and attempting to influence policy in that area. The earliest examples in France, in the nineteenth century, were generally organised at a local level, and for humanitarian purposes, and these developed into 'pressure groups' which tried to influence Parliament under the Third and Fourth Republics. Since the 1950s, the term 'interest group' is usually preferred, and more recently the women's movement and the anti-nuclear phenomenon have been analysed as 'social movements'.

The parliamentary stage of the legislative process is normally the culmination of a lengthy process of activity in Ministries and other extra-parliamentary locations, including formal consultative organs – the numerous 'Conseils Supérieurs', 'Comités Nationaux' and 'Comités d'usagers' specialising in a particular field. The tendency during the Fifth Republic has been to attempt to influence the Executive, not only because it dominates Parliament, but also because important areas of policy are often the result of routine decision-making, through the exercise of the pouvoir réglementaire. Interest groups operate in a Fifth Republic system which can be described as statist pluralism, where public policy is the product of State interpretation of a public interest which transcends sectional interests. Groups espousing these have therefore to be brought into conformity with societal standards, and this often leads to a collusive relationship between some interest groups and the Government, alongside the conflictual one sometimes leading to dramatic protest demonstrations.

This ambivalent aspect of interest group activity and the associated phenomenon of their fragmentation, was shown in the area of agriculture by their relationship with the post-1981 Left-wing government. The agriculture minister said: 'Le syndicalisme négocie et contexte, l'Etat décide'. But French governments tend to

treat agricultural interests with indulgence and four farmers'
groups were quick to express the wish to work in harmony with the
new Government:

1 *Fédération nationale des syndicats d'exploitants agricoles*
  (FNSEA) the main agricultural interest group;
2 *Assemblée permanente des chambres d'agriculture* (APCA);
3 *Centre national des jeunes agriculteurs* (CNJA);
4 *Confédération nationale de la mutualité, du crédit et de la
  coopération agricoles* (CNMCCA)

They were joined by a newly-formed *Confédération nationale
syndicale des travailleurs–paysans* (CNSTP) which was Socialist-
oriented and which received 7 per cent of votes nationally in the
first elections to Chambers of Agriculture to be held by
proportional representation in 1983. But the Communist-leaning
small peasants' group *Mouvement de défense des exploitants
familiaux* (MODEF) and the conservative *Fédération française de
l'agriculture* (FFA) maintained their distance from the government.

This kind of adversary relationship is evident, firstly, in groups
representing business interests and industrial employers – the
Conseil national du patronat français (CNPF) was often critical of
Right-wing governments in the 1970s, and organisations defending
the interests of *petites et moyennes entreprises* were particularly
hostile to the post-1981 Left government – and secondly in the case
of employees' unions (*syndicats ouvriers*). The latter were legalised
only in 1884 and tended to be antiparliamentary in attitude,
suspicious of politicians and political groupings, and determined to
work out their own political orientation. However, the movement
was divided from its origins on whether relations with political
groupings should be based on close cooperation or complete
autonomy, on how far workers should control the means of
production, distribution and exchange, and on how far direct
action should go – a concerted general strike to break the capitalist
system was advocated by some groups, but the extreme version of
insurrection was remembered as a failure in 1870–1.

Differences such as these ended all chance of a general Labour
movement, and the loose confederations established in the
twentieth century reflected divisions between the reformist and the
revolutionary strategy, and between classical nineteenth-century
unionism stressing wages and conditions, and a more modernist
approach, originally of Catholic inspiration, which advocated a
restructuring of industrial and economic units in the interests both

of the participants and the wider community. The four main confederations in contemporary France are, in descending order of membership:

1 CGT (*Confédération générale du travail*): the link with the Communist Party is strong at middle levels, and the CGT has been called the 'transmission belt' (*courroie de transmission*) of the PCF.

2 CFDT (*Confédération française démocratique du travail*): split from the CFTC in 1964, and became more explicitly Socialist in 1970; in favour of the self-management (*autogestion*) of industrial units.

3 FO (*Force ouvrière*): split from the CGT in 1948, hence its full title of CGT–FO; moderate, European-minded, and in favour of negociated agreements in a spirit of democratic socialism.

4 CFTC (*Confédération française des travailleurs chrétiens*): founded in 1919 and inspired by the social teaching of the Catholic Church though now not so explicitly Catholic; weakened by the 1964 split when the new CFDT took most of its members; favours worker participation in management.

The fragmentation of present-day French trade unions is compounded by the existence of categories of employees organised into autonomous unions outside these four confederations. A small *Confédération des Syndicats Libres* links many independent anti-strike unions, and in the field of education the *Fédération de l'Education nationale* (FEN) has been dominant since its foundation in 1948. Although each of the main four confederations came to include a union representing white-collar workers and middle management, their inability to adapt totally to this growing phenomenon in the 1920s and 1930s led in 1944 to the establishment of the CGC (*Confédération générale des cadres*). In the 1970s and 1980s this confederation considerably extended its recruitment among lower management and became more self-assertive in the face of declining real income levels. These developments led to a change of name in 1981 to *Confédération générale de l'encadrement*, but the former initials CGC still persisted.

Organisational fragmentation, slowness to adapt to changing economic circumstances in some fields, and the inability to mobilise more than a fifth to a quarter of the total workforce (though the proportion is healthier in the public sector and service industries) have meant that French unions remain uncertain about the ends and means of their activity in the area of what is usually called *'la vie sociale'*. Moreover, these weaknesses persisted in the 1980s at a time when unions might have been expected to make some gains in power and influence, helped by sympathetic legislation, particularly the various elements of the *'loi Auroux'*, introduced by the post-1981 Left government.

Bibliographical guidance

On political parties and groups in general, the following are recommended:

D.S. Bell (ed.), *Contemporary French Political Parties* (Croom Helm, 1982)
F. Borella, *Les partis politiques dans la France d'aujourd'hui*. 4th ed. (Seuil, 1981)
'Douze ans de la vie des partis 1969–1981' in *Regards sur l'actualité*, nos. 71–2, (La Documentation Française, 1981)
P. Lavigne, 'Retour au régime des partis sous la Vᵉ République?' in G. Conac *et al.* (eds) *Itinéraires – études en l'honneur de Léo Hamon* (Economica, 1982)
'Les élections législatives de juin 1981', *Supplément aux Dossiers et Documents*, (*Le Monde* June 1981) pp. 50–8: Prises de position des leaders des grands partis politiques; entretiens avec les dirigeants des grandes centrales syndicales.

On parties of the Right, the appropriate sections of the above books and of books on the Giscard and Mitterrand Presidencies are suggested, as well as the following:

J.-C. Colliard, 'The Giscardians', and P. Lecomte, 'The political forces of French Conservatism', both in Z.A. Layton-Henry (ed), *Conservative Politics in Western Europe* (Macmillan, 1982)
P. Crisol, and Y. Lhomeau, *La machine R.P.R.* (Fayolle, 1977)
Pouvoirs no. 28 (1984); number devoted to Le RPR
D. Seguin, *Les nouveaux Giscardiens* (Calmann-Lévy, 1979)

There is more in the way of recent books on parties of the Left, and the following selection is recommended:

J.-P. Brunet, *Histoire du P.C.F.* (PUF, 1982)
A. du Roy, and R. Schneider, *Le roman de la rose* (Seuil, 1982)
Intervention nos. 5–6 (août – sept. 1983) 'Les socialistes croient-ils à leurs mythes?'
R.W. Johnson, *The Long March of the French Left* (Macmillan, 1981)
J. Kergoat, *Le parti socialiste* (Le Sycomore, 1983)

G. Lavau, *A quoi sert le Parti communiste français?* (Fayard, 1981)
N. Nugent and D. Lowe, *The Left in France* (Macmillan, 1982)
P. Robrieux, *Histoire intérieure du Parti communiste*, 4 vols (Fayard, 1980–4
Y. Roucaute, *Le parti socialiste* (Huisman, 1983)
D. Tartakowsky, *Une histoire du P.C.F.* (PUF, 1982)
J. Touchard, *La gauche en France depuis 1900* (Seuil, 1981)

On economic interest groups (trade unions and employers' organisations) see:

J.A. Basso, *Les groupes de pression* (PUF,1983)
A. Bergounioux, *Force ouvrière* (PUF, 1982)
M. Branciard, *Syndicats et partis*, vol, 2, *1947–81* (Syros, 1982)
H. Hamon and P. Rotman, *La deuxième gauche – histoire intellectuelle et politique de la C.F.D.T.* (Ramsay, 1982; paperback Seuil, 1984)
C. Harmel, *La C.G.T. 1947–81* (PUF,1982)
H. Landier, *Demain, quels syndicats?* (Livre de Poche, 1981)
H. Landier, *Les organisations syndicales en France* (Entreprise Moderne de l'Edition, 1980)
G. Lefranc, *Visages du mouvement ouvrier français*, part 3 (PUF, 1982)
G. Lefranc, *Les syndicats*, 11th ed.(PUF, 1981)
R. Mouriaux, *La C.G.T.* (Seuil, 1982)
Pouvoirs, no. 26 (1983), number devoted to 'Le pouvoir syndical'
M. Tozzi, *Syndicalisme et nouveaux mouvements sociaux* (Editions ouvrières, 1982)

Illustrative texts and linguistic exercises

Texte 6.1 L'AGNEAU DU SEIGNEUR

Mise en situation

Le Quotidien de Paris était après 1981 un des organes les plus incisifs de l'Opposition de droite. Dans cet article, Philippe Dufay décrit le rôle de Lionel Jospin, premier secrétaire du Parti Socialiste dont le siège national se trouve à 10, rue de Solférino, à Paris. Plusieurs références sont expliquées à la fin du texte.

*   *   *

PS: Parti socialiste. Fondateur: François Mitterrand, éternel. Directeur gérant: Lionel Jospin, 45 ans. Le vieil étudiant aux boucles grises tient la boutique Solférino depuis 350 jours hier. Exactement, depuis le 24 janvier 1981: soit dix ans après son entrée au parti, aussitôt le congrès d'Epinay. 350 jours, dont 200 à la tête d'un parti au pouvoir, et l'homme n'apparaît pas à proprement parler comme une 'bête' politique. Il n'a qu'une ambition déclarée: comme le garçon de café de Sartre, Jospin joue à être le premier secrétaire du PS. Mitterrand, Jospin: après le père, le grand frère, avancent certains. *Balivernes*, la révolution du 10 mai rend les deux hommes, les deux gestions, incomparables. A quoi sert aujourd'hui Lionel Jospin? Le patron reste Mitterrand. L'exécutif: c'est Mauroy. Le Parlement: c'est Joxe et Mermaz. La voix de son maître: c'est Delanoé et Estier. Les négociations avec le PC: c'est Poperen et Debarge. Réponse: le parti, c'est lui. Question: mais à quoi sert le chef d'un parti, quand ce parti est au pouvoir? Réponse: *rayer les mentions inutiles*: de super-attaché de presse, de courroie de transmission; de gardien des réliques; de chef de station au métro Solférino. Jospin, bien sûr, les trouve toutes inutiles. Inadmissibles. Il les raye. Le coup du 'super-godillot', on le lui a fait dès le départ. Il a répondu cinquante fois: 'ni *parti godillot*, ni courroie de transmission'. Le parti doit être 'une force de proposition', 'la conscience – bonne ou mauvaise – du gouvernement'.

Son principal 'job' de chef – il le reconnaît souvent – c'est d'"expliquer': expliquer d'abord aux socialistes la politique du gouvernement; au gouvernement les états d'âme des socialistes, et aux Français l'action des socialistes au pouvoir.

Il fallait un séraphin
En entrant en politique, l'ancien *énarque*-diplomate devenu universitaire est resté maître assistant: il est l'homme des TD, pas celui des programmes. On a dit qu'il avait été 'porté dans un fauteuil' à la tête du PS. C'était en fait une chaire. Jospin n'est pas un porte-parole. C'est un interprète. Il jospine du Mitterrand; celui d'avant et d'après le 10 mai, l'ancien et le nouveau Mitterrand, ce qui n'est pas toujours évident ... Dans la bergerie de la rue de Solférino, le vieux loup a soigneusement choisi son agneau. L'agneau du Seigneur. Le chef de l'Etat a préféré l'aube de Jospin à la bouteille de Poperen. Mitterrand a peut-être, sur ce point, influencé Giscard dans son choix de prendre François Léotard à la tête du PR. Les monstres politiques s'offrent ainsi des jeunes gens 'clean', dont la dialectique politique passe par l'enthousiasme et le jogging.

La jospination est une alchimie qui transforme les plus vieux mensonges en vérité vécue, et donne aux ficelles du pouvoir l'accent de la sincérité. A cet exercice, ni le *teigneux* Joxe, ni le sectaire Mermaz, n'auraient pu sans doute se plier. Il fallait un séraphin.

La jospination suit une géometrie dans l'espace. L'homme est, en effet, le lieu géometrique entre l'Elysée, Matignon, le parti, le groupe et les Français. Avec l'Elysée, s'il conserve le privilège d'absorber encore chaque jeudi un petit déjeuner, il *avale surtout des couleuvres*. A lui de les dégurgiter ensuite sous forme de bouillie présentable aux militants. La liste est longue: ventes d'armes, politique africaine, politique économique, affaire des *putschistes* ...

Le ministre du parti

En fait, la gesticulation jospinatoire consiste – en tandem avec Matignon –(bien qu'inavouée, l'alliance Jospin–Mauroy est une réalité indéniable) à jouer les essuie-glaces, les essuie-problèmes, entre le 'château' et la rue de Solférino. Seul le groupe, pour sauver la face du parlementarisme, et de par la rugosité de son chef, peut perturber ce ballet. Guerre des 'J'*, peaux de banane sous les ballerines de l'étoile (Cf. l'affaire des généraux), mais Dieu le père veille à pourfendre au besoin l'archange noir . . .Avec les Français, pas de problème: Lionel Jospin est un ministre comme les autres: le ministre du parti. Point. Il passe à la TV et participe comme ses (faux) pairs aux campagnes sur le terrain.

Ministre du parti. L'image n'est pas seulement valable pour les citoyens téléspectateurs, ignorants par définition. A Lionel Jospin revient la tâche de gérer le ministère de la rue de Solférino, et notamment de garantir l'homogénéité de la machine PS: c'est-à-dire de couper les têtes – à tout point de vue repoussantes – de *l'hydre des courants*. Comme son maître, Jospin chasse donc le rocardien, et surveille les CERES. Il pousse, à Paris, Quilès contre Sarre†, et décourage les offensives souterraines des amis de Rocard après la démission-scandale du ministre de la Coopération‡.

Est-ce à dire qu'il *tient vraiment son monde*? Du moins lui en donne-t-on largement les moyens. Puissamment soutenu, il reste vigilant, conscient que dans cette gymnastique, il demeure plus un point d'articulation qu'un véritable membre.

Patron patronné, comme les yaourts, Lionel Jospin a-t-il *une date limite de fraîcheur*? Quels sont son taux d'usure et ses possibilités de recyclage? Pour l'instant, autre fusible du président, il s'apprête, comme Mauroy, à affronter le 'court-jus' des municipales, et prépare le prochain congrès du parti. Quitte après à lâcher sa chère 'singularité' pour rejoindre les 'quarante' au sein du gouvernement.

SOURCE: Article écrit par Philippe Dufay paru dans *Le Quotidien de Paris*, lundi 10 janvier, 1983.

Exploitation du texte

1   Expliquez en quelques mots les expressions en italique.

2   Faites une analyse textuelle générale, en vous appuyant éventuellement sur l'approche suggérée dans l'Annexe A (p. 23).

3   A partir de votre analyse générale, faites une étude plus détaillée de l'emploi

---

*Une référence au prétendu combat entre Pierre Joxe, Président du groupe socialiste à l'Assemblée Nationale, et Lionel Jospin.

†Il s'agit du conflit entre Paul Quilès (mitterrandiste) et Georges Sarre (CERES) pour devenir chef de file de l'Union de la gauche à Paris aux élections municipales de 1983. Quilès gagna cette bataille, mais ne réussit pas à évincer Jacques Chirac de son poste de Maire de Paris.

‡Il s'agit de Jean-Pierre Cot, démissionnaire en décembre 1982.

de métaphores
de néologismes
de jeux de mots

4 Expliquez les allusions dans les expressions suivantes:

il est l'homme des TD
Le Parlement: c'est Joxe et Mermaz
la voix de son maître: c'est Delanoë et Estier
entre le 'château' et la rue de Solférino

Actualisez éventuellement les références nominatives.

5 Rédigez une description du rôle de Lionel Jospin en tant que premier
secrétaire du PS, comme s'il la faisait lui-même dans un rapport.

6 Donnez quelques détails sur une ou plusieurs des politiques suivantes
pendant la première période de la Présidence de François Mitterrand:

vente d'armes
politique africaine
politique économique
affaire des putschistes

Texte 6.2   Le financement des partis politiques

Mise en situation

Le Figaro, vieux journal libéral et bourgeois, fut acheté en 1975 par le
groupe de presse dirigé par Robert Hersant, et devint un organe redoutable
de la droite politique. Cet article parut en novembre 1982.

*   *   *

La découverte de bureaux d'études qui *auraient servi* à financer
indirectement le parti communiste par l'intermédiaire des municipalités
qu'il contrôle, a, une fois de plus, fait resurgir le problème du financement
occulte des partis politiques. Et, une fois de plus, on a assisté à une
débauche de propositions vertueuses tendant à assurer la 'transparence' de
ce financement, soit en obligeant les partis à publier la liste de leurs
généreux donateurs et le montant de leurs contributions, soit en les faisant
financer par l'Etat, soit par une combinaison de ces deux procédés.

Sur le principe de la publicité des ressources des formations politiques,
on ne peut, bien sûr, qu'être d'accord du point de vue moral. Mais très
sceptiques aussi sur son application pratique. On l'a bien vu ces jours
derniers encore lorsque M. Marchais a affirmé que le PC vivait
exclusivement des *cotisations de ses militants,* des souscriptions qu'il lance
périodiquement, des *ristournes* que lui versent ses parlementaires sur leurs
indemnités et des bénéfices de la fête de l'Humanité. Tout le monde sait
bien que les sommes ainsi recueillies, pour importantes qu'elles puissent
être, sont une goutte d'eau par rapport aux dépenses que nécessite son
activité. Et ce qui est vrai du PC l'est aussi des autres formations de gauche

ou de droite. Aucune d'entre elles ne sera totalement sincère dans la déclaration de ses ressources, parce qu'il y aura toujours des dons, qui, politiquement, sont embarrassants à justifier. Le CNPF, par exemple, a souvent contribué à financer des partis ou, plus précisément, les campagnes électorales de certains dirigeants de partis qui n'étaient pas forcément des partis de droite. Certains industriels également. Quand on est un parti qui fait profession d'anticapitalisme ce sont là des cadeaux que l'on accepte en fermant pudiquement les yeux sur leur provenance mais que l'on n'avoue pas volontiers. A moins de mettre une police politico-financière – avec tous les risques de manipulation, de provocation ou au contraire de complicité que cela comporte – chargée d'apprécier le train de vie de chaque parti et de lui demander de justifier l'origine des sommes correspondantes, on ne voit pas très bien comment on pourrait parvenir à obtenir une *transparence* acceptable. Même les pays où existe une tradition de tout 'mettre sur la table' comme les Etats-Unis, n'y arrivent pas totalement. Et Dieu sait qu'une telle tradition ne correspond guère à notre tempérament national et aurait bien du mal à s'implanter chez nous.

Autre solution envisagée: le financement des partis sur fonds publics ce qui, à en croire les promoteurs de ce système, permettrait une *moralisation de la politique*. M. Giscard d'Estaing, dès 1974, avait lancé cette idée et en 1979 il avait fait déposer, après consultation des partis, un projet de loi en ce sens par M. Raymond Barre. Là encore les intentions sont sans doute pures et louables, mais le principe même et la réalisation sont pour le moins sujet à controverse.

Sur le principe tout d'abord, on peut objecter que, la fiscalité étant ce qu'elle est, il n'est peut-être pas indispensable d'ajouter un poste supplémentaire de dépenses au budget de l'Etat qui en a déjà plus qu'assez. D'autant que l'ensemble des partis politiques en France regroupe, en comptant large, un million d'adhérents et qu'il n'y a aucune raison d'obliger quinze millions de *contribuables* à payer une cotisation à des formations en lesquelles ils ne se reconnaissent pas. La *politique politicienne* n'a déjà pas tellement réputation chez nous pour qu'il soit nécessaire de 'braquer' davantage contre elle le *'pays réel'* et d'accentuer ainsi un clivage déjà suffisamment marqué. Un sondage de l'IFOP à la fin de 1979 faisait apparaître que 42 pour-cent des personnes interrogées étaient hostiles à un système de financement par l'Etat des partis contre 19 pour-cent seulement de favorables. En revanche lorsque les consultations sur ce sujet furent entreprises en 1978–1979, les partis – à l'exception du parti communiste –se déclarèrent plutôt favorables au principe. Pardi! Mais bien entendu, ils se séparèrent sur les modalités et le projet fut, en fin de compte, retiré. Les modalités d'un tel système ne sont en effet pas faciles à *mettre au point*. Que l'on proportionne l'aide de l'Etat au nombre de suffrages obtenus aux élections politiques (législatives essentiellement) et l'on est accusé – et c'est objectivement vrai – de favoriser les formations qui ont déjà *pignon sur rue*. Mais comment faire autrement si on ne veut pas provoquer la prolifération de *groupuscules plus ou moins 'bidons'* attirés par la perspective d'une subvention d'Etat? A moins, là encore, de sombrer dans l'arbitraire et de distribuer la manne à la tête du client ou, ce qui revient à peu près au même, en fonction de critères inévitablement subjectifs.

On peut faire observer du reste que, d'une certaine manière, l'aide officielle aux partis politiques existe déjà chez nous en dehors même du remboursement d'une partie des frais électoraux accordé aux candidats qui obtiennent plus de 5 pour-cent des suffrages exprimés. Cette aide est constituée par la *prise en charge* sur les crédits des assemblées du traitement de deux collaborateurs pour chaque parlementaire. Bien sûr, il ne s'agit pas d'une subvention versée aux partis mais d'un avantage accordé personnellement aux députés et sénateurs. Mais très souvent les crédits ainsi distribués sont en fait attribués à des permanents de partis, lesquels se trouvent de la sorte en mesure de réaliser des économies non négligeables.

Les moeurs et les lois

Quant aux justifications morales d'un financement des formations politiques par l'Etat, elles apparaissent fort contestables si l'on en juge du moins par ce qui se passe dans les pays où ce financement existe. L'argument mis en avant est que le financement officiel mettra un terme, ou en tout cas, freinera le financement occulte par les caisses noires d'industriels, les ristournes de bureaux d'études, les 'gestes' de gouvernements ou de 'partis frères' étrangers, etc.

On aimerait pouvoir y croire. Mais, au printemps dernier, en Allemagne fédérale, éclatait un scandale politico–financier: deux membres du gouvernement de M. Schmidt étaient accusés d'avoir favorisé le réemploi à des conditions fiscalement très avantageuses par un important groupe industriel du produit de la vente d'actions opérée par ce groupe. Les *pots-de-vin perçus* ne l'étaient pas pour le compte des ministres eux-mêmes mais allaient dans les caisses de leur parti. D'autre part, à l'occasion de cette affaire, sont ressortis plusieurs *dossiers* de subventions d'industriels à des oeuvres charitables – subventions qui, à ce titre, étaient en partie déductibles des bénéfices imposables – alors que les 'oeuvres charitables' en question étaient en fait des *succursales camouflées* des principaux partis politiques allemands. Or, en Allemagne, l'Etat subventionne officiellement les partis; leurs ressources doivent être publiées et les Allemands passent, à tort ou à raison, pour être plutôt moins portés sur les 'combines' que nous. Il est donc pour le moins probable que l'aide officielle aux partis n'empêcherait pas plus chez nous qu'en RFA le recours à des moyens de financement clandestins.

Alors que faire? C'est un peu triste à dire, mais le mieux est encore peut-être de ne rien faire. Bien sûr, on peut toujours faire voter une loi qui instituerait un contrôle des ressources et un plafond des dépenses des formations politiques et qui accorderait une participation de l'Etat à ces dépenses. Cela donnerait bonne conscience à quelques idéalistes sincères mais cela ne changerait guère – sauf pour les contribuables invités à verser une *obole* supplémentaire – la situation actuelle. Dans ces conditions, il est peut-être inutile d'ajouter à l'immoralité existante des procédés auxquels recourent les partis pour se procurer des subsides, l'immoralité supplémentaire qui consisterait pour eux à violer délibérément la loi qu'ils auraient fait voter. 'Lorsqu'on veut changer les moeurs et les manières, il ne faut pas les changer par les lois', disait Montesquieu. Le conseil est toujours valable.

SOURCE: Article écrit par Pierre Thibon, paru dans *Le Figaro*, 17 Novembre, 1982.

Exploitation du texte

1 Expliquez en quelques mots le sens des expressions en italique.

2 Faites une analyse textuelle générale, en vous appuyant éventuellement sur l'approche suggérée par l'Annexe A (p. 23).

3 A partir de votre analyse générale, faites une étude plus détaillée de la structure de l'argumentation dans le texte:

    sur le plan des idées
    sur le plan des conjonctions

4 Quel serait, à votre avis, le meilleur système de financement des partis politiques dans une démocratie de type occidental?

5 Imaginez, en tant que journaliste, plusieurs questions à poser à Lionel Jospin sur le thème du financement des partis politiques.

Exercices de comparaison et d'application

1 Formulez un prospectus annonçant la création d'un nouveau club politique et invitant le public à y adhérer. Indiquez, par exemple, le titre, les raisons de votre initiative, ce que vous combattez, ce que vous proposez, des slogans et mots d'ordre susceptibles de mobiliser l'opinion en votre faveur.

2 Rédigez une dissertation sur l'évolution d'un des partis politiques français depuis 1958.

3 Expliquez l'existence du multipartisme dans la France contemporaine.

4 Tracez l'évolution des deux grandes 'coalitions' de partis dans la France d'aujourd'hui.

5 Ecrivez une dissertation de 1200 à 1500 mots sur le sujet suivant: 'L'échiquier syndical d'aujourd'hui, malgré son étonnante diversité, reflète clairement l'évolution historique et les problèmes contemporains.'

7
Parliament

The framers of the 1958 Constitution were clearly decided on the place which Parliament would occupy in the new institutional structure. They wanted to retain it as the organisation composed of the people's elected representatives, and as the body which, in the final analysis, decided whether the Government should continue in office, both of which are characteristic features of Western parliamentary democracy. But they wanted to avoid a state of affairs where Governments were overthrown frequently (*un régime d'assemblée*), as happened during the Fourth Republic and to a lesser extent during the Third Republic. De Gaulle accepted that political parties had their particular function, but not that the traditional forum in which they operated should dominate the political system. His view was that the concept of the separation of powers, a long-established tenet of Western democracy, should be used to establish where Parliament stood in relationship to the Executive, and to distinguish clearly their respective functions. This method of proceeding, characterised by a determination to achieve an institutional structure through clear, watertight constitutional rules was called '*le parlementarisme rationalisé*', a phrase first applied to similar attempts in new European states created after the First World War.

One such provision was that the standing orders (*règlements*) of each of the parliamentary assemblies – the *Assemblée Nationale* (the Lower House) and the *Sénat* (the Upper House) – were to be subject to the approval of the Constitutional Council (Article 61). The 1958 Constitution went into some detail concerning the internal working of Parliament, because members of Fourth Republic Parliaments had exploited gaps and contradictions in constitutional provisions in order to gain the upper hand over Governments. The 1958 Constitution lays down exactly when Parliament has the right to be in session, which contrasts with the Fourth Republic Parliament's right to sit when it considered this necessary.

1 Ordinary sessions are from 2 October for 80 days, and from 2

April for not more than 90 days (Article 28) – less than half the year.

2 Parliament meets by right on the second Thursday after it has been elected, for 15 days (Article 12).

3 Parliament sits by right when Article 16 is in operation, as in 1961, and is convened, if necessary, to hear a message from the President (Article 18).

4 Extraordinary sessions can be called by the Prime Minister, and no time limit is imposed on these; they can also be called at the request of a majority of the National Assembly, but if so, they end after the predetermined agenda is completed, and in any case after 12 days (Article 29).

In the period 1959–82, 23 extraordinary sessions were requested by the Prime Minister in order to finish government business. Only one was at the request of a majority of deputies – in 1979 to discuss 'problems of information and employment'. An example of de Gaulle's cavalier treatment of Parliament, verging on contempt, was when he refused in 1960 to grant a request by a majority of deputies to discuss agricultural problems. He did this by claiming that those who had rural constituencies would be acting not in the national interest, but according to an 'imperative mandate' which in the 1958 Constitution is void (Article 27). Article 27 also tries to curb parliamentary absenteeism by providing that a deputy can vote on behalf of another only in exceptional circumstances; Article 26 concerns the concept of parliamentary immunity, which is a normal feature of democratic representation.

But one aspect of the 1958 Constitution which represented a dramatic break with the practice of parliamentary regimes, and which came about because of de Gaulle's belief in the need for the separation of powers, was the extension of the principle of *incompatibilité*. It is usual in a parliamentary democracy to prevent, for example, the clash of interests which would arise from simultaneously holding national political office and office in, say, the judiciary, the armed forces, or in State industry. De Gaulle, however, insisted that it should also be constitutionally impossible to be at the same time a member of the Government and a member of a parliamentary assembly. A person who, by appointment or election, is included in both categories has to choose in which one he or she will remain. It was not uncommon for members of Gaullist governments to use their prestige to win seats in the National Assembly, with no intention of leaving the Government. This was especially true after 1962 when the existence of a Gaullist majority in Parliament meant that de Gaulle's obsession with the separation of Executive and Legislature no longer had a basis. In such cases, and in cases where a person is elected deputy, and then accepts a Government appointment, an alternate or running partner (*suppléant*) takes over the seat in the National Assembly. This is merely one of many new elements in the system of parliamentary elections in the new regime.

Legislative elections in the Fifth Republic

In 1958, and in all subsequent elections, members of the National Assembly were elected according to a system which is officially called *scrutin uninominal majoritaire à deux tours*. The two important features of this system (though not new in the history of French electoral systems) are that a second electoral round is held if necessary and that instead of electing several members in a *département* according to the proportion of votes cast for lists of candidates (the Fourth Republic system), the new system is based on single-member constituencies. These had to be specially created, and for the elections to the seventh Parliament in 1981, there were 491 constituencies in metropolitan France and overseas, but the number has varied since 1958 because of decolonisation and administrative boundary changes. Constituencies were drawn in 1958 on the basis of the 1954 census and in such a way as to reduce Communist representation in Parliament, but a bigger distortion was caused by population movements over time which, by 1981, had given the largest constituency (Bouches-du-Rhone, 10th) an electorate of 189 383 and the smallest (Lozère, 2nd) one of 26 251. There have been adjustments for changes in *département* boundaries, but France has no mechanism for the automatic review of constituency sizes.

As with presidential and other elections, legislative elections are conducted in a strict legal framework, which lays down rules on candidate eligibility, the closing date for candidacies, the repayment of a part of election expenses, on which there is no legal ceiling, the format of the ballot paper (*bulletin de vote*) and candidates' propaganda, and the use of radio and television. In 1981, both coalitions in the outgoing Assembly were given 90 minutes before the first round, and smaller parties not represented were given seven minutes, broadcast simultaneously on radio and television. Citizens can vote from the age of 18 if they are registered, though this right can be taken away in cases of mental incapacity or serious crime, as in most democracies. To promote

secret voting, a voting booth (*isoloir*) in polling stations was
introduced by law in 1913, but abuses and manipulations are not
unknown, especially in Corsica and the West Indian overseas
départements. Postal voting was abolished in 1975, but voting by
proxy is possible: the 1978 law which allowed French citizens
resident abroad to register in any town of 30 000 or more
inhabitants led to quasi-corrupt practices and was abrogated in
1982. The average number of candidates in the first round of
legislative elections since 1958 is about twelve, and the name of
each candidate must be accompanied on the ballot paper, in smaller
letters, by that of his or her *suppléant*. To maximise support,
parties often try to present a *suppléant* who makes up a balanced
'ticket' with regard to age, sex and profession, or to achieve an
urban–rural mix. The fact that a *suppléant* can take over a seat if
an elected member of the Assembly cannot continue means there
are fewer by-elections (*élections partielles*) and anti-government
sentiment has less opportunity to show itself.

   To be elected on the first round, a candidate must receive 50 per
cent plus one of the valid votes (*suffrages exprimés*), provided this
is not less than 25 per cent of registered electors. If this does not
happen, there is a run-off (*ballottage*) in a second round a week
later – both rounds are traditionally on a Sunday. Some first-round
candidates do not renew their candidature for reasons of party
coalition agreements, but there is a legal hurdle, which has been
raised twice. From 1958 a candidate had to receive 5% of valid
votes cast; from 1966, this became a number equivalent to 10 per
cent of registered voters, and from 1976, a number equivalent to
12.5 per cent of registered voters (a compromise on the 15 per cent
first suggested). The candidate in the second round who receives
the highest number of votes is declared elected. It can happen that
there is only one candidate in the second round, if, say, the only
other candidate to clear the 12.5 per cent hurdle withdraws in
accordance with a national agreement between parties. Legally the
sole candidate needs only one vote to be elected, but what usually
happens (and there were 10 such constituencies in 1981) is that the
opposing groups call upon their supporters to cast blank or void
votes, which are duly counted; if there were more of them than
there were valid votes for the only candidate, the resulting
embarrassment could be politically exploited.

   Elections to the Senate (316 seats in 1983) are by an indirect
system. A different third of the Senate is elected every three years
by an electoral college in each *département* which consists of all the
deputies representing its constituencies, all *conseillers généraux*

PARLIAMENT 169

(members of the council of the *département*), and a number of representatives from each commune depending on its size, but favouring smaller communes and therefore rural interests. The electoral college meets in the *chef-lieu* of the *département*, and within the space of one day chooses the Senators. For *départements* entitled to no more than four senators, the method is the two-round majority one, including *suppléants*, with the possibility of new candidates for the second round. For the fourteen *départements* with five or more Senators, however, a one-round proportional representation method is used.

The debate on the respective merits of a majority system and a proportional representation system is long-standing in European democracies, and is complicated by the fact that there are variants of each, and especially of proportional representation. This debate is still very much alive in France, though it is not one to arouse great passion: politicians are caught between advocating proportional representation which would be more equitable, and accepting the advantages which a majority system usually gives. Support for proportional representation appeared, for example, in the presidential campaigns of Giscard and Mitterrand (number 47 of the latter's 'Cent dix propositions') but the 1982 Corsican regional elections by proportional representation showed the confused picture which this system can produce. An element of proportional representation for the 1986 legislative elections was mooted in 1982 and the system was used in direct elections to the European Parliament, the first of which were held in 1979. For these the whole country formed one constituency, and lists contained 81 candidates, equal to the number of *représentants* to be chosen (the word *député* is applied only to members of the National Assembly). Seats were allocated proportionately according to votes cast for each list, provided this was at least 5 per cent of the total. The novelty of the system in 1979 may have led an exceptionally large number of electors (5.3 per cent of those who voted) to cast void votes by mistake – they put into the envelope which goes into the ballot box a Giscardian election address which showed a list of 81 candidates as well as policy proposals, instead of the proper voting paper. The supervisory commission said they were valid and initially gave a Socialist seat to the Giscardians.

Organisation of Parliament

The National Assembly elects a President for the whole of a Parliament – five years is the full term – and the Senate does so each time after a third of its members have been elected – once every three years (Article 32) – though there have been only two Presidents of the Upper House since 1947. These Presidents have considerable prerogative powers outside the Parliamentary context: they each appoint three members of the Constitutional Council (Article 56), three members of the Haute Autorité de la Communication Audiovisuelle, established in 1982, and can refer a law to the Constitutional Council before promulgation, for a decision on its constitutionality (Article 61). They can disagree with a Government decision that an amendment or draft law suggested by Parliament is out of order, and the Constitutional Council may be called upon to decide (Article 41), though this happened only 41 times in the National Assembly between 1958 and 1981. The President of the Senate becomes temporary President of the Republic if this office falls vacant (Article 7), though he cannot invoke the provisions on referendum or dissolution. The Presidents of each assembly ensure their smooth functioning, and are helped by a bureau of members of the assembly in question, acting as vice-presidents, secretaries and auditors.

Parliamentarians can be members of special purpose all-party groups (*intergroupes*), some of long standing, but the setting up of official political groups in each assembly is closely regulated. Members can be either registered as belonging to a particular group, for which the minimum number is 30 in the National Assembly and 15 in the Senate, or as attached (*apparenté*) to a group, or as attached to no group (*non inscrit*). Parliamentary groups normally contain all the members in each assembly of specific political parties, but the concept of group predated that of party and the Senate has amorphous groups on the Right; in the National Assembly, parties which have not enough deputies to form a group on their own sometimes, if they feel sufficiently close politically, join together to constitute a group.

The advantage of being in a group is that their members sit on the committees (*commissions*) of each assembly, in proportion to the size of the groups. One of the ways in which the 1958 Constitution limited Parliament's powers was in providing (Article 43) that instead of the Fourth Republic system of powerful self-perpetuating committees watching over, and usually inhibiting, the work of each Government department, each draft law should be examined by a separate, specially constituted committee which would disband when its work was done. But what happened was that permanent committees (*commissions permanentes*) which in Article 43 were to be used only if the Government or Parliament did not ask for a special committee, became the more frequent forum for examining draft laws.[1] They were however limited to six in number for each assembly, to avoid the Fourth Republic situation. Proceedings in each committee are private and not published, which allows a more technical, less demagogic approach to be adopted, and committees frequently take evidence and advice from experts, professional organisations, and the 'Higher Committee' in the appropriate field, as well as from the Government minister concerned; the Constitutional Council decided in October 1981 that they could meet outside parliamentary sessions. In 1981, the Left-wing government tried to break the convention whereby the chairmanship of all permanent committees is held by a member of the parliamentary majority, but the offer of two committee chairmanships to the Opposition was in the end refused.

Parliamentary majority

In the Fourth Republic, governments were constituted on the basis of the willingness of parties to come together on an agreed compromise programme after elections in which they had emphasised to the electorate the distinctive nature of their own programme. The resulting coalition governments were not only fragile and liable to collapse over basic differences of approach to issues, but also far from representative of electors' wishes expressed through the ballot-box. In the Fifth Republic, the reality of a Parliamentary 'majority' was a corollary of the development of a presidentialist regime. In November 1958, voters had only an image to go on – that of de Gaulle as the potential saviour of France from unthinkable chaos. When they came to vote in November 1962, they had the experience not just of occasionally reshuffled governments under different Prime Ministers which had survived without a stable parliamentary majority (this, after all, they had had in 1951 and 1956), but also of an institutional set-up which was clearly stamped as 'Gaullist' or 'Fifth Republic', in the way it made policy and in the ideological underpinning of that policy.

The executive pre-eminence of the President of the Republic in the Gaullian interpretation, his control over policy, and his importance relative to the Prime Minister implied the necessity of a parliamentary majority to give support to the government's policies – a government party, or group of parties in close cooperation, owing its election to the attractiveness for voters of the past record of the President and Government, and willing to support them in future. In the Fifth Republic, being in power has come to mean winning not only a Presidential election, but a parliamentary one as well; and the emergence of a presidential majority, as the following shows, whether from a presidential election (E) or a referendum (R) has had in normal times (ignoring the two referenda on Algeria) implications for the majority in Parliament supporting the Government:

1962 (R)   Parliamentary majority for the first time, after the ensuing elections.
1965 (E)   Government reshuffle, partly to take account of a growing 'legislative' Gaullism.
1969 (E)   Enlargement of parliamentary majority to include some Centrists.
1972 (R)   Change of Prime Minister and government reshuffle to take account of a more self-assertive conservative Gaullist parliamentary majority.
1974 (E)   Enlargement of parliamentary majority to include Radicals and remaining Centrists, to compensate for some Gaullist hesitation.
1981 (E)   Dissolution of National Assembly and new Left parliamentary majority.

The conclusion can be drawn that however dominant the Presidency is within the executive function, it is always circumscribed by the accountability of the Government to Parliament, and the need for a supportive majority in the latter. These two factors have led to the Fifth Republic, 25 years after its foundation, being called 'semi-presidential'.

Government accountability to Parliament

Even when it has no stable automatic majority, the Government has considerable constitutional powers (pp. 127–8) to get through Parliament those policies which require legislation. But the National Assembly can, by passing a motion of censure, oblige a Government in which it has lost confidence to submit its resignation to the President (Article 50). A motion of censure may be put at any time (*'motion de censure spontanée'*), except when there is a temporary President, even if it means delaying the end of a parliamentary session (Article 51). But the conditions laid down are strict (Article 49-2): it must be signed by at least a tenth of deputies; the vote on it must be at least 48 hours after it was put down – this allows members to reflect on the possible consequences of their act; the motion is passed only if it receives the votes of a majority of members of the whole Assembly and not just a majority of those actually voting. It the motion is not carried, those who signed it cannot sign another in the same session, unless it is one which arises in the context of the main way in which the Government asks for an expression of confidence from the National Assembly. This is when, in accordance with Article 49-3, the Government text (or part of a text, as the Constitutional Council decided in 1979) is regarded as accepted unless a motion of censure, as outlined above, is carried within 24 hours (*'motion de censure provoquée'*). It has been argued that there are two other ways which amount to the Government's putting something as a matter of confidence, which of course the National Assembly can refuse:

1   Article 49-1: The matter put to the Assembly is in the form of the Government's programme, or a 'declaration of general policy'; it is voted upon and if it is not carried, the Government must submit its resignation to the President.
2   Article 44-3: The procedure of the *vote bloqué* (page 128) can be used by a Government to get an expression of confidence, especially where its own majority needs to be kept within bounds, and this can be refused by the Assembly.

The only time a 'spontaneous' motion of censure was carried in the National Assembly was in October 1962, at a time when the Government had no stable automatic majority; and it was really President de Gaulle who was the object of censure for having decided (in theory on the Government's suggestion) to change the method of Presidential election by referendum and not in the way which the Constitution lays down for its own revision, in Article 89. Prime Minister Pompidou tendered his resignation, but de Gaulle dissolved the Assembly and did not accept the resignation until he was ready to reappoint Pompidou after the ensuing elections, 23 days later. Motions of censure put down judiciously, if unsuccessfully – as on 25 occasions between 1959 and 1981 – can, as in other Western parliamentary democracies, be a way of focussing public attention on the alleged deficiencies of the Government. But the existence since November 1962 of a Government majority in the National Assembly has meant that it has never been denied an expression of confidence. A majority which is less than totally automatic, however, as was the case on some issues in 1976–81, leads a Government to modify its legislative proposals accordingly, and not tempt fate too far.

As well as being the means to ensure the basic principle of Government accountability in the sense of its remaining in office, Parliament also makes the Government accountable in the sense of having to answer for the way in which it performs its executive function.

Questions in Parliament

As part of its effort to watch over government activity, each assembly of the French Parliament offers the possibility of written or oral questions to Government ministers, and to the latter it is obliged to devote one sitting a week (Article 48). These periods at one extreme enable members merely to elicit information which the Government has at its disposal, and at the other extreme to attempt to cause the Government political embarrassment and provoke changes of policy. Oral questions can be ones which merely receive a reply ('sans débat') or ones, virtually extinct since 1981, where other members may contribute for 20 minutes to a discussion ('avec débat'). In 1969, questions on matters of current concern were introduced, to be taken first in the sitting; these developed in 1974 into 'questions to the Government' every Wednesday afternoon –since 1981, 45 minutes are granted to the Majority, and 40 to the Opposition. But the efficacy of parliamentary questions is limited by the fact that not all are answered – in 1981, 13 897 written questions and 115 oral questions were put, but only 8932 and 86 respectively received a reply; the picture is not as bleak as it appears, however, since delays in answering questions will mean that a large number of replies appear in the following year's statistics.

Committees of inquiry and scrutiny, and parliamentary delegations

Parliament can watch over Government activity by setting up investigatory committees on a specific matter. The Senate or National Assembly can establish a *commission d'enquête* to look into a matter, provided it is not *sub judice*, and report back to it. In the period 1959–81, the National Assembly set up 16 such committees – all, as it happened, after 1971. Examples in 1981–2 were committees to look at hill farming, and to report on the *Service d'action civique*, a nebulous security force still purporting to act with the degree of autonomy which it had under de Gaulle and Pompidou; parliamentary investigation led to its being declared illegal. *Commissions de contrôle* can look into the running of public undertakings or services: there were four in the National Assembly during 1959–81, an example being the examination of the financial management of the social security scheme in 1978.

Both kinds of committee are normally dominated by the parliamentary majority, which can lead to Government interference in their work. Their deliberations, for which they are allowed up to six months, are private, and they can oblige witnesses to attend; their conclusions are made public unless the assembly in question decides otherwise.

A method of watching over Government executive activity by permanent parliamentary bodies developed when the 1972 law reorganising the ORTF – the State broadcasting authority –included the setting up of a small *délégation parlementaire* of 14 parliamentarians, which the Government was obliged to consult on important aspects of broadcasting. The formula was largely followed in 1979, for delegations in both Senate and National Assembly to oversee the effect of European Community legislation on the French Parliament's function, and in 1982 on planning; and in 1980, joint ones to look at population policy in the light of recent law reforms which might affect it, and in 1982 on *'communication audiovisuelle'*.

The legislative function

In a republican regime, Parliament alone had the power to make laws, but in France, this principle has been subject to derogations. In the Third Republic, the practice of delegating this power in specified areas to the Government for a fixed period was accepted from 1918 onwards; in the Fourth Republic, legislative power was exercised by the National Assembly, not by both assemblies, but a Constitutional ban on delegation was circumvented; the 1958 Constitution restored legislative power to the whole Parliament (that is, the National Assembly and the Senate) and allowed its delegation to the Government in specified areas for a fixed period (Article 38). But the major innovation of the Constitution in this sphere was its strict limitation of the areas where legislation is necessary (*le domaine de la loi*), everything else being dealt with by executive orders. The Constitutional Council decides in cases of uncertainty.

From the Government's point of view, the *domaine de la loi* defines areas where it must put its policies as draft laws before Parliament;[2] from Parliament's point of view, it defines areas where it can pronounce on Government proposals by accepting or rejecting draft laws, and where it has some degree of initiative of its own, in accordance with Western democratic tradition. The areas listed in Article 34 are those of basic concern to citizens and to the State: they have been aptly summarised by a facetious modification of the motto of the French Republic as '*Liberté, Egalité, Propriété, Fiscalité*'. To this Article 34 list must be added areas from other parts of the Constitution:

1 human rights (Preamble)
2 the status of the judiciary (Article 64)
3 the creation of new territorial units of government (Article 72) e.g. regions
4 the organisation of overseas territories (Article 74)

Parliamentary initiative in the areas covered by legislation comes from the basic right of amendment (Article 44) and from the right, shared with the Government, to propose draft laws. But both are subject to the severe constraint that they must not have financial implications – they must not reduce public revenue or increase public expenditure (Article 40). Moreover, in common with the situation in other parliamentary democracies, draft laws suggested by members of Parliament (*propositions de loi*) have only a small chance of becoming laws, unless the Government adopts them, though it must be admitted that they are often for media consumption rather than serious attempts to tackle a problem.

The 1958 Constitution also divided laws into various categories, some of which were new and subject to different procedures. For example, an organic law (*loi organique*) was necessary to establish the details of many Constitutional principles; an enabling law (*loi d'habilitation*) allows the Government to govern by ordinances (Article 38). But limitations on Parliamentary freedom are particularly heavy when it is a matter of the procedure laid down for a finance act (*loi de finances*) by which the national budget is approved. The Prime Minister must put these first to the National Assembly, and both assemblies have to operate to a strict timetable with an overall limit of 70 days. It is in this context particularly that Article 40 (see above) stifles parliamentary initiative.

The process for ordinary laws (Article 45) is designed to reduce the delay which could occur (and frequently did in the Fourth

Republic) when the National Assembly and Senate modify each other's text of a draft law by amending it before sending it back. To avoid this situation, to which the word *navette* was applied, the Fifth Republic Constitution provided that after two readings in each assembly (or if the Government declares the matter urgent) a joint committee of equal numbers from each assembly (*commission mixte paritaire*) tries to establish an agreed text to put to both assemblies. But if this is not possible, the Government asks the National Assembly to make the final decision.

The legislative programme can be heavy – in the two years after July, 1981, 235 laws were passed, of which three were enabling laws and 71 were ratifications of international agreements.

The Senate

Constitutional provisions such as the one just mentioned, together with the National Assembly monopoly in the matter of censuring the Government, and differences in the method of electing members of each assembly, confirm the fundamentally inferior position of the Senate in the 1958 Constitution, in keeping with twentieth century trends in bicameral systems. But the assumption in 1958 that the Senate, with its assured rural and conservative majority, would support the Government proved wrong. Senate opposition to de Gaulle culminated in fierce hostility to attempts to restructure it in the 1969 referendum. It became aware of the need to improve its public image, but it was not until Giscard's Presidency that the Senate came to be seen as a sometimes indispensable ally of the Government in the latter's relations with an increasingly refractory majority in the National Assembly. After 1981, the Senate was disposed, despite its Centre–Right majority, to cooperate with the Left-wing government in most areas of policy, and beginning in March 1982, it was granted an hour per month of 'questions to the Government'. It was comforted by President Mitterrand's acceptance of the virtues of a bicameral system in the face of some of his more radical supporters – he, like many others politicians, had taken refuge in the Senate when he had no National Assembly seat between 1958 and 1962.

Economic and Social Council

The *Conseil économique et social* established by the 1958 Constitution (Articles 69–71) was the most recent in a series of consultative socio–professional bodies which date back to 1925.

The Government has to consult it on economic planning matters, and may do on other subjects, and the Council itself may draw the Government's attention to problems of a social or economic nature. It is organised in seven specialised sections, aiming to promote collaboration between the different professional groups which make up its membership of 200, of whom a third are Government appointed. It has a marginal role in the legislative function, but continues in the hope that its numerous reports and studies will have some effect on parliamentary thinking during the consideration of draft laws, before consigned to some ministerial pigeon-hole.

Parliament in the system: decline

The conventional wisdom among politcal scientists is that in the twentieth century, the role of Parliament in the decision-making processes of government has been eroded. This declining salience of elective assemblies in the case of France is seen in four main areas, where its previous position of monopoly no longer applies. The French National Assembly is no longer the only institution to achieve its political legitimacy through universal suffrage, and the most significant reduction in its prestige was in the direct election of the President from 1965, as well as in the use of the referendum in the early years of the Fifth Republic. Secondly, the National Assembly is no longer the deciding factor in the political composition of governments. The Government appointed by the President has not always felt under an obligation, even in cases where it could count on a majority, to put its policy programme to the Assembly or Senate soon after taking office. Thirdly, the proportion of Government members who are of parliamentary origin has been on average about four-fifths, and Parliament no longer monopolises the career path to government posts, which was the case before 1958. Fourthly, the area of legislation is no longer delineated by Parliament, but by Constitutional provisions, principally Article 34.

In 1958, Parliament retained control of the process of Constitutional change, but only just. The Government committee responsible for the actual drafting of the new Constitution included four senior party politicians of the Fourth Republic with the title of Minister of State, and Parliament laid down conditions as to the nature of the Constitutional modifications which it was widely agreed were necessary. But the new Constitution, which came to be interpreted in a permissive way where the Government was concerned, was on the contrary subject to restrictive interpretations in the case of Parliamentary prerogatives. An example was in 1959 when, in the context of oral questions, Parliament tried to revive the previous practice of *interpellation* which usually amounted to a requirement for the Government to explain its actions in the particular matter under discussion. But the Constitutional Council ruled that Parliament was forbidden to do what it was not expressly permitted to do.

Parliamentary supervision of economic planning became more and more tenuous, and its ability to influence budgetary decisions declined as the Government became more skilled in manipulating the budgetary process. Sometimes the Government decrees needed to implement laws passed by Parliament were issued after several years' delay, and then only because of extra-parliamentary pressure – an example was the *'loi Neuwirth'* on contraception, of December 1967. The existence during the 1960s of a stable automatic Parliamentary majority which supported the Government meant that the role of the parliamentarian became reactive rather than active, but developments during the 1970s may have gone some way to halt the decline of Parliament seen in its relationship to the Executive.

Parliament in the system: renewal?

The desire of Giscard d'Estaing as President for the removal of tension (*décrispation*) in political life led him to introduce reforms which gave back to Parliament some of the initiative it had lost in the previous 15 years. The most important was to modify Article 61 to allow 60 deputies or 60 senators to refer a matter to the Constitutional Council; another was to begin the 'constitutional custom' of devoting an hour a week, at first, to 'questions to the Government'. Also, Parliament regained some measure of budgetary control which the Government had usurped; committees of enquiry and scrutiny, with a stronger legal framework, were used more frequently; and the power to make amendments to draft laws (within the limits of Articles 40, 41 and 44) was employed by Parliament to regain some legislative initiative, especially during 1976–81, when the majority behind Barre's government was not always cohesive. Giscard's attempt to increase Opposition involvement in political life (he was greatly struck by the un-French image of Harold Wilson as Prime Minister and Edward Heath as Leader of the Opposition standing side by side at Pompidou's funeral) did not achieve results, but Giscard tried to please

Parliament – and of course broaden his support – by giving parliamentarians temporary 'missions' to study a particular problem.

Given that the flouting of Parliament's rights and prerogatives was one of the Left opposition's main complaints, it was natural that President Mitterrand and his colleagues should wish to continue the policy of Parliamentary revival begun under Giscard. In July 1981, he said: *'Fini, je l'espère, cet abus des votes bloqués ou de ces lois réputées adoptées par le subterfuge de la "non-censure"'*, referring to Articles 44-3 and 49-3. And yet the latter was used four times in 1982, and the Government asked for powers to govern by ordinance on Social Security matters.

The main reason for Parliament's revival after 1981 was that, although the Socialist Party had a majority by itself in Parliament, without having to rely on Communist or Left Radical support, most Socialist deputies considered themselves very much as local activists and defenders of either doctrinal values or specific electoral promises, rather than automatic supporters of government policies, especially those aspects influenced by considerations of holding power. There were no revolts in the years immediately after 1981 which threatened the Government's existence, but serious differences over, for example, the defence budget, energy policy, fiscal measures and the amnesty of those involved in the 1961 putsch in Algeria, were very public and sometimes had to be defused by concessions. The renewal of Parliament in the 1980s is necessarily dependent on contingent developments of this nature, which have to cope with the constraints of the institutional system set up in 1958.

Bibliographical guidance

The following books are recommended as further reading on the French Parliament:

N. About, *Profession: deputé* (Flammarion, 1981)
P. Avril, *Les Français et leur Parlement* (Casterman, 1972)
J.-M. Benoit, *Chronique de décomposition du PCF* (Table Ronde, 1979): despite its title, most of the book is devoted to the author's account of his constituency campaign in the 1978 elections.
P. Birnbaum *et al. Réinventer le Parlement* (Flammarion, 1977)
J. Bourdon, 'Les Assemblées parlementaires sous la Ve République', *La Documentation Française, Notes et Etudes Documentaires*, no. 4463-4 (avril, 1978)

M. Cotta, 'Partis et Parlement sous la Ve République', in *Pouvoirs*, no. 4 (1978)

F. Goguel, 'Sur la réhabilitation du bicamérisme en France', in *Mélanges –études en l'honneur de Léo Hamon* (Economica, 1982)

'Les Parlements sous la Cinquième République', special number of *Revue Française de Science Politique* (février, 1981)

J.-C. Masclet, *Un député pour quoi faire?* (PUF, 1982)

J. Mastias, *Le Sénat de la Ve République – réforme et renouveau* (Economica, 1980)

R.-G. Schwartzenberg, *La droite absolue*, Part II (Flammarion, 1981)

Illustrative texts and linguistic exercises

Texte 7.1   Les idées constitutionnelles du Général de Gaulle

Mise en situation

Le contexte historique du discours de Bayeux est décrit dans la 'mise en situation' du Texte 1.1. Après s'être étendu sur le caractère unique des Français en matière politique, le Général de Gaulle évoque brièvement les dangers de la dictature et explicite dans cette deuxième partie de son discours ses idées constitutionnelles.

*   *   *

Il suffit d'évoquer cela pour comprendre à quel point il est nécessaire que nos institutions démocratiques nouvelles compensent, par elles-mêmes, les effets de notre *perpétuelle effervescence politique*. Il y a là, au surplus, pour nous une question de vie ou de mort, dans le monde et au siècle où nous sommes, où la position, l'indépendance et jusqu'à l'existence de notre pays et de notre Union française *se trouvent bel et bien en jeu*. Certes, il est de l'essence même de la démocratie que les opinions s'expriment et qu'elles s'efforcent, par le suffrage, d'orienter suivant leurs conceptions *l'action publique* et la législation. Mais aussi, tous les principes et toutes les expériences exigent que les pouvoirs publics: législatif, exécutif, judiciaire, soient nettement séparés et fortement équilibrés et qu'au-dessus des *contingences politiques* soit établi un arbitrage national qui fasse valoir la continuité au milieu des *combinaisons*.

Il est clair et il est entendu que le vote définitif des lois et des budgets revient à une Assemblée élue au suffrage universel et direct. Mais le premier mouvement d'une telle Assemblée ne comporte pas nécessairement une clairvoyance et une sérénité entières. Il faut donc attribuer à une deuxième Assemblée, élue et composée d'une autre manière, la fonction d'examiner publiquement ce que la première a pris en considération, de formuler des amendements, de proposer des projets. Or, si les grands courants de politique générale sont naturellement reproduits dans le sein de la Chambre des Députés, la vie locale, elle aussi, a ses tendances et ses droits. Elle les a dans la Métropole. Elle les a, au premier chef, dans les territoires d'Outre-mer, qui se rattachent à l'Union française par des liens très divers. Elle les a dans cette Sarre à qui la nature des choses, découverte par notre victoire, désigne une fois de plus sa place auprès de nous, les fils des Francs. L'avenir des 110 millions d'hommes et de femmes qui vivent sous notre drapeau est dans une organisation de forme fédérative, que le temps précisera peu à peu, mais dont notre Constitution nouvelle doit marquer le début et *ménager le développement.*

Tout nous conduit donc à instituer une deuxième Chambre, dont, pour l'essentiel, nos Conseils généraux et municipaux éliront les membres. Cette Chambre complétera la première en l'amenant, s'il y a lieu, soit à réviser ses propres projets, soit à en examiner d'autres, et en faisant valoir dans la confection des lois ce facteur d'ordre administratif qu'un collège purement politique a forcément tendance à negliger. Il sera normal d'y introduire, d'autre part, des représentants des organisations économiques, familiales, intellectuelles, pour que se fasse entendre, au-dedans même de l'Etat, la voix des grandes activités du pays. Réunis aux élus des assemblées locales des territoires d'Outre-mer, les membres de cette Assemblée formeront le Grand Conseil de l'Union française, qualifié pour délibérer des lois et des problèmes intéressant l'Union; budgets, relations extérieures, rapports intérieurs, défense nationale, économie, communications.

Du Parlement, composé de deux Chambres et exerçant le pouvoir législatif, il va de soi que le pouvoir exécutif ne saurait procéder, sous peine d'aboutir à cette confusion des pouvoirs dans laquelle le Gouvernement ne serait bientôt plus rien qu'*un assemblage de délégations.* Sans doute aura-t-il fallu, pendant la période transitoire où nous sommes, faire élire par l'Assemblée Nationale Constituante le Président du Gouvernement provisoire, puisque, sur la table rase, il n'y avait aucun autre procédé acceptable de désignation. mais il ne peut y avoir là qu'une disposition du moment. En vérité, l'unité, la cohésion, la discipline intérieure du Gouvernement de la France doivent être des choses sacrées, sous peine de voir rapidement la direction même du pays impuissante et disqualifiée. Or, comment cette unité, cette cohésion, cette discipline, seraient-elles maintenues à la longue, si le pouvoir exécutif émanait de l'autre pouvoir, auquel il doit faire équilibre, et si chacun des membres du Gouvernement, lequel est collectivement responsable devant la représentation nationale tout entière, n'était, à son poste, que *le mandataire d'un parti*?

C'est donc du Chef de l'Etat, placé au-dessus des partis, élu par un collège qui englobe le Parlement mais beaucoup plus large et composé de manière à faire de lui le Président de l'Union française en même temps que celui de la République, que doit procéder le pouvoir exécutif. Au Chef de l'Etat la charge d'accorder l'intérêt général quant au choix des hommes avec l'orientation qui se dégage du Parlement. A lui la mission de nommer les ministres et, d'abord, bien entendu, le Premier, qui devra diriger la politique et le travail du Gouvernement. Au Chef de l'Etat la fonction de promulguer les lois et de prendre les décrets, car c'est envers l'Etat tout entier que ceux-ci et celles-là engagent les citoyens. A lui la tâche de présider les Conseils du Gouvernement et d'y exercer cette influence de la continuité dont une nation ne se passe pas. A lui l'attribution de servir d'arbitre au-dessus des contingences politiques, soit normalement par le Conseil, soit, dans les moments de grave confusion, en invitant le pays à faire connaître par des élections sa décision souveraine. A lui, s'il devait arriver que la patrie fût en peril, le devoir d'être le garant de l'indépendance nationale et des traités conclus par la France.

Des Grecs, jadis, demandaient au sage Solon: 'Quelle est la meilleure Constitution?' Il répondait: 'Dites-moi, d'abord, pour quel peuple et à quelle époque?' Aujourd'hui, c'est du peuple français et des peuples de l'Union française qu'il s'agit, et à une époque bien dure et bien dangereuse! Prenons-nous tels que nous sommes. Prenons le siècle comme il est. Nous avons à mener à bien, malgré d'immenses difficultés, une rénovation profonde qui conduise chaque homme et chaque femme de chez nous à plus d'aisance, de sécurité, de joie, et qui nous fasse plus nombreux, plus puissants, plus *fraternels*. Nous avons à conserver la liberté sauvée avec tant et tant de peine. Nous avons à assurer le destin de la France au milieu de tous les obstacles qui se dressent sur sa route et sur celle de la paix. Nous avons à déployer, parmi nos frères les hommes, ce dont nous sommes capables, pour aider notre pauvre et vieille mère, la Terre. Soyons assez *lucides* et assez forts pour nous donner et pour observer des règles de vie nationale qui tendent à nous *rassembler* quand, sans relâche, nous sommes portés à nous diviser contre nous-mêmes! Toute notre Histoire, c'est l'alternance des immenses douleurs d'un peuple dispersé et des fécondes grandeurs d'une nation libre groupée sous l'égide d'un Etat fort.

SOURCE: Charles de Gaulle, 'Discours prononcé à Bayeux', *Discours et Messages*, vol. 2, 1946-58 (Plon, 1970).

Exploitation du texte

1 Expliquez en quelques mots le sens des expressions en italique.

2 Expliquez les allusions dans les expressions suivantes:

l'Union française
cette Sarre à qui la nature des choses...désigne une fois de plus sa place auprès de nous.
la période transitoire où nous sommes
le sage Solon

3 Résumez les arguments en faveur de la Deuxième Chambre qui existe dans le système bicaméral de la plupart des démocraties occidentales.

4 Jusqu'à quel point les principales dispositions de la Constitution de 1958 reflètent-elles les idées constitutionnelles du Général de Gaulle exprimées dans le discours de Bayeux? Quels Articles spécifiques de cette Constitution sont esquissés dans le discours de Bayeux?

Texte 7.2 Le premier tour d'une élection législative

Mise en situation

Nicolas About (né en 1947) maire de Montigny-les-Bretonneux (Yvelines) et médecin, fut élu député de la Majorité (UDF) au deuxième tour des élections législatives de 1978, dans une circonscription (Yvelines, 8e) qui était jusque-là le fief de Jacqueline Thome-Patenôtre (MRG). Il perdit son siège en 1981.

*   *   *

Dimanche 12 mars 1978. Je me lève à 6 h 30, prêt à affronter cette journée qui sera longue. En tant que maire de Montigny-le-Bretonneux, je dois présider à l'ouverture du premier bureau de vote, celui de la mairie. J'y accueille les représentants des différents candidats et c'est machinalement que je leur indique leurs responsabilités; mon esprit est ailleurs, il voyage d'une commune à l'autre de la circonscription où *je me présente*. Les fatigues et la tension de la campagne n'ont pas contribué à rendre mon sommeil paisible et le poids de mes paupières facilite mon évasion. Vers 11 h 30, je cours avaler quelque chose à la maison et m'assoupis quelques instants.

20 heures. 'Y a-t-il encore dans cette salle un électeur inscrit qui demande à voter?' *Les scrutins sont clos.* Les résultats vont tomber rapidement et, vers 22 heures, je saurai que la majorité est minoritaire à Montigny-le-Bretonneux. Mon collègue Wagner, RPR, *député sortant*, est *en ballottage*. Les Ignymontains, dans une faible majorité, n'ont pas fait confiance à ses idées, ils ont voulu également lui montrer qu'ils n'appréciaient pas de ne l'avoir jamais vu dans leur commune. Et s'ils avaient tout simplement exprimé leur mécontentement et condamné la société de liberté et de progrès pour laquelle je me bats? Mais l'heure n'est plus à l'analyse. Il me faut repartir rapidement pour connaître les premiers résultats de la huitième circonscription des Yvelines. Je file, nerveux et tendu, vers mon quartier général de Rambouillet. Ma femme, aussi nerveuse que moi, est à mes côtés. Ma voiture avale les kilomètres de la Nationale 10 et nous pénétrons quinze minutes plus tard dans la grande salle de l'institut que dirige mon *suppléant*. Ce n'est pas l'ambiance des grands soirs, les visages sont inquiets, l'éclairage est sinistre. Sur les murs, d'immenses feuilles de papier où sont inscrits les résultats des communes dont le dépouillement est terminé. Ces chiffres ont fait parfois beaucoup de kilomètres avant de venir s'inscrire en rouge, bleu, noir et vert sous le nom de chaque candidat. D'autres ont été *crachés par le téléphone mural*.

Les premiers résultats, rapidement additionnés, montrent que Mme Thom-Patenôtre est en tête de la gauche et Jean-Pierre Gérard en tête de la majorité. Il me faut pourtant *faire bonne figure*. Bernard m'appelle de la sous-préfecture, il est dans le bureau des *Renseignements généraux* et il connaît les résultats avant nous. Sa voix est rassurante, nous rattrapons notre retard sur le RPR dans les bureaux de vote des communes importantes et plus particulièrement de la ville nouvelle. Tout est possible en ces moments où la nuit est bien entamée, où ce n'est encore ni tout à fait hier ni tout à fait demain.

Au fur et à mesure que les résultats tombent, Jean-Pierre Gérard voit peu à peu ses espoirs du début de soirée se transformer en craintes. Un quart d'heure plus tard, nouveau coup de fil de la sous-préfecture: c'est gagné pour moi! De peu, mais gagné. Je m'y rends rapidement pour saluer mon concurrent malheureux. Nous n'avons pas grand-chose à nous dire. Il est déçu, je le comprends. Je ne suis pas triomphant, je n'ai parcouru que la moitié du chemin. Le plus dur reste à faire et je suis fatigué. En arrivant au quartier général, B. Moulin prend le micro et lit un communiqué qui paraîtra demain dans le presse régionale: 'Jean-Pierre Gérard remercie les électrices et les électeurs qui lui ont fait confiance le dimanche 12 mars. En vertu des accords conclus en septembre 1977 entre les diverses formations politiques de la majorité, il leur demande de voter dimanche prochain pour Nicolas About, candidat unique de cette majorité au deuxième tour des élections législatives.' Les visages se détendent, les verres tintent, les bravos s'envolent, nous avons franchi la première étape avec un score largement supérieur à ceux réalisés par mes prédécesseurs. Raymond Barre vient de tirer la leçon de ce premier tour: 'Les Françaises et les Français ne se sont pas laissé abuser par les promesses démagogiques par lesquelles l'opposition espérait les séduire.' C'est court, net et précis. Dans la huitième circonscription, Jacqueline Thome-Patenôtre perd des points. J'ai créé la surprise, et le verdict populaire a tranché en ma faveur en ce qui concerne la majorité. Le second tour sera difficile, la campagne commence à cet instant.

J'ai passé une longue journée d'anxiété et une bonne partie de la nuit à travailler. C'est au petit matin que je salue mes amis et rentre à Montigny prendre quelques heures de repos.

SOURCE: Nicolas About: *Profession: député* (Flammarion, 1981) pp. 46–9.

Exploitation du texte

1 Expliquez en quelques mots les expressions en italique.

2 Rédigez une lettre que M. Wagner, député RPR sortant en 1978 (6ᵉ circonscription des Yvelines), aurait pu écrire pour répondre à un de ses électeurs qui se plaignait de ne l'avoir jamais vu dans sa commune.

3 Nicolas About nous présente le communiqué que M. Gerard, devancé par lui, remit à la presse après le premier tour. Rédigez le communiqué que M. About aurait pu publier le même soir.

4 Sur le modèle de la réaction de M. Barre aux résultats du premier tour en 1978, formulez celle qu'aurait pu avoir un leader de la Gauche.

Texte 7.3   Une question d'actualité

Mise en situation

Les séances de questions d'actualité à l'Assemblée Nationale offrent une tribune de choix à l'opposition pour apostropher le gouvernement. Un député RPR en profita le 30 juin 1982 pour essayer de déconcerter le Premier Ministre (Pierre Mauroy) et le gouvernement, à la suite d'articles de presse qui faisaient état d'une prétendue conversation téléphonique entre M. Ralite, le Ministre communiste de la Santé, et M. Krasucki, membre du Bureau politique du PCF et alors secrétaire général adjoint de la CGT. Plusieurs allusions sont expliquées dans les Notes en bas de chaque page.

*   *   *

M. ROBERT-ANDRÉ VIVIEN: Monsieur le Premier ministre, avant de vous poser ma question, je souhaite, au nom de l'opposition, que vous rappeliez certains de vos ministres à un minimum de décence (*Exclamations sur les bancs des socialistes*), singulièrement M. Delors...

M. JEAN-CLAUDE GAUDIN: Très bien!

M. ROBERT-ANDRÉ VIVIEN: ...qui, depuis quelques jours, traduit, à travers son excitation, son emportement (*Rires et exclamations sur les bancs des socialistes*), les préoccupations que tout ministre des finances aurait à sa place en voyant la France au bord de la faillite. (*Mêmes mouvements*)

Mais, monsieur Delors, ce n'est pas une excuse suffisante pour traiter les membres de l'opposition de 'braillards fascistes'.* (*Très bien! sur les bancs du RPR et de l'UDF – Exclamations sur les bancs des socialistes et des communistes*)

M. JACQUES DELORS (*ministre de l'économie et des finances*):   Pas tous!

PLUSIEURS DÉPUTÉS DU RPR ET DE L'UDF: C'est scandaleux!

M. ROBERT-ANDRÉ VIVIEN: Je veux vous rappeler, monsieur Delors, que c'est au sein de nos groupes – M. Savary,† mon camarade de guerre, compagnon de la Libération en est témoin – qu'on compte le maximum d'hommes qui se sont battus, pendant la Résistance, sans attendre que la Russie leur en donne l'ordre, comme certains! (*Protestations sur les bancs des communistes et des socialistes*)

C'est dans nos rangs que l'on trouve le maximum de déportés, comme M. Fossé, M. Mauger et bien d'autres.

PLUSIEURS DÉPUTÉS SOCIALISTES.   C'est grotesque!

M. ROBERT-ANDRÉ VIVIEN: Il est indigne d'un membre d'un gouvernement de la République de se laisser ainsi emporter, comme il était indigne, monsieur le Premier ministre, de dire à M. Madelin tout à l'heure‡ que vous n'aviez

*Le ministre de l'Economie et des finances avait, quelques minutes auparavant, utilisé cette expression pour qualifier ceux qui l'interrompaient.
†Alain Savary, ministre socialiste de l'Education nationale.
‡Pierre Mauroy avait refusé de répondre à la question d'Alain Madelin (UDF – Ile et Vilaine) qui lui demandait s'il allait mettre en demeure les communistes 'de choisir entre le soutien au gouvernement et le soutien à la CGT'. Le Premier ministre reprochait en outre la 'goujaterie' d'Alain Madelin à l'egard de Nicole Questiaux, qui venait d'être remplacée au Ministère de la Solidarité Nationale.

pas envie de répondre à un député. Je vous rappelle que, durant les vingt-trois premières années – ô combien bénies! – de la Vᵉ République, l'opposition d'alors a usé largement de son droit de contestation et de critique du Gouvernement.

Puisque vos réponses ne m'ont pas satisfait, c'est au nom du groupe RPR que je vous repose la question, d'une façon très précise et dans votre intérêt. (*Exclamations sur les bancs des socialistes et des communistes –Applaudissements sur les bancs du RPR et de l'UDF*)

L'irresponsabilité des 'braillards gauchisants', pourrais-je dire (*protestations sur les bancs des socialistes et des communistes*), ne cachera pas votre embarras pour répondre à un député de la nation. Que vous n'ayez 'pas envie' de lui répondre est indigne d'un Premier ministre. (*Très bien! Très bien! sur les bancs du RPR et de l'UDF*)

Vous prétendez qu'il s'agit d'une médiocre opération de presse. Je vous rappelle, monsieur le Premier ministre, car vous semblez l'avoir oublié quelques instants, la lettre et l'esprit de la Constitution, qu'évoquait lundi dernier M. Michel Debré – approuvé en cela par M. Delors – Constitution dont vous vous servez, ô combien! en recourant à des 'magouilles' (*exclamations sur les bancs des socialistes et des communistes*) dignes de la IVᵉ République. Mais ce n'est pas l'objet de ma question.

M. LE PRÉSIDENT: Monsieur Vivien, veuillez en venir à votre question!

M. ROBERT-ANDRÉ VIVIEN: Je suis en train de l'exposer, monsieur le président!

M. LE PRÉSIDENT: Plus personne ne sait de quoi vous parlez! Je vous rappelle que vous avez la parole pour poser une question d'actualité. (*Rires et applaudissements sur les bancs des socialistes et des communistes – Protestations sur les bancs du RPR et de l'UDF*)

M. ROBERT-ANDRÉ VIVIEN: Si vous aviez le temps de retourner dans votre circonscription, comme mes collègues de l'opposition et moi-même...

M. GILBERT SÉNÈS: Il se croit à Médrano:*

M. ROBERT-ANDRÉ VIVIEN: ...vous auriez été suffoqué de constater l'étonnement, l'indignation des Français devant la révélation faite par un hebdomadaire paraissant le lundi, comparé par le beau-frère du Président à *Libération*† – je n'ai d'ailleurs jamais compris pourquoi (*Rires sur les bancs du RPR et de l'UDF*) – et reprise par la quasi-totalité de la presse quotidienne.

Les Français ont ainsi pu mesurer la déférence, la soumission, la platitude d'un membre du Gouvernement, grâce aux indiscrétions d'un autre membre du Gouvernement que vous avez chassé tout en lui rendant un éloge funèbre qui nous a tous sidérés. (*Rires sur les bancs du RPR et de l'UDF*).

PLUSIEURS DÉPUTÉS SOCIALISTES ET COMMUNISTES: Et la question?

M. ROBERT-ANDRÉ VIVIEN: Car pourquoi avoir renvoyé un ministre aussi bon et aussi compétent?

---

*Ancien cirque parisien aujourd'hui démoli.

†Roger Hanin avait établi un parallèle entre la revue d'extrême-droite *Minute*, et *Libération*, un journal d'extrême-gauche en reprochant à ce dernier d'être 'fasciste'. Interview publié dans les colonnes du *Figaro Magazine* le 19 juin 1982.

L'un de vos journalistes disait hier à TF1 que Mme. Questiaux avait plus fait sur le plan social que l'ensemble des gouvernements de la IVe et de la Ve République en quarante ans. Il ne donne pas dans l'excès! Vous avez 'jeté' Mme Questiaux, et vous avez bien fait. (*Rires sur les bancs du RPR et de l' UDF – Vives protestations sur les bancs des socialistes et des communistes*)

Je vous rappelle, monsieur le Premier ministre, que, en vertu de l'article 31 ou 32 – je ne me souviens plus exactement – de la loi sur la presse de 1881, il était loisible à M. Ralite de démentir et qu'il peut citer en justice l'ensemble des quotidiens qui ont relaté cette conversation.

M. Madelin, par gentillesse, ne l'a pas rappelée. (*Rires et exclamations sur les bancs des socialistes et des communistes*)

Soucieux du règlement, monsieur le président, je n'ai pas voulu vous passer le 'bobineau' que nous avons là, où l'on entend un ministre de la République s'incliner platement, en demandant pardon de déranger, à l'un des apparatchiks – numéro un peut-être – de la CGT, ce fossoyeur du travail et de l'économie française. (*Vives protestations sur les bancs des socialistes et des communistes*)

M. PAUL BALMIGÈRE: Salaud!

M. ROBERT-ANDRÉ VIVIEN: On se croirait à Valence* en vous entendant. (*Mêmes mouvements*)

M. PAUL BALMIGÈRE: C'est dégueulasse!

M. ROBERT-ANDRÉ VIVIEN: Monsieur le Premier ministre, voyez le sectarisme de votre majorité! Elle interdit à un député de l'opposition de s'exprimer.

UN DÉPUTÉ SOCIALISTE: Il est saoul!

M. ROBERT-ANDRÉ VIVIEN: Lorsque, tout à l'heure, M. Madelin, avec beaucoup de pudeur (*Exclamations sur les bancs des socialistes et des communistes*) et de réserve, a fait allusion aux écoutes, l'opposition a hurlé. (*Mêmes mouvements*)

M. LE PRÉSIDENT: S'il vous plaît, monsieur Vivien, finissons-en!

M. PIERRE MAUGER: Laissez-le parler, monsieur le président!

M. ROBERT-ANDRÉ VIVIEN: Monsieur le Premier ministre, je voudrais vous citer ce qui est sans doute pour vous la Bible, à savoir un ouvrage de M. Mitterrand, *Ma part de vérité*, publié en 1969. A la page 33, je lis: 'Parce que nous n'étions pas dans la ligne, Pierre Mendès-France, Gaston Defferre et moi-même, qui appartenions au Gouvernement, nous étions l'objet des pires suspicions et nos communications téléphoniques étaient passées au crible'. Le président du conseil était M. Guy Mollet†. Ce n'était pas Chaban-Delmas, Chirac ou Barre. Je l'ai rappelé en 1973.

J'en viens donc à ma question. (*Rires et exclamations sur les bancs des socialistes*)

Ma question – et cela répondra au souhait de M. le président – sera très précise et appellera une réponse par oui ou par non: monsieur le Premier ministre, la conversation entre Jack Ralite, ministre de la santé, et M. Krasucki, secrétaire général – adjoint, alors – de la CGT, révélée par la

---

*Ville ou se tint le Congrès extraordinaire du PS après la victoire de mai–juin 1981.
†Socialiste; Président du Conseil des Ministres 1956–7.

presse, est-elle exacte? (*Applaudissements sur les bancs du RPR et de l'UDF*)

M. LE PRÉSIDENT: La parole est à M. le Premier ministre.

M. PIERRE MAUROY (*Premier ministre*): Monsieur le président de l'Assemblée nationale, mesdames, messieurs les députés, il y a quelques mois nous avons abordé ce problème, qui en est un, au niveau de l'Etat et au niveau des citoyens: le problème des écoutes téléphoniques.

Quelle était la réaction sur tous les bancs? C'était d'exiger que, dans une démocratie comme la démocratie française, il n'y ait plus d'écoutes téléphoniques de quoi que ce soit, et que personne ne puisse se fonder sur des écoutes téléphoniques pour porter des attaques contre les uns ou contre les autres. Voilà quelle a été la décision du Gouvernement.

M. ROLAND HUGUET: Très bien!

M. LE PREMIER MINISTRE: Nous avons mis en place une commission qui a été présidée par le Premier président de la Cour de cassation. A cette commission participaient plusieurs magistrats, les représentants des plus grands corps de l'Etat, et, je crois, trois ou quatre parlementaires, dont des parlementaires qui siègent sur vos bancs.

Le rapport de cette commission m'a été remis par le Premier président de la Cour de cassation il y a huit jours. J'enverrai ce rapport à l'ensemble des députés. Il a été rendu public. C'est un hommage au Gouvernement d'avoir supprimé les écoutes téléphoniques et, sur ce point-là, de n'avoir pas fait ce qu'avaient fait ses prédécesseurs. Voilà la réalité! (*Vifs applaudissements sur les bancs des socialistes et sur les bancs des communistes –Exclamations sur les bancs du RPR et de l'UDF*)

M. GABRIEL KASPEREIT: Vous dites n'importe quoi! Cela n'a rien à voir!

M. MICHEL NOIR: Alors, c'est oui ou c'est non?

M. LE PREMIER MINISTRE: Nous nous en tiendrons à cette politique. Quant à la question posée par M. Robert-André Vivien, je considère qu'il n'est vraiment pas acceptable (*protestations sur les bancs du RPR et de l'UDF*), ni pour l'Assemblée nationale, ni pour le Gouvernement, qu'il y ait un tel dévoiement des questions posées dans cet hémicycle. (*Vives protestations sur les mêmes bancs*)

PLUSIEURS DÉPUTÉS RPR: Cela vous gêne!

M. LE PREMIER MINISTRE: C'est également une sorte de dévoiement de reprendre ce qui est écrit par un certain hebdomadaire...

M. GABRIEL KASPEREIT: C'est dans tous les journaux!

M. LE PREMIER MINISTRE: ...qui déverse régulièrement des insanités sur les uns et sur les autres.

Dans ces conditions, le Gouvernement ne répondra pas (*protestations sur les bancs du RPR et de l'UDF*)...

M. GABRIEL KASPEREIT: Vous avouez!

M. LE PREMIER MINISTRE: ...et je demande instamment et solennellement à M. le président de l'Assemblée qu'à la prochaine conférence des présidents* soit

*La Conférence des Présidents des deux assemblées est responsable du fonctionnement intérieur du Parlement.

posé le problème général du caractère que doivent revêtir les questions posées par les uns et par les autres. (*Applaudissements sur les bancs des socialistes et des communistes – Protestations vives et prolongées sur les bancs du RPR et de l'UDF*)

M. PIERRE MAUGER: Quel aveu!

M. JACQUES MARETTE: C'est scandaleux!

M. GABRIEL KASPEREIT: C'est une honte!

M. JACQUES TOUBON: Le Gouvernement doit répondre aux questions qui lui sont posées!

M. LE PRESIDENT: Je vous en prie, mes chers collègues!

PLUSIEURS DÉPUTÉS RPR ET UDF: On s'en va!

M. ROBERT-ANDRÉ VIVIEN: Je demande la parole, monsieur le président!

M. LE PRÉSIDENT: La parole est à M. Robert-André Vivien.

M. ROBERT-ANDRÉ VIVIEN: Monsieur le président, je vous remercie de m'avoir permis de répondre au Gouvernement, qui vient de nous informer qu'il ne répondrait pas aux questions qui le dérangeaient.

Jamais, depuis quatorze mois, l'opposition n'a posé de questions sur les problèmes privés concernant le Gouvernement. La déclaration de M. le Premier ministre est d'une extrême gravité. Il entend imposer – et je vous fais confiance, monsieur le président, ainsi qu'à l'opposition, pour qu'il n'en soit pas ainsi – les questions auxquelles il lui plaira de répondre. Je constate qu'il n'a pas répondu à ma question, alors qu'une réponse par oui ou par non suffisait. Nous considérons donc que la converstion relatée est exacte, ce qui met en péril les institutions de la V⁰ République.

(*Applaudissements sur les bancs du RPR et de l'UDF – Les députés du RPR et presque tous les députés de l'UDF* se lèvent et quittent l'hémicycle*)

M. YVES DOLLO: L'opposition fait son numéro!

SOURCE: *Journal Officiel de la République Française: Débats parlementaires – Assemblée Nationale 1981–82* pp. 4074–5: Première Séance du Mercredi 30 juin, 1982.

Exploitation du texte

1 Expliques le sens des expressions suivantes:

   braillards fascisants
   des 'magouilles'
   le 'bobineau'
   un des apparatchiks
   salaud!
   cet hémicycle

2 Qu'est-ce qui dans cet extrait indique qu'il s'agit de français parlé?

3 Faites une liste des expressions utilisées dans cet extrait pour s'en prendre à un adversaire politique. Essayez de trouver un antonyme pour chaque expression.

*Seul Emmanuel Hamel (UDF Rhône) est resté à son banc.

4 Supposez que M. Vivien décide de poser sa question sous forme de question écrite. Rédigez ses remarques préliminaires et sa question précise, ainsi que la réponse écrite du Premier Ministre.

5 Faites la comparaison entre cet extrait d'une séance à l'Assemblée Nationale et une représentation théâtrale. Trouvez un ou plusieurs exemples des phénomènes suivants: tirades, onomatopées, apartés, interjections, mouvements de foule, figuration, personnages secondaires, personnages 'à l'arlésienne' (c'est-à-dire dont on parle beaucoup mais qu'on ne voit jamais).

Exercices de comparaison et d'application

1 Quelles étaient les déficiences du 'regime d'assemblée' de la Quatrième République auxquelles la Constitution de 1958 voulait remédier dans le nouveau regime?

2 (i) Quels sont les arguments pour et contre le système électoral majoritaire et la représentation proportionnelle?

(ii) Quel serait le systeme électoral optimum pour les élections législatives et senatoriales?

3 Un livre publié en 1977 s'intitulait *Réinventer le Parlement*. Pourquoi cette réinvention paraissait-elle alors nécessaire?

4 En prenant les Articles de la Constitution de 1958 que vous jugez nécessaires, reformulez-les pour inverser l'érosion du pouvoir parlementaire sous la Cinquième République.

8
Politics at the Local Level

Apart from institutions on the national level which provide a basic framework for political, economic and social life, the central authority of a state needs to be present throughout its territory to maintain internal order, to apply laws, and to ensure that the general interest – at its most stark, the survival of the state –prevails over the interest of groups, classes or geographical areas. The setting up of a local administrative machinery, however, raises fundamental questions. Firstly, there are considerations regarding the optimum size of administrative units, and the number of levels or tiers which are needed below national level. Secondly, there are problems concerning the status of the persons and bodies at the head of the local administrative units. Here, two broad concepts are evoked:

1 decentralisation, where responsibility for local administration is given to locally designated bodies, which have as much independence as is compatible with the general interest of the state; in a state organised as a federation, for example, the degree of independence of constituent units is high.
2 deconcentration, where a representative acting on behalf of the state, and subject to its control, is responsible at local level for carrying out the decisions of the central authority; in the interests of efficiency, officials charged with implementing government decisions are not concentrated in the capital, but geographically dispersed; there remains, however, a centralisation of decisionmaking, and a strong hierarchy of power.

It was the benefits of the latter approach which appealed to the French Revolutionaries in the years following 1789, and particularly to the group who came to be known as *Jacobins*. After a period of confusion, they eventually opted for centralisation as a means of imposing a rational, uniform system to replace the confused one which had developed over several centuries of the *ancien régime*, and to ensure the supremacy of the principles on which the new Republic was founded. They divided France into new territorial units called *départements*; there were 83 at first, but subsequent annexation and subdivision increased the number – the splitting of Corsica into two *départements* in 1975 brought the total in metropolitan France to 96. The boundaries were fixed with some regard to previous provincial boundaries, and to the position of a major town, which became the *chef-lieu* of the *département*. It was in these in 1800 that Napoleon, continuing as First Consul and Emperor the centralising approach associated with the Jacobins, established a system of prefects (*préfets*). They were appointed by the state and were responsible for carrying out government orders; under them in the hierarchy were sub-prefects (*sous-préfets*) in subdivisions called *arrondissements* – between three and five in a *département*. Sub-prefects passed orders to the mayors of towns and villages, each of which was called a *commune*, whatever its size. The basic outline of this system survives in present-day France, though the substance has been modified in several significant ways.

Local elections

Originally, not only the heads of the three levels of administrative units mentioned, but also their advisory councils were appointed by the government. Gradually, changes were made as democracy made progress with the introduction of universal adult suffrage for men in 1884 and for women in 1944, applying not only to national legislative elections but also to elections to the *conseil municipal* of the *commune* and the *conseil géneral* of the *département*. Soon after the beginning of the Third Republic, the legal framework of a limited degree of local administrative responsibility was established, and the principle of electing the mayor and his assistants (*adjoints*), even in medium and large towns, was accepted.

A member of a *conseil général* (there are over 3500 *conseillers généraux* in all) represents *communes* grouped into a *canton*, which is a subdivision of an *arrondissement*. All traces of the *canton* as a unit in the administrative hierarchy between *arrondissement* and *commune* have virtually disappeared; the *canton* is important now only as an electoral area and elections to the *conseil géneral* are *élections cantonales*. They take place every three years, when half the council members are elected for a six-year term. The system in 1982 was a two-round single member one, like that for parliamentary elections, but without a *suppléant* for each candidate, and this factor traditionally gave a high frequency of by-elections. A future reform of the system for cantonal elections was part of the post-1981 Left government's suggestions for introducing some measure of proportional representation into the electoral process at local and national level.

The latter consideration was also a significant element in the decision to introduce a new system for the 1983 elections to the councils of *communes* (*élections municipales*), though it added to the complexity of an already complex system. The total number of members of each *conseil municipal* is fixed by law according to the size of the population – in 1983 this was between nine and 63, with just over 500000 in all – but an important point is that they are elected at the same time, for a six-year term (1977,1983,1989...). The electoral system varies with the size of the commune:

1 Those with fewer than 3500 inhabitants. Candidates group themselves in lists containing as many names as there are seats available, but electors are free to indicate which order they prefer (*vote préférentiel*) and to make their own list by combining names from different lists (*panachage*). A further degree of latitude is granted in communes of fewer than 2500 inhabitants, where individual candidatures are allowed and an elector can put in the ballot box a voting paper which has fewer names than the number of seats available (*une liste incomplète*) or which contains names of people who are not even candidates. Individual members are elected on the first round by an absolute majority, that is, if their names appear on more than 50 per cent of valid ballot papers cast, and seats remaining in the second round go to those receiving most votes.

2 Those with more than 3500 inhabitants. Electors must vote for complete lists, and neither *vote préférentiel* nor *panachage* is allowed; if a list obtains more than 50 per cent of votes in the first round, it is allotted half the seats available, while the other half is distributed proportionately among all lists which received at least 5 per cent of votes cast, including of course the one which got the first half of the seats; in the absence of an absolute majority for one list, all lists which received at least 10 per cent of votes cast in the first round may go through to the second round; an added complication is that names from a 'minor' list getting between 5 per cent and 10 per cent of first-round votes (or getting more than 10 per cent but not wanting to go forward as a separate list) can be grafted on to a 'major' list, after removing some of the original names, in order to

maximise its electoral appeal in the second round; after the second round, half the seats are allotted to the list obtaining most votes, with the other half being distributed as above. In Paris, each *arrondissement* now has a council with limited powers which it exercises in conjunction with the *Conseil de Paris*; the same system also applies to Lyon and Marseille.

Elections to *conseils municipaux* have become increasingly political. This is partly because electors vote more and more on national issues, using municipal elections as a 'mid-term' opportunity to express dissatisfaction with the central government. But it is also because some aspects of national politics are increasingly reflected at local level. Firstly, although smaller communes – over 90 per cent have fewer than 2000 inhabitants –usually have councils composed of 'independents', elected either as *'sans étiquette'* or on lists with names such as *'action locale'*, larger towns and cities have become miniature examples of the bipolarisation of national politics. The electoral system operating in municipal elections before 1983 meant that in communes of more than 30000 people there was no opposition, and all seats were captured by a list which was usually regarded as either Left or Right. Even with a new law which applies the same system to all communes above 3500 inhabitants, attention is focussed on how far control of towns above 30000 changes hands.

Secondly, the presidential aspect of national politics is reflected in local politics, again particularly in large towns. A list of candidates is less likely to be identified in the public mind by the name of a political party or coalition than by that of the politician who heads it. He receives, as potential mayor, the same kind of approval by the electorate as does a future President of the Republic. The 1884 law which provided for the election of a mayor and his *adjoints* at the first meeting of a new council, like a miniature National Assembly, still applies, but the political reality is different.

Thirdly, the attention of political parties in the Fifth Republic is more directed to local affairs. They are better organised at the local level than previously; and holding the *mairies* of a significant number of the larger towns can add another dimension to a political party in various situations. Party success in local politics can serve as:

1 Compensation for being excluded from national governments, e.g. PCF 1947–81.

2 Compensation for a decline in popularity even when
   participating in national governments, e.g. Radicals from the
   period of the First World War to the 1960s; PCF after 1981.
3 The first stage of an attempt to change the system at national
   level, e.g. the Gaullist party (RPF) 1947–53.
4 Reinforcement of a sudden success at national level, e.g. the
   Gaullist party during the 1960s.
5 An indication of revitalisation prior to national success, e.g. the
   PS in the 1970s.

To say, however, that there has been a politicisation of local
politics is to evoke the whole question of centre–periphery
relations, which has assumed a high degree of saliency in the Fifth
Republic.

Centre–periphery relations

The centralised administrative system perfected during the Jacobin
–Napoleonic era was well adapted to the gradual industrialisation
and modernisation which France experienced during the following
century and a half. Local administration adapted remarkably well,
and its fragmented nature – there were over 38000 communes in the
nineteenth century – enabled it to ride out the frequent changes of
regime in Paris. The Third Republic, once firmly established, was
self-confident enough to extend the system of electing a mayor to
towns of over 6000 people, and to replace the close political
supervision characteristic of the Second Empire by a more subtle
form of control.

As public services developed in the nineteenth century, they were
progressively taken over by the state in the interests of efficiency
and were supervised by government departments through a system
of field services. Local elected representatives (*élus locaux*)
assumed the role of intermediaries between their electors and
government departments, and their political influence was in
theory circumscribed by central authority, and, after 1945, by
national economic planning. However, although there were clear
differences between rural and urban communes, the local political
apparatus in general had achieved a degree of sophistication under
the Third and Fourth Republics in its dealings with the central
authority and its representatives, the prefects, which enabled the
centralised system to continue without intolerable strain. The
relationship between the prefect and the mayors in his *département*
was obviously a complex one, but large towns had inevitably gained

some freedom of manoeuvre in local matters. The supervision (*tutelle*) by central government was somewhat relaxed over the years in important areas, and in any case could often be alleviated by a network of personal contacts maintained by a politician holding a plurality of elective office (*cumul des mandats*), of which the classic example has always been those of mayor and parliamentary deputy.

The question of centre–periphery relations, however, came to be starkly posed when France experienced a period of rapid economic expansion during the two decades after the mid-1950s. Economic modernisation during this time emphasised land use planning (*aménagement du territoire*) and created the need for greater coordination of activity within a rapidly expanding urban framework – rural depopulation (*exode rural*) boosted the urban population from 53 per cent of the total in 1946 to 70 per cent in 1968. However, the traditions of centralisation were so strong that this coordinating role was firmly located within the state machinery, including its local representatives, the prefects. The *Commissariat au Plan*, which had existed since 1945, set about integrating the new factors of urban growth into the overall national economic plan, aided from 1963 by the *Délégation à l'Aménagement du Territoire et à l'Action Régionale* (DATAR), usually controlled by the Prime Minister, and from 1965 by a new 'superministry', the *Ministère de l'Equipement*. A better coordination of the activities of central government departments and local economic forces was ensured by the prefect in each *département*, who became '*la seule autorité départementale bénéficiaire des délégations ministérielles*'. Moreover, 21 of them became regional prefects in regions established in 1964 to try to increase the efficiency of national economic planning, particularly investment decisions. It was by measures such as these, mainly concerned with functional efficiency, that Gaullist governments in the Fifth Republic approached the growing problem of centre–periphery relations and thereby brought to the fore, firstly, the possibility of some recasting of administrative boundaries, but more importantly, the whole notion of decentralisation.

Administrative boundaries

The fact that there are, in the 1980s, over 36000 basic units of local government in France has frequently raised questions about how compatible such a fragmentation of local interests can be with contemporary political and administrative realities. The rapid growth of conurbations since 1945 not only accentuated the disparities between rural and urban communes, but meant that the boundaries of the latter were inconsistent with new settlement patterns, and this aggravated the tensions created by urban growth. These merely added to the difficulties which smaller communes had long encountered in providing – even with state financial aid – the level of public services necessary to modern life.

Since 1890, *communes* had been able to create joint organisations for the provision of a single common facility, but a more important step was when a 1959 law allowed them to do this by setting up a *syndicat intercommunal à vocation multiple* (SIVOM), and by 1980 this formula applied to just over half of all French *communes*. Developments in the 1960s tackled the administrative problems of urban growth in two ways: firstly, by allowing the creation of *districts* in conurbations, to provide a limited range of joint facilities according to locally perceived needs; this formula was successful in bringing considerable rationalisation to administration and planning in the Paris area in the 1960s, and by 1980 there were 152 districts covering five million people. Secondly, between 1968 and 1973, *communautés urbaines* were imposed on nine conurbations of more than 50000 inhabitants –Lyon, Bordeaux, Lille, Strasbourg, Dunkerque, Le Creusot, Le Mans, Cherbourg and Brest – with well-defined structures and powers, in relation to their constituent *communes*.

The establishment of new towns in the Paris region cut across existing *commune* boundaries, and the necessary cooperation was usually effected by a *syndicat communautaire d'aménagement*. A 1971 law encouraged the merger of *communes* by providing financial incentives, but ten years later only some 600 mergers had taken place, and the strength of resistance to this destruction of a separate identity was recognised when the post-1981 Left government promised the abrogation of this law.

Communes in France remain the basic unit of local political life, the focus of the ordinary individual's attention in formulating many political demands, even the object of his or her affective attachment. No French government would contemplate, and no French parliament would approve, a law which entailed the kind of wholesale restructuring of administrative boundaries which was done in France two centuries ago, and in some other Western countries much more recently. In contemporary France, a *commune* of average size and above is an increasingly complex organisation: it collects, saves, spends and lends money; it sells goods and services, runs social organisations and pays wages (*le personnel communal* in France totals over 500000 people); it is involved in employment and housing policy, negotiates with economic interest groups, and enters into contracts with the State. For all this, it needs specialised technical and administrative staff if it is not going to be subject to a de facto *tutelle technique*, whereby reliance on technical expertise provided by government departments – often the *Direction Départementale de l'Equipement* (see Texte 8.1) – reduces what little power it has. Above all, it needs to be headed by a mayor conscious of his responsibilities and able to devote time and effort to carrying them out with the help of *adjoints* if it is not to be oppressed by a *tutelle financière* of indebtedness.

The increasing complexity of local administration inevitably raised the question of how tasks were to be distributed between different levels of local government, and whether the region, as a new echelon with political responsibility, as well as a context for coordinating local economic activity, would enhance the momentum of modernisation. But answers to these questions depended on how far the concept of decentralisation entered into the tissue of contemporary French politics, countering the centuries-old basis on which the nation state had been run.

Decentralisation

Reforms in the 1960s continued and reinforced trends towards restructuring the framework of economic activity, aimed at making France outside Paris less of a 'desert', as Gravier called it in his pioneering book.[1] This involved locating administrative procedures in the *départements* and in the new programming regions, and associating local socio–professional élites with them. But to call this 'decentralisation', as some Gaullists did, was to extend too far the meaning of a term which nevertheless had always lacked precision. Since the general interest of the State was conceived in widely divergent ways, decentralisation could be a rallying cry for technocrats who regarded a centralised system as inefficient, for Gaullists who considered that the State could rediscover its historic role only if national energies were mobilised, and for political radicals who wanted a permanent shift in the locus of political decision making.

Political parties have in general been slow to incorporate the notion of decentralisation, however interpreted, into their doctrine. Within the Gaullist ranks a strong body of opinion led by Michel Debré persistently pointed out that it could spell the end of France as a unitary state; and the value of the PCF's official support for decentralisation from the early 1970s was limited by the survival of well-entrenched instincts in favour of a strong central authority. Opinion in groups in the political Centre, however, and in the Radical Party (particularly Jean-Jacques Servan-Schreiber in his 1973 book *Le pouvoir régional*) was more receptive; and Michel Rocard, whose book *Décoloniser la province* (1967) was the plea of a political radical and a technocratic moderniser, reinforced moves within the Socialist Party, after he joined it in 1974, towards a clear commitment to political decentralisation.

Giscard as President commissioned the 1976 report by Olivier Guichard 'Vivre ensemble', on the development of local responsibilities, but little became of it apart from minor changes to local government financing. François Mitterrand, however, outlined in his 1981 Presidential campaign (nos 54 and 57 of his *Cent dix Propositions*) a policy package in which he said '*la décentralisation de l'Etat sera prioritaire*'. The programme of the post-1981 government included proposed laws on:

1 the rights and liberties of *communes*, *départements* and regions (approved March 1982);
2 the respective powers of the State and of local government (approved January 1983);
3 the reform of local government finance;
4 the legal and professional status of local government employees.

The application of this legislation represented profound changes in the context of politics at the local level, and particularly in the role of the prefect, who was given the new title of '*Commissaire de la République*'. He now no longer acts as the executive officer in the *département*, in the sense of initiating and closely monitoring each separate decision-making process; this function is transferred to the president of the *conseil général*, who is an elected representative, and he has at his disposal some of the technical and administrative staff formerly attached to the prefect. The allocation of these had to be done by written agreement, and there were instances of a physical separation of the two staffs in the former prefecture. The second major innovation is the abolition of the '*a priori*' *tutelle* which was the legal basis of state supervision of communes, and despite gradual dilution, had been a source of irritation to local politicians when it stifled innovation. The new *Commissaire de la République*, however, as the representative of the State, has powers not just to coordinate, as the prefect did, activities of government departments in his area apart from education and law, but to exercise independent managerial responsibility over them in the context of local needs. In this way, the post-1981 government claimed it had established the appropriate degree of deconcentration of power to make decentralisation of political decision-making meaningful. An *'a posteriori' tutelle* remains in that local government acts which are *ultra vires* can, as before, be overturned by judicial review; a retrospective financial scrutiny is possible, but by a new system of *Chambres régionales des comptes*; and the State retains its ultimate power of mediation in case of conflict at local level. But the reforms were radical enough for the Mauroy government to claim to have brought about *'une révolution tranquille'*. Right-wing critics, on the other hand, were convinced that decentralisation would lead to overspending by local government no longer subjected to *a priori* scrutiny, to a greater politicisation of its decisions, and to an increase in regional disparities: they argued that even though *communes* get a lump sum (*dotation globale d'équipement*) to spend more or less how they wish, it amounts to a survival of the *tutelle* if the government keeps it low in the interests of national economic policy.

Regions and regionalism

The laws on decentralisation applied also to regions, and the regional prefect became a *Commissaire de la République à la Region* with increased authority to facilitate the task of harmonising central government and regional wishes, analogous with the new degree of deconcentration at *département* level. Similarly, the president of the *conseil régional* became responsible for the executive function in the region, with staff at his disposal. It was necessary to try to defuse the problem of growing Corsican demands for autonomy by giving the island a special status which recognised its cultural identity, and by holding direct elections to the *Assemblée de Corse* in 1982. Plans to hold direct elections to choose mainland regional councils at the same time as the 1983 municipal elections were deferred.

The post-1981 regional reforms go some way to satisfying long-standing demands made by the various strands of the regionalist movement, in that by granting some measure of autonomy in political decision making, they recognise that regions have an identity separate from the State and from the *départements*.

However, the regions thus exalted after 1981 were those which had been created in 1964 as *circonscriptions d'action régionale* to promote local economic coordination. They were groupings of *départements* often of widely unequal demographic and economic weight, sometimes cutting across the boundaries of historical regions which had managed to maintain a separate cultural identity even in the face of strenuously fostered national consciousness.

Large parts of France, for example Brittany, Alsace and 'Occitanie', were not French in sentiment or language until well into the nineteenth century; regionalism up to the Second World War was characterised by cultural nostalgia, and sometimes maintained by a vague folk memory of the Counter-revolution of the 1790s. After 1945, regionalists who espoused the cause of decentralisation to promote economic efficiency and prevent political alienation, urged that the region, however defined territorially, was a more appropriate framework than the much larger number of *départements*. Efforts in Brittany to foster regional economic activity at the same time as a politico-cultural consciousness were particularly successful, to judge by the degree to which they provoked central government hostility. In the 1960s in many areas, 'cultural' regionalism and 'political' regionalism tended to converge in their opposition to central authority, and this surfaced as a strong element in the 1968 'events'. It was to defuse this hostility and to mobilise conservative but hitherto non-Gaullist *notables* behind the regime that de Gaulle proposed, in the unsuccessful 1969 referendum, that the region should have slightly increased powers, and a council of delegates from socio-professional bodies, *conseils généraux* and *conseils municipaux*, plus the deputies representing constituencies in the region.

The Gaullist fear that directly elected regional assemblies would impugn the unity of the State also inspired the 1972 regional reform which replaced each *Commission de dévelopement économique régional* (CODER) of 1964, by a consultative *Comité économique et social* and a separate *Conseil régional* composed of elected (though not directly elected) representatives. In general, however, the new regional councils had enough power to undertake a clear if difficult integrative task at local level, and enough prestige to become the locus of a growing regional political consciousness. Regional political elites can be said to have emerged, who did not necessarily regard national elective office as the next career step. This focus on local political life as a worthy activity in its own right was increasingly strong on the Left, and was consistent, for example, with opinion in the Socialist Party favouring *autogestion* in political life – *'la gestion, si possible directe, par les citoyens, de leurs propres affaires'.*[2] It was against the background of such developments that the *Ministère de l'Intérieur* became in 1981 the *Ministère de l'Intérieur et de la Décentralisation*. Some claimed, even before the 1981 *septennat* of Mitterrand had run half its course, that decentralisation was the single most important achievement (*'la grande affaire'*) of his Presidency.

The post-1981 government was also interested in the cultural aspects of regionalisation, and Jack Lang, the Minister of Culture appointed in 1981, addressed himself to the question of how far a qualitative change in French cultural life depended on *'la mise en oeuvre d'une politique de dynamisation du tissu culturel régional, (...) le soutien des initiatives locales et l'épanouissement des différences linguistiques et culturelles dont la France est riche'*. He wanted also to encourage cultures which were not territorially defined – immigrant workers, refugees, and the Jewish, Gypsy and Armenian communities. The problems associated with cultural regionalisation within the wider context of decentralisation are that centrifugal tendencies threatening the unity of the French state will be reinforced, and that in any case linguistic and cultural regions do not coincide with the administrative regions inherited from the 1964 reforms: Basque, Flemish and Catalan are spoken only in part of single *départements*, whereas *'Occitanie'* covers 31 *départements* in six regions. These discrepancies have been used by some as an added argument for a federal Europe of regions.

Associations and local politics

Taken in conjunction with its decentralisation policy, the establishment of a *Ministère du Temps Libre* and a *Ministère de la Solidarité Nationale* by the post-1981 government was an indication that it intended to adopt a different approach to people's relationship with each other and with the institutional structures which surround them. But the long-standing phenomenon of associations in France had already shown that people were only imperfectly moulded into a collective national unity, and instead were prone to give their loyalty to participatory sub-groups.

Non-profit making associations experienced a remarkable expansion of numbers beginning in the mid-1960s. They are regulated by a law dating from 1901, but this was updated after 1981 by the new *Ministère du Temps Libre*, which reported that there were 350 000 associations in France. Clearly, only a minority of this total have aims which are specifically political, but their existence is based on, and helps to maintain, the belief that in some way voluntary associations approach problems in a more creative, less hidebound way than traditional parties and political groups.

Associations traditionally exist to fill a gap in the public or private provision of facilities, particularly in sport and the wider cultural context; but it is not uncommon for these activities to merge into the assertive stance of more overtly political associations, which seek change on a specific issue, for example, by demanding public facilities or improvements in services. Associations pressing demands in quantifiable terms – limitation of increases in rents, local rates and public transport fares – are analogous to trade union action on a national level in defence of their members' standard of living, and this leads them either to cooperate closely with local trades' councils formed of local branches of employees' unions, or to seek some form of national coordinating framework themselves.

On the other hand, following the pioneering work since the mid-1960s of *Groupes d'Action Municipale* (GAM) in Grenoble, the recent trend is for more and more associations to pursue qualitative aims in defending and improving the urban environment by bringing pressure on the *conseil municipal* for full consultation on planning matters. They wanted to counter the stifling effect which local government, backed by an omnipotent State, was seen as having on civil society (*la société civile*), and to restore the element of personal autonomy which traditional collective action on behalf of broad-based socio–economic categories had of necessity reduced. In this, the associational phenomenon often became the preserve of the new salaried middle classes, especially in the burgeoning suburbs where close-knit social networks were lacking. The expansion of local associations has added a new dimension to politics at the local level, in that local government is increasingly obliged to conduct its business on the basis of a dialogue with these partners (*interlocuteurs*). Moreover, national politicians have had to adjust to the reality that participation in a local association is often more meaningful to individuals than mobilisation through a political party; they have promised to give the elected officers of associations (*élus sociaux*) a better deal regarding their rights, for example, of access to local government officials.

Some commentators have seen in the associational phenomenon an encouraging trend towards the establishment of sufficiently weighty countervailing forces (*contre-pouvoirs*). These would be a factor in the healthier balance between the State and *la société civile* which itself would be a measure of the success of the *'révolution tranquille'* claimed for the decentralisation policies of the post-1981 government.

Bibliographical guidance

On centre–periphery relations and local government in general, the following are recommended:

M. Arreckx, *Vivre sa ville* (Table Ronde, 1982)
J.F. Auby, *Le Commissaire de la République* (PUF 1983)
Autrement no. 47 (1983), number devoted to 'Le local dans tous ses états'
R. Beaunez, and P. Boulais, *Cadre de vie – des municipalités innovent* (Editions Ouvrières, 1983)
A. Gautier, *Des socialistes à visage ouvert – les élus PS en Haute-Garonne* (Privat, 1982)
P. Gremion, 'Crispation et déclin du jacobinisme' in H. Mendras, (ed); *La sagesse et le désordre en France 1980* (Gallimard, 1980)
J. Hussonois, *Les technocrates, les élus et les autres* (Editions Entente, 1978)
A. Merquiol, and A. Caussignac, *Le maire, le conseillers municipaux vous parlent* (Litec, 1983)
P. Poutout, *L'heure du citoyen* (France-Empire, 1983)
Pouvoirs, no. 24 (1983) number devoted to 'Le Maire'
R. Pronier, *Les municipalités communistes – bilan de trente ans de gestion* (Balland, 1983)
P. Richard and M. Cotten, *Les communes françaises d'aujourd'hui* (PUF 1983)
M.A. Schain, *French Communism and local power* (Frances Pinter, 1984)
V. Wright and J. Lagroye (eds) *Local government in Britain and France* (Allen & Unwin, 1979) published in French as *Les structures locales en Grande-Bretagne et en France* (La Documentation Française, Notes et Etudes Documentaires, oct.1982)

On decentralisation and regionalisation, see for example:

J. Baguenard, *La décentralisation territoriale* (PUF 1980)
P. Bernard, *L'Etat et la décentralisation* (La Documentation Française, Notes et Etudes Documentaires, mars 1983)
J. Chevallier, *et al. Le pouvoir régional* (PUF 1982)
J.-J. Dayries, and M. Dayries, *La régionalisation*, 2nd ed., updated (PUF 1982)
F. Dupuy, and J.C. Thoenig, 'La loi du 2 mars 1982 sur la décentralisation' in *Revue Française de Sciences Politiques* (décembre, 1983)

Le Monde, série *Dossiers et Documents,* no. 107, 'La Décentralisation'
(jan. 1984)
Pouvoirs no. 19 (1981) number devoted to 'Régions'
J.E. Vié, *La décentralisation sans illusion* (PUF 1982)

On specific regions:

Y. Guin, *Histoire de la Bretagne de 1789 à nos jours* (Maspéro, 1982)
M. Nicolas, *Histoire du mouvement breton* (Syros, 1982)
J.-P. Richardot, *La France en miettes* (Belfond, 1976)
Vanina, *Corse, la liberté, pas la mort* (Acratie, 1984)

Illustrative texts and linguistic exercises

Texte 8.1   Compte rendu d'une réunion d'un conseil municipal

Mise en situation
La commune de Nointel, de quelques cinq cents habitants, se trouve dans le
département du Val d'Oise, à une trentaine de kilomètres de Paris. Ce
compte rendu d'une des réunions mensuelles de son conseil municipal en
1982 donne une idée des préoccupations de la vie publique à échelon local.
Une liste des abbréviations se trouve à la fin du texte.

DEPARTEMENT du VAL-D'OISE

ARRONDISSEMENT de PONTOISE

CANTON de BEAUMONT-SUR-OISE

Tél. 470.01.41

REPUBLIQUE FRANCAISE

LIBERTE - EGALITE - FRATERNITE

MAIRIE DE NOINTEL

95590 PRESLES

COMPTE RENDU DE LA REUNION DU CONSEIL

MUNICIPAL DU 24 SEPTEMBRE 1982

Etaient présents : M. ANCELEET, Maire
                     M. DE TOLLENAERE,
                     Mme LE GIZL Adjoints
Mmes. LANCHEC - PLAINE
MM. BOSCH - BUTLER - FOURNIER - FAUCHIER
MAGNAN - HURON - PENVEN -

Le procès-verbal de la précédente
séance est adopté à l'unanimité.

CONCOURS D.D.E. - TRAVAUX RUE EDOUARD BECUE
AVENUE DE VERDUN

Monsieur le Maire rappelle que les travaux de
la Rue Edouard Bécue et de l'Avenue de

Verdun ont été surveillés par la
D.D.E. et qu'il y a lieu de régler les
honoraires qui seront calculés à raison
de 2,90 F par habitant suivant une convention.

Le Conseil Municipal donne avis favorable à la
convention proposée.

VOIRIE LE LOTISSEMENT "CLOS THERESE"
CLASSEMENT DANS LE DOMAINE COMMUNAL

Une demande a été adressée par les
habitants de la Rue du Clos Thérèse,
afin que celle-ci soit reconnue dans la
voirie communale.

Monsieur le Maire rappelle la convention
établie avec la Société A.I.G.V.
dans laquelle il était stipulé que la
rétrocession de la voirie serait
acceptée après un examen de l'état
de la voirie par la D.D.E.

Une lettre a été adressée à
Monsieur l'Ingénieur des T.P.E. qui va
procéder à cette vérification. Si
l'état est reconnu correct le dossier
d'enquête publique pourra être lancé.

TRAVAUX D'ASSAINISSEMENT 1ère TRANCHE

Monsieur le Maire rappelle qu'à
l'ouverture des plis de l'appel d'offres le
montant des travaux s'élevaient à
1.574.000 F au lieu de 1.300.000 F prévus
à l'origine par la D.D.E.

Il y a donc lieu de passer un avenant, et de
solliciter un emprunt complémentaire de
274.000 F.

Le Conseil Municipal,

Après en avoir délibéré,

Donne son accord afin de passer un avenant
au Marché; Mandate le Maire afin de
solliciter un emprunt complémentaire
dont les annuités seront prises en
charge dans le cadre du Syndicat
d'Assainissement de PERSAN-BEAUMONT.

REGLEMENT DU Ier ACOMPTE DES TRAVAUX
D'ASSAINISSEMENT.

Afin de régler le plus rapidement
possible l' Entreprise BARRIQUAND le Conseil
Municipal vote une ouverture de crédit
d'un montant de 304.265 Frs qui sera prévue
au Budget supplémentaire 1982, article
21361/1.

TRAVAUX DE REMISE EN ETAT AVENUE DE LA GARE

A la remise en état de l'Avenue de la Gare,
Monsieur l'Ingénieur de la D.D.E. avait
soumis aux membres de la Commission des
Travaux que cette rue supportant une très
grande circulation, elle pouvait être
renforcée par un apport de grave ciment.
La Commission des Travaux ayant émis un
avis favorable, le Conseil Municipal confirme
cette décision et afin de régler ces
travaux d'un montant de 50.000 F, donne
mandat à Monsieur le Maire pour solliciter
un emprunt.

MARCHE CONSTRUCTION D'UN COLLECTEUR D'EAUX
USEES ET D'UN BASSIN DE RETENUE

Monsieur le Maire soumet au Conseil Municipal,

le marché de construction d'une canalisation
d'eaux pluviales et d'un bassin de retenue qui
doit être réalisée dans les terrains acquis
par la Commune (CIMENTS FRANCAIS).

Le Marché s'élève à 348.203,67 F à
prélever   sur   une   enveloppe   de   500.000   F
subventionnée à raison de 150.000 Frs,
emprunt pour le complément soit 350.000 F.

Le Conseil Municipal donne avis favorable au
Marché, et donne pouvoir au Maire afin de
solliciter un emprunt.

ACQUISITION DE L'ORANGERIE ET DE LA NOUVELIE
MAIRIE

Monsieur le Maire rappelle qu'une subvention a
été sollicitée dans le cadre du Contrat
Régional des Feux Vallées. Le dossier ayant
pris du retard, il y a lieu de réaliser un
emprunt de 550.000 F à court terme auprès du
Crédit Coopératif, afin de régler le plus
rapidement possible le vendeur.

Le Conseil Municipal,

Après avoir pris connaissance de la convention
à intervenir entre la Banque Française de
Crédit Coopératif et la Commune, donne mandat
à Monsieur le Maire pour signer la dite
convention.

SUBVENTION B.A.S.

Le Conseil Municipal vote une subvention
complémentaire de 4.200 F pour le B.A.S. qui
sera prévue au Budget supplémentaire 1982,
article 657.

OUVERTURE DE CREDIT

Afin de régler le plus rapidement possible
l'acquisition de la débroussailleuse, le
Conseil Municipal vote une ouverture de crédit
de 1.899,24 F qui sera prévue au Budget
supplémentaire 1982, article 2147/2.

FOSSE RUE DU LAVOIR

Au cours des travaux du fossé, Madame FIACRE
avait demandé que l'entrée de la propriété de
son fils soit faite du côté mur de sa
propriété, il lui a été donné satisfaction.

D'autre part, elle demande la création de deux
accès supplémentaires.

Le Conseil Municipal ne donne pas son accord.

CONVENTION ENTRE LA COMMUNE ET LA STE H.L.M. - CONTROLE TECHNIQUE DES TRAVAUX D'ASSAINISSEMENT

Monsieur le Maire expose au Conseil Municipal
qu'il y a lieu de désigner un technicien pour
la surveillance des travaux d'assainissement
dans le lotissement.

Il suggère qu'il soit fait appel à la D.D.E.
et donne connaissance des conditions de
règlement.

Le Conseil Municipal,

Considérant que les réseaux d'assainissement
réalisés dans le cadre du lotissement, sont
destinés à être repris dans le réseau
communal,

Décide,

de demander le concours de la D.D.E.
de fixer le montant de la rétribution soit
0,3% du montant réel des travaux,

Autorise,

Le Maire à signer une convention avec la
Société H.L.M. qui s'engage à rembourser la
Commune des frais de contrôle.

PRIX DES PLACES FORAINS FETE COMMUNALE

Le Conseil décide de ne pas augmenter les prix
des places des forains.

AMENAGEMENT MAIRIE

Le Conseil prend connaissance des plans de la
Nouvelle Mairie dressés par Monsieur DROIT
Architecte.

LIEU DE VOTE

En raison des travaux de transformation qui
vont avoir lieu à la Mairie, le bureau de vote
est transféré à la Salle Municipale

RECENSEMENT 1982

Il est donné connaissance du recensement de la
Commune vérifié par l'I.N.S.E.E.

Nombre d'habitants 1975 :   508

   "   "   1982 :   471

TROTTOIRS AVENUE DE PARIS

Monsieur BUTLER souligne que les trottoirs de l'Avenue de Paris ont été enfoncés avec le passage des engins et des camions.

L'Entreprise doit les remettre en état.

CHATEAU

Une correspondance avait été adressée par Monsieur le PRINCE MURAT concernant les projects pour l'utilisation du Château et du Parc.

Le Conseil Municipal ayant pris connaissance de cette lettre et n'ayant aucune objection à soulever, il va être pris contact avec Monsieur le PRINCE MURAT afin de préciser certains points concernant la Commune (Assainissement etc.....).

REMERCIEMENTS

Il est donné lecture des remerciements concernant le versement de subventions.

L'ordre du jour étant épuisé, la séance est levée à 23 heures.

LE MAIRE

Notes
DDE: Direction Départmentale de l'Equipement
TPE: Travaux Publics de l'Etat
HLM: Habitation à Loyer Modéré
INSEE: Institut National de la Statistique et des Etudes Economiques
BAS: Bureau d'Aide Sociale

Exploitation du texte

1 Relevez toutes les phrases ayant comme sujets 'Monsieur le Maire' et 'le Conseil Municipal', et dressez la liste des verbes qui y figurent. Quels sont les rôles respectifs du Maire et du Conseil, d'après votre étude de ces verbes?

2 Quelle est la structure typique des phrases ayant comme sujet 'le Conseil Municipal'?

3 Commentez la fréquence relativement élevée de l'expression 'il y a lieu de ...' et de constructions impersonnelles ('il' avec verbe au passif) dans ce texte.

4 Expliquez le sens des expressions suivantes:

Plis, appel d'offres, convention, avenant, places des forains, honoraires, montant, ouverture de crédit, régler, prélever sur, enveloppe, subventionner, rétribution, à raison de.

5 Rédigez la lettre qu'auraient pu écrire les habitants de la Rue de Clos Thérèse, précisant les raisons pour lesquelles ils veulent que celle-ci soit incluse dans la voirie communale.

Text 8.2 Conseils de quartier contre féodalités politiques

Mise en situation

La décentralisation n'est pas la solution à tous les maux à en croire ce jugement d'un animateur d'association à Orléans, interviewé par un journaliste du *Monde*; celui-ci décrit d'abord l'environnement qui donna lieu à la création de l'association de locataires.

*   *   *

Il n'y a pas si longtemps on montrait du doigt le quartier des Salmoneries, un carré d'immeubles *rébarbatifs*, coincés entre deux voies rapides dans la banlieue orléanaise, à Saint-Jean-de-la-Ruelle. Un quartier avec ses 1500 habitants qui accumulait les problèmes sociaux (15 pour-cent environ de chômeurs, 40 pour-cent de familles étrangères); la délinquance, les expulsions étaient le lot quotidien. Aujourd'hui, le quartier est en train de *faire peau neuve*. La population s'est prise en main, et retrouve sa dignité.

A l'origine de ce renouveau, une association de locataires. Avec l'aide d'une équipe d'éducateurs, la compréhension de la municipalité de Saint-Jean-de-la-Ruelle, et la participation de l'office d'HLM d'Orléans, une opération 'Habitat et Vie sociale' a été lancée. Fait exceptionnel; les habitants, après une large *concertation* avec leur association, ont défini eux-mêmes les grandes lignes de la rénovation de leur quartier, les modifications architecturales à apporter dans les parties communes comme dans leur propre appartement, prouvant que l'urbanisme n'est pas seulement l'affaire des spécialistes.

Nous avons interrogé M. Serge Corfa, un des responsables de l'association des locataires des Salmoneries:

– La décentralisation a-t-elle facilité la tâche de rénovation de votre quartier?
– La décentralisation n'est pas encore arrivé jusqu'à notre niveau; nous n'en percevons pas les effets. Elle a profité jusqu'ici aux élus, qui possédaient déjà un certain pouvoir. Le 'cercle' du pouvoir ne s'est pas encore élargi; l'exercice des responsabilités n'a pas encore été étendu à de nouvelles couches de la population, à de nouveaux groupes de pression. On s'est contenté de renforcer le pouvoir des élus, ce qui n'est pas toujours forcément une bonne chose ...
– Pourquoi?
– La concertation n'existe pas 'au naturel'. Ce n'est pas un réflexe chez bien des élus – qu'ils soient de droite ou de gauche – comme dans l'administration, et qui raisonnent toujours en termes de pouvoir. Dans notre association, certains ne parlent pas le français, le niveau ne dépasse pas le certificat d'études. Nous ne savions pas exprimer nos besoins, et il nous a fallu éviter l'écrasement. Les élus, l'administration ont besoin d'avoir en face d'eux des *interlocuteurs* qui leur ressemblent, c'est-à-dire des *technocrates*. Face à des gens qui ont un langage simple, ils sont dépassés ... Nous avons donc appris à *faire des dossiers*, et plus ces dossiers étaient épais, plus nous avons été respectés.
– Vous êtes vraiment très critique ... Et pourtant, la décentralisation est en train de modifier bien des habitudes *contraignantes* entre Paris et la province ...
– La décentralisation de la commune vers les quartiers, c'est-à-dire là où les gens vivent, est absolument nécessaire. Pour de multiples raisons, d'efficacité notamment, la mairie reste le lieu central de décision. Mais les élus perdent souvent le contact avec la réalité des quartiers à cause de la politique ...
– Vous êtes donc favorable à la création de conseils de quartier?
– Oui, à partir des associations qui existent sur place. Les associations ne sont pas toujours rentables financièrement, mais elles le sont socialement: ne vaut-il pas mieux que cent personnes aient la possibilité de s'exprimer surtout en milieu populaire plutôt que dix? Ces conseils auraient un pouvoir de décision sur l'environnement immédiat, avec des moyens de gestion. Nous pouvons aussi gérer l'animation, et pourquoi pas les dégâts occasionnés dans le quartier: ce serait un bon moyen de 'responsabiliser' les gens ... La participation des habitants, c'est vrai, varie en fonction des pôles d'intérêt; celle des associations aussi.
C'est pourquoi je pense qu'il faut se garder de créer des structures trop 'figées', de vouloir tout institutionnaliser. Sinon, on va 'fabriquer' à nouveau de 'petits élus', avec leurs 'petits pouvoirs', bref on risque de créer de nouvelles *féodalités*.

SOURCE: Article paru dans *Le Monde*, le 9 février, 1983.

Exploitation du texte

1 Expliquez en quelques mots le sens des expressions en italique.

2   Rédigez la lettre d'une association de résidents au sujet des problèmes de leur quartier, adressée aux élus de leur commune et reprochant à ceux-ci de ne rien faire pour remédier à la situation.

3   Le conseil municipal se défend d'être éloigné des 'nouvelles couches de la population'. Imaginez la lettre qu'il envoie en réponse à celle de l'association de résidents.

4   Rédigez les statuts d'une association de résidents ou de locataires du genre de celle animée par l'interviewé dans cet article: objet; dénomination; siège; durée; composition; administration; modification des statuts; dissolution.

5   Quels seraient les arguments pour et contre la création de 'conseils de quartier'?

Texte 8.3   Un arrêté préfectoral

Mise en situation

Cet arrêté préfectoral, affiché sur les panneaux d'information des mairies, précise les formalités à remplir pour se faire inscrire sur les listes électorales et pouvoir bénéficier du droit de vote.

                *   *   *

RFPUBLIQUE FRANCAIS

PREFECTURE DU DEPARTEMENT DU VAL D'OISE

REVISION ANNUELLE

DES

LISTES ELECTORALES

Le Préfet, Commissaire de la République du
Départment du Val d'Oise, Chevalier de la
Légion d'Honneur

Vu le Code électoral
Vu la circulaire de M. le Ministre
    d'Etat, Ministre de l'Intérieur
    et de la Décentralisation, No.
    69.352, du 31 juillet 1969 mise à
    jour le 1er juin, 1982, relative à
    la révision des listes électorales
Vu le décret No. 75.605 du 8 juillet,
    1975
Vu la loi No. 75-1329 du 31 décembre,
    1975
Sur la proposition de M. Le Secrétaire-
    Général du Val d'Oise,

ARRETE :

Article Premier - Les opérations de révision
    des listes électorales auront lieu dans
    toutes les communes du départment du Val
    d'Oise dans les délais figurant ci-dessous.

Article 2 - M. le Secrétaire-Général du Val
    d'Oise, MM. les sous-préfets, Commissaires-

Adjoints de la République des Arrondissements
de MONTMORENCY, ARGENTEUIL, et PONTOISE, Mmes.
et MM. les Maires sont chargés, chacun en
ce qui les concerne, de l'exécution du
présent arrêté qui sera publié dans toutes
les communes du département.

Fait à Cergy-Pontoise, le 9 août, 1982

Le Préfet, Commissaire de la République
Pour le préfet
Le Secrétaire-Général par Intérim

J.-M. JANILLAC

DELAIS

DEMANDES D'INSCRIPTION - jusqu'au dernier jour
ouvrable de Décembre 1982 inclus

RECLAMATIONS - du 11 Janvier au 20 Janvier
1983 inclus

En application des dispositions de l'article
L.9 du Code Electoral

L'INSCRIPTION SUR LES LISTES ELECTORALES EST
OBLIGATOIRE

Conditions à remplir pour être inscrit sur les
listes électorales
IL FAUT A LA FOIS
-Etre de nationalité francaise
-Etre majeur (il suffit d'avoir 18 ans avant
 le 1er Mars 1983)
-N'être ni interdit ni frappé
 d'une incapacité prévue par la loi
 (incapacité perpétuelle ou temporaire
 consécutive à certaines condamnations),
 ni frappé d'indignité nationale

EN OUTRE, POUR ETRE INSCRIT DANS UNE COMMUNE,
IL FAUT
-Soit y posséder son domicile réel tel qu'il
est déterminé par le Code Civil;
-Soit y avoir sa résidence réelle et effective
de 6 mois (avant le 1er Mars, 1983);
-Soit y être inscrit pour la cinquième fois
sans interruption au rôle d'une des quatre
contributions directes ou au rôle des
prestations en nature et déclarer vouloir
exercer ses droits électoraux dans la
commune;
-Soit y exercer en qualité de fonctionnaire
public assujetti à résidence obligatoire
(aucun délai de résidence n'est exigé).

Pièces à fournir à l'appui des demandes
  d'inscription

Pour les HOMMES, l'une des pièces suivantes:
-Livret militaire, livret de famille,
 carte d'identité, passeport en règle,
 ancienne carte d'électeur.
-Pour les FEMMES, l'une des pièces suivantes:
-Livret de famille, carte d'identité,
 passeport en règle, ancienne carte d'électeur.

-A défaut de la carte d'identité ou d'un
 passeport en règle, les femmes célibataires
 devront présenter, si possibile, le livret de
 famille des parents.

NUL NE PEUT ETRE INSCRIT SUR DEUX LISTES ELECTORALES
-Toute personne qui aura   réclamé et obtenu
 son   inscription sur deux ou plusieurs listes sera
 punie des peines prévues par l'article L.86
 du Code Electoral (1 mois à 1 an de prison et
 une amende de 360 à   3.600 F).

```
-Des contrôles sont effectuées pour découvrir
et poursuivre les infractions à la loi.
```

```
LES DEMANDES D'INSCRIPTION SONT RECUES EN
MAIRIE AUX HEURES HABITUELLES D'OUVERTURE DES
BUREAUX
```

Exploitation du texte

1 Quelles sont les formules et expressions qui, selon vous, doivent figurer dans tout arrêté préfectoral, quel que soit son objet?

2 Pourquoi la forme de tout document juridique de ce type est-elle si figée?

3 Vous présentez une émission de radio consacrée au droit de vote: l'objet de l'émission est d'informer le grand public quant à ses droits et ses responsabilités. Expliquez quelles sont les conditions à remplir pour pouvoir s'inscrire sur les listes électorales.

4 Expliquez en quelques mots les expressions suivantes:
arrêté; décret; circulaire; loi; jour ouvrable; frappé; pièces; à défaut de; indignité nationale; présent; ci-dessous; Code Civil.

Exercices de comparaison et d'application

1 Quels sont les arguments pour et contre le système selon lequel les communes constituent l'unité de base de l'administration territoriale de la France?

2 Indiquez les grandes étapes de l'histoire du mouvement régionaliste en France.

3 Préparez un débat sur les atouts et les dangers de la décentralisation en France.

4 Secrétaire de mairie d'une commune de quelques 5000 habitants, vous rédigez le compte rendu d'une réunion du conseil municipal de manière à souligner les préoccupations de la vie publique locale.

5 Retracez l'évolution, depuis 1981, de l'idée de l'élection des conseils régionaux au suffrage direct.

9
Rights, Issues and Prospects

The French Revolution of 1789 was above all the assertion that human rights ought to be defended against the use of arbitrary power, and the picture of France as a haven for those who are the victims of the arbitrary exercise of power, and as the country of human rights, survives in international opinion. But in the second half of the twentieth century, Western democracies can be said to have derogated in practice from the highest standards of protection of human rights to which in theory they subscribed. This was because they came to perceive that the major threat to their value systems, or in starker terms to regime survival, came not from defeat in war, but from the activities of internal groups whose ideological dissent was too great for institutions to absorb. In France, derogations in this sphere serve to reinforce the vigilance of groups for whom the 1789 Declaration of the Rights of Man remains a real point of reference, and to underline the fact that imperfections exist in the array of dispositions by which individual rights are intended to be defended.

The Constitutional Council

President Giscard said in his January 1977 press conference that the President of the Republic is *'le garant des institutions'*, and *'le protecteur des libertés des Français'*. In saying this, he was stressing the non-political aspects of the Presidential function, and presumably had in mind the provision that the President is guarantor of the independence of the judiciary (Article 64) and that the judiciary is *'gardienne de la liberté individuelle'* (Article 66). But much of what the President can do in this domain is carried out indirectly through the Constitutional Council, one of the most important innovations of the 1958 Constitution. The nine members of the Constitutional Council are appointed for a nine-year non-renewable term of office. A third of the members are appointed each by the President of the Senate, the President of the National Assembly, and by the President of the Republic, one of whose

221

nominees chairs the Constitutional Council. Former Presidents of the Republic are members by right, but only ex-President Coty attended regularly from 1959 to his death in 1962; Vincent Auriol objected that its role was too restricted, and de Gaulle apparently considered that participation would be a loss of status. Giscard said he would attend only if it were a matter of defending the institutions of the Republic, and Mitterrand declared as early as 1982 that he would never exercise his right. The expiry of the mandate of a nominee of each of the institutional heads means a renewal every three years of a third of the Council, three members having been appointed originally in 1959 for only three years, and another three members for six years. The renewal in 1983 confirmed how the three institutional heads, but particularly the President of the Republic, can make appointments which may well introduce a political element (see *Texte* 9.1) into the Council's activities, which cover two main areas.

The first of these is the original one of regulating the new institutions established by the 1958 Constitution, and especially of ensuring the maintenance of the new balance between Parliament and Government, one of the major principles of the new Constitution. For this reason, organic laws, that is, those which put broad constitutional rules into detailed effect, and Parliamentary standing orders, had to have the prior approval of the Constitutional Council (Article 61-1), because any latitude in the interpretation of these, as well as of Article 34 limiting the *domaine de la loi*, may well have led to a drift back to the practices of the Fourth Republic. Other important parts of its role as institutional regulator are those of acting as a consultative body on measures taken by the President under Article 16, and of ensuring that referendums and elections on the national level are conducted properly; it resolves conflicts in this area (*le contentieux électoral*), and in the application of the principle of *incompatibilité*. The number of alleged irregularities referred to the Constitutional Council is often a reflection of the degree of contentiousness with which a legislative election has been fought, though it must be said that most cases tend to arise from constituencies in Corsica or the West Indian overseas *départements*. In extreme circumstances, a new constituency election can be required – this happened in four cases after the 1981 elections. The role of institutional regulator gave the Constitutional Council the reputation in the 1960s of a timid instrument at the disposal of the Executive in its efforts to establish firmly the principles of the new regime.

However, from 1971, the Constitutional Council began to assert greater independence not only in favouring Parliament against the Government in deciding what came under the *domaine de la loi*, but also by becoming active in another major area, that of protecting the rights and freedoms of individual citizens. Whereas organic laws and Parliamentary standing orders have to be referred to the Council for prior approval, ordinary laws may be referred before they take effect if there are doubts about their constitutionality; this may be done (Article 61-2) by the President of the Republic, the Prime Minister, the President of either chamber of Parliament, and, since 1974, by 60 deputies or 60 senators. The latter amendment was a considerable extension of the means by which Parliament could exercise its supervisory function, but even before 1974, the Constitutional Council had begun to make decisions (against which there is no appeal) on the basis of explicit reference to individual rights entrenched in the Preamble to the 1958 Constitution, where 'the French people solemnly proclaims its attachment to human rights as defined in the 1789 Declaration, and confirmed and added to by the Preamble to the 1946 Constitution'.

The Constitutional Council reaffirmed the right, for example, to:

1 freedom of association without prior consent by the authorities (1971);
2 equality of treatment on fiscal matters (1973);
3 equality before the law (1975);
4 privacy, by rejecting wide police powers to search vehicles (1977);
5 a fair hearing, in that one's lawyer should not be excluded from court for disturbing the proceedings (1981);
6 fair compensation, even where expropriation is in the public interest (1982).

In the first five cases mentioned, the Council's objection in the name of individual rights struck at the very basis of the proposed law, which was dropped. The last case quoted obliged the Left-wing government to rewrite parts of its law on nationalisation, and provoked criticism from Socialist and Communist deputies that the Constitutional Council was an instrument of the pre-1981 Majority, just as the 1983 appointments to the Council were attacked as being an undisguised attempt to redress the balance. President Mitterrand, however, defended it against the most vehement of Socialist attacks in 1982, as did Gaston Defferre, who, as Socialist parliamentary leader from 1974 to 1981, had fully exploited the opportunity given to Parliament by the 1974 reform to refer ordinary laws to the Constitutional Council, thereby helping it to achieve the prominent role it now has in the defence of individual rights.

Rights and freedoms

The significant part played by the Constitutional Council in defending rights goes a long way to counter certain weaknesses. Some of these are, firstly, that its procedural rules do not allow the publication of the reasoning behind the decisions, or of dissenting opinions; secondly, that there is no constitutional review possible after a law has been promulgated; thirdly, that private individuals cannot refer a matter to it. They have to rely on judicial review by the *Conseil d'Etat* of the administrative consequences of a law, or since 1973, through the medium of their parliamentary representative, on the intervention of the French Ombudsman (the *Médiateur*) in defence of rights denied by maladministration. Moreover, the politicisation of the Constitutional Council is less a function of the method of nomination – it was the advent of *le fait majoritaire* in 1962 which introduced the possibility of pro-Executive bias – than of the length of time taken for *alternance* to apply in the Fifth Republic.

The political dominance in the 1960s of a closely-knit group of Gaullists compounded the worsening of the situation with regard to human rights and civil liberties; this degradation was seen in the use of detention without trial during the Algerian war, to which the Fifth Republic regime added internment, torture, and in 1963 a special *Cour de sûreté de l'Etat* with military judges. This was set up to try crimes against the State by Right-wing terrorists of the *Organisation de l'Armée Secrète* (OAS) hostile to Algerian independence, but it was kept in existence until Mitterrand abolished it in 1981, carrying out a pledge contained in the 1972 Socialist and Communist Joint Programme for Government. The 23-year dominance by Gaullists and their Giscardian successors led not only to a spoils-system (*système des dépouilles*) characterised for example by favouritism in the promotion of civil servants and diplomats – and which the post-1981 government was accused of applying in its turn[1] – but more importantly to denial of rights and liberties by close governmental supervision of radio and television, by electronic surveillance of anti-Gaullist politicians and journalists, by the existence of a 'parallel' police force (the *Service d'Action Civique*, disbanded in 1982), and by the application of pressure on the judiciary in the exercise of their functions. Rights and liberties, especially freedom of information, which are fundamental to democratic values came to rest less on the range of directly enforceable constitutional principles (*le bloc de la constitutionnalité*) than on the expectations of the people. Liberal trends in the first half of Giscard's Presidency were overtaken by a resurgence of authoritarianism after 1978, epitomised by a law in February 1981 called '*Sécurité et liberté*', which in its extension of police powers at the expense of judicial authority was condemned by most lawyers.

The post-1981 administration took important steps to halt the erosion of human rights and civil liberties. Apart from the abolition of the *Cour de sûreté de l'Etat*, these included the extension to individuals of the right to refer a matter to the European Human Rights machinery, the ending of the death penalty for murder, and the clarification of immigrants' rights by some reduction of arbitrary police powers which a growing climate of racism in France had allowed to flourish. Public susceptibilities on the presence of immigrants, North Africans particularly –Chilean and Vietnamese refugees were generously admitted – and on worsening crime rates had to be taken into account by politicans urging greater protection of human rights. The distaste for authoritarian measures which led to the dilution of the '*Sécurité et liberté*' legislation was tempered by realistic admission that the quality of public life, including law and order, was deteriorating.

The media

It was in the area of information, however – the press and broadcasting – that the Left felt that an intolerable erosion of individual rights had taken place during the first 23 years of the Fifth Republic. De Gaulle discovered during the Second World War the immense power of mobilisation and persuasion through radio, and by 1958 concluded that broadcasting was a vital national resource to be kept under State control. Radio and television journalists came to be regarded as a different kind from those working for the press; in the early days of the Fifth Republic, radio chiefs had their offices inside the Ministry of Information, to save time for both sides; and peripheral radio stations were taken under partial control, while at the same time the State monopoly of broadcasting within France was strictly maintained.

The close State supervision of broadcasting within this monopoly was paralleled by the increasing concentration of the press under the control of a small number of Press groups, headed by people sympathetic to Right-wing governments. Developments in the 1950s and 1960s in the regional press also, marked the end of an era in which most newspapers set up after the Liberation operated in a spirit of ideological commitment to radical reforms. In such a situation, which is not unknown in other Western democracies, the defence of rights and freedoms rests on the existence of a small-circulation independent press and the professional integrity of journalists as a whole. The Mauroy government, however, decided in 1983–4 to give legislative underpinning to its opposition to press concentration, particularly the empire controlled by Robert Hersant, but this initiative provoked controversy and even misgivings among the Government's supporters during Parliamentary debates.

One of the promises of Mitterrand's Presidential campaign was to free the media and establish a clear independence from Government control. The State monopoly of broadcasting was ended, but the number of local radios which were already operating illegally was too great for the available wavebands, and a system of licensing, with partial State aid, was introduced in 1983; listeners in Paris, for example, then had the choice of about thirty radio stations, of which five belonged to the State organisation, which was itself restructured for the fifth time since 1945.

The desire to separate clearly the media from State power led to the setting up of the *Haute Autorité de la communication audio-visuelle*, which became responsible for appointing the chairmen of the various state radio and television companies, for maintaining overall programming standards, and for the licensing of local radios and the provision of radio and television services by means of optical fibre cabling, plans for an extensive network of which were approved by the Council of Ministers at the end of 1982. The *Haute Autorité* was criticised as being merely a different, more subtle, means of State supervision of broadcasting, but Opposition complaints of media domination by Left-wingers through, for example, 'action committees' of trade unions, rang hollow given the situation obtaining from 1958 to 1981. The view that it is logical and somehow democratic to promote through radio and television the view for which a majority of electors voted, appears well-entrenched in contemporary French politics, despite the negative implications of this for rights and freedoms.

Issues

Considerations of the rights and civil liberties of individuals, and of individuals in groups, as well as questions of values for the whole polity, are present not only in broad-ranging political programmes and comprehensive *projets de société* inspired by ideologies, but also within the narrower confines of specific issue areas. The study of these has assumed greater importance in political science, to complement insights gained from the analysis of traditional institutional structures, parties and groups.

Participation

General de Gaulle saw participation as a kind of middle way between capitalism and Communism; it would be a measure of the social reconciliation of antagonistic groups which he regarded as a necessary basis for his ultimate aim of a strong, independent State. But the vagueness of the concept could signify that employees had a share of the profits of the company (*intéressement*) or that they shared the exercise of powers of management (*cogestion*). Many non-Marxist Left-wingers were attracted in the late 1950s by the innovatory nature of the Gaullist vision of social reform; '*gaullisme de gauche*' was influential in the early years of the Fifth Republic, and a factor in the acceptance of the new regime by a broad range of public opinion.

Moves to apply the idea, however, met with opposition from conservative Gaullist elements – Pompidou disagreed strongly with de Gaulle on the matter – and hostility from the trade unions. The attitude of the latter was reinforced by the failure of a move to introduce voluntary profit-sharing in 1959, and the limitations of an obligatory scheme in 1967, when the Government emphasised that '*la participation ne veut être en aucune manière la cogestion*'. In 1968, de Gaulle urged participation as a solution to the problems he considered to have been responsible for the 'events' of May and June, but Pompidou later alienated Gaullist reformism by his antagonism to the concept.

The idea of industrial units as social organisations was taken up as part of Giscard's initial commitment to reform, but this interest led to little except a law in 1977 which somewhat increased employees' rights to information in the context of the 'social impact' (*bilan social*) of industrial plants. A plan for the obligatory distribution to employees of 5 per cent of a company's shares became the voluntary distribution of 3 per cent, and a contemplated participation in the exercise of power was limited to managerial staff.

The post-1981 administration extended employees' rights, and the trade unions' role, in matters of representation (two members of the board of a nationalised industry), information, and collective bargaining, but the rights and power of bosses in the private sector were not diminished. Participation remains a principle which questions the authoritarianism of corporate control and makes bold promises of economic democracy. In the 1980s, it is still visible as a minor strand of Gaullist party (RPR) doctrine, and inspires small groups on the periphery of Gaullism who are attracted by a middle way towards social and political reform.

Autogestion

Autogestion, which is inadequately translated as self-management, or as workers' control, postulates a new social and economic, and therefore political, structure, and has its origins in anarcho-syndicalism (see page 36). It summarised in May-June 1968 many of the disparate aspirations for democracy in economic as well as political life which had grown into a revolt against the abuses of hierarchy and a call for power to be exercised at the basic level – the industrial plant, the neighbourhood, the university, the classroom. The word was incorporated into documents within the PSU but this party did not officially call for *autogestion* until 1972. It was the CFDT which was the first mass organisation to espouse *autogestion* in 1968, and two years later called it 'one of the pillars of socialism', the others being democratic planning, and the socialisation of the means of production. It was necessary, and perfectly possible, not to *'produire plus'* or *'produire mieux'*, but *'produire autrement'* by giving workers control over their own fate. The experience of the Lip factory in Besançon which for some months after June 1973 assembled watches without bosses or supervisors was, for some, a proof that *autogestion* worked, but for others a confirmation that there were contradictions between *autogestion* and economic planning – that the cooperative or self-management approach was inappropriate for the large-scale industrial complexes in existence today.

The *Parti Socialiste* in the early 1970s thought of *autogestion* as merely improving the efficiency of public sector undertakings by giving workers more managerial responsibilities, but, spurred on by the CERES faction which considered that 'socialism from below' would complement 'socialism from above', and after the attempts at doctrinal renewal of the *Assises du Socialisme* (1974) and the PS Conference on *autogestion* (1975), the party seemed to be adopting *autogestion* as a major element of its policy, distinct from that of the PCF on the one hand, and social democracy and the Right on the other. But when the PCF after much hesitation was converted to what it called 'national autogestion', reference to the concept was quietly dropped by the PS, which during the 1977 talks to update the Joint Programme for Government realised that if *autogestion* was applied, the Communist-dominated CGT would control future nationalised industries. A small *'Union pour l'autogestion'* faction in the PS, headed by Christian Pierret, became hopelessly divided at the end of the 1970s, and after 1981, only the original minimalist interpretation survived to reinforce the policy of giving workers more share in management and wider legal rights.

Autogestion remains an important area of socialist political thinking outside the PS, particularly in the PSU and the CFDT –the so-called *'deuxième gauche'*; and Robert Lafont, the most influential of the intellectual inspirers of regionalism, linked this movement with the desire for *autogestion* in a seminal work in 1976: *Autonomie, de la région à l'autogestion*.

Consumerism

The post-war economic recovery of Western Europe was sufficiently advanced by the second half of the 1950s for firms to gear production more to the individual consumer and to enter a new competitive field where product marketing assumed a greater importance. But in this new 'consumer society', reactions inevitably grew against the excesses of competitive marketing, and a consumer movement dedicated to the defence of consumer interests and rights (*consumérisme*), made its tentative appearance in the 1960s. Consumers grouped together to tackle manufacturers, suppliers and the authorities, and a whole range of general and specialised defence groups was eventually established to protect the individual's right to full information on what the market offered and to conduct specific campaigns concerning products.

What became the most prestigious of the general organisations at national level, the *Union fédérale des consommateurs* (UFC), made its mark in the 1960s by a successful attack through its journal *Que choisir?*, on exaggerated claims made by several manufacturers on behalf of their mineral water; subsequent successful campaigns by this and other organisations were launched against, for example, private beaches, marine pollution, cases of inaccurate labelling and harmful additives, and in the early 1980s hormones in veal. In the 1960s also, the Government was obliged to try to regulate competition more, and to take account of the role of consumers in national economic activity; in 1967 the *Institut National de la Consommation* (INC) was set up, as a state body to advise the government on technical and legal aspects, and to spread information on consumer affairs through the medium of television. Giscard introduced a localised system, *Boîte Postale 5000*, to adjudicate small claims by individual consumers against manufacturers and suppliers, and extended the consultative role of consumers in the public sector.

The rights of consumers were in general reinforced under the impetus of a Minister of Consumer Affairs during the period 1981–3, with attention being given to legal backing, and to the regional coordination of the many different kinds of consumer organisations. There were also plans to foster competition, from which it was assumed the consumer would benefit, by modifying the *Loi Royer* of 1971 which had slowed the development of large-scale retailing in order to protect smaller businesses. Such moves may allow wider sections of the population to take fuller advantage of their rights as consumers and make *consumérisme* less of a middle-class phenomenon.

Ecology
Sensitivity to the concept of a global ecological balance was a product of nineteenth century scientific advance, but the realisation that this could be seriously upset, to the detriment of human welfare, was dramatically underlined by a spate of atmospheric nuclear testing in the 1950s. The ecological movement which sprang up in the 1950s and 1960s was a mixture consisting of those people who understood from a more scientific viewpoint the dangers on an international level to the global ecosystem – for example, *Les Amis de la Terre*, founded in 1970 – and those concerned with threats to the more immediate environment within the national context – for example, the *Fédération française des sociétés de protection de la nature*. This latter strand stressed the dangers of pollution and other harmful effects of a consumer-oriented growth economy, called for *'des options non productivistes'*, and created a climate of opinion leading to the setting up of a *Ministère de l'Environnement* in 1971, regarded by many as a mere palliative because of the acute economic constraints in which it had to work.

Both of the above-mentioned strands of the movement were evident in the radical programmes of May–June 1968, and both of them combined to considerable effect in opposing, from 1971 onwards, the building of nuclear power stations and of establishments to recycle nuclear waste. The growth, not only of the complexity of the issue in the context of national energy policies, but also of the number of different organisations within the wider movement led ecologists to become candidates in local elections, in parliamentary elections from 1973, and in the Presidential elections of 1974 (Dumont) and 1981 (Lalonde).

Ecologists, like most single-issue groups, resisted efforts to assimilate them into the system of parties or broader coalitions of interests, and maintained a strict independence with regard to established parties, though there remained strong temptations within the movement to form an 'ecology party'. Ecologist supporters tend to split two or three to one in favour of the Left in the second round of elections, partly because, among major parties, it is only in the Socialist Party that the views of the ecological movement have gained significant acceptance, and 1983 saw the first meeting of the national council of a pro-government *'Alliance écologique'*.

Electoral support for ecology candidates fell in 1981 to less than 4 per cent in the first round, after being near 5 per cent in the 1979 European elections. They had some success after 1981, however, in being granted representation on the *Conseil supérieur de la sécurité nucléaire*, and in the slowing down of plans to supply a larger proportion of France's energy requirements from nuclear sources, though France is well ahead of the rest of Europe in the number of nuclear reactors in service or under construction. The nuclear question (*le nucléaire*) continues to be the main potential unifying focus for often disparate groups which, lacking common aims and methods, or the common denominator of class solidarity, can only mobilise mass support around opposition to specific projects, or in operations like the *'Etats généraux sur le nucléaire'*.

Prospects

By contrast with an often turbulent past, the image of French politics in the 1980s is more reassuring to the observer who wishes to assess political stability and the regime's chances of survival. The Third Republic was built on a 'republican synthesis' of contending groups which did not however survive the tensions caused by dissentient forces in the 1930s and the shock of military defeat. The Fourth Republic emerged from the experience of the Resistance, but without the support of Gaullists and Communists it was unable to survive acute political crises. The Fifth Republic gained rapid acceptance among a majority of public opinion and more grudging acceptance by Left-wing politicians, but by the 1970s, it was possible to speak of a consensus on the institutional structure of the regime.

The stability which this support provided was reinforced in 1981, when power passed into the hands of the Left without jeopardising the institutional equilibrium. The regime, it was argued, had established a synthesis between the republican and authoritarian traditions which the French state reflected at various times over two centuries. Commentators claim that whereas over much of this period the process of political change and modernisation in France was convulsive rather than incremental, future political change will be effectively contained within institutions underpinned by a high degree of political legitimacy. A further element of regime support is provided by the existence of a wide consensus on basic values –the maintenance of the rule of law, freedom of conscience, the sovereignty of Parliament and free elections to it, and State-guaranteed minimum welfare provision.

However, like all industrialised states at the end of the twentieth century, France inevitably needs to adapt to changing circumstances and faces problems which may prove less than perfectly amenable to traditional solutions. Major changes in the objective conditions confronting Western society pose questions which require not merely a delicate application of economic regulators, but often a stark political choice between ideological alternatives. A renewed concern with ideology, provoked by deepening economic crisis, could see the breakdown of constraints placed on ideological conflict by the Fifth Republic synthesis. Just as a lack of support for the Fourth Republic regime in the 1950s jeopardised economic expansion and modernisation, so with the last quarter of the twentieth century, the economic problems of the oil crisis and world recession could be seen as influencing politics by reducing the number of options available. The liberal values on which Giscard called, in order to bring '*décrispation*' to French politics, proved in the 1970s to be an inadequate basis on which to build a system which could reduce glaring inequalities and respond to social imperatives as well as to private satisfaction.

Therefore, while it is true that the idea of France as the archetype of a centrifugal political system with a fragmented political culture has had to be revised and refined, there are important aspects of the political culture and institutional structure of France which remain to provoke doubts about the future. For example, although nobody seriously suggests that France might break up, as people were suggesting in the mid-1970s that the United Kingdom might dissolve into its constituent units, the French state is still hostile to groups which by their nature or objectives could exist and operate beyond its control. The extinction of Breton cultural identity in the nineteenth century is matched in the 1980s by the attempted suppression of Corsican separatism; and the policy of decentralisation could mean that the territorial basis of conflict is revived.

Constitutional crisis and change?

It is frequently argued that the intensity of ideological conflict in French politics was reduced by party acceptance in the 1970s of the desirability of *alternance*, and by its realisation in 1981. No longer, it was claimed, could discontents accumulate in a basically conservative society until catharsis was inevitable in the form of revolutions, or of upheavals falling short of national revolution, as in 1848, 1870–71, and 1968.

But the 'presidentialist' regime which emerged at the end of the 1960s from de Gaulle's constitutional practice and the 1962 amendment made the Presidency a factor which increased the possibility of constitutional crisis, instead of one which, as the 1958 text made clear (Article 5), was the means for resolving such crisis. Moreover, the associated phenomenon of *le fait majoritaire* meant that any case of *alternance* was also more likely to precipitate a constitutional crisis, or at least pose constitutional questions to which the Constitution itself provides no ready-made answers.

The problem would become acute in two principal ways: firstly, if an incumbent President (or his political heir) enjoying the support of a parliamentary majority was defeated by an Opposition Presidential candidate; the latter as the new President dissolves the 'hostile' Assembly, but the ensuing elections fail to return a majority favourable to the new President. This would have happened in 1981 if Mitterrand's strategy had not succeeded. It is unlikely, however, that such a *'double alternance'* would not come about in the above circumstances, unless the electorate perversely rejected the logic of the post-1962 Fifth Republic and, having elected a President, refrained from giving him the supportive majority in the Assembly which the logic of the system requires. A second set of circumstances is much more likely to bring about a constitutional crisis: this is where an existing Parliamentary majority supporting a President and 'his' Government becomes a minority after legislative elections. It was this situation which almost happened in March 1967, seemed about to happen in March 1978, and which was postulated from 1981 onwards, for the end of the Assembly elected in that year. It remains an unresolved question in the Fifth Republic system, provoked by the 'presidentialist' nature of the regime, and about which many political commentators have speculated.

The most extreme of the possible outcomes are the least likely. These are:

In the President's favour:

1 The President invokes Article 16, ostensibly because the institutions of the State are under serious and immediate threat, and their proper functioning is interrupted, but in effect as the first stage of a *coup d'état* ending parliamentary democracy.

2 The President asks the people (Article 11 – he has to wait until Parliament is in session) to approve either a different regime – a 'Sixième République' where for example the Government was not responsible to Parliament – or a major modification of the Constitution of the Fifth Republic. De Gaulle after all did the first in the September 1958 referendum, and attempted the second successfully in October 1962 and unsuccessfully in April 1969.

In Parliament's favour:

3 Parliament (both Chambers) accuses the President of high treason (Article 68) and he is tried by a *'Haute Cour de justice'* made up of parliamentarians (Article 67). High treason appears to have no strict legal definition, and as history shows, political considerations play a large role. It has been argued that, in the appropriate political circumstances, high treason could apply to cases 1 and 2 above.

4 Parliament (both Chambers) asks the people (Article 89) to approve either a different regime – a 'Sixième République' where the President no longer had the new powers given to him in the 1958 Constitution – or a major modification of the latter by removing, for example, Article 16 powers.

Within these extremes, however, there is a whole range of possible outcomes, depending on the precise nature and impact of unpredictable factors such as the international political situation, internal economic circumstances, the salience of social conflict, and the composition of the new parliamentary majority. The latter would be crucially affected by the degree to which an admixture of proportional representation to the electoral system led to the presence of small groups in the National Assembly which held the balance of power, especially if these constituted a *groupe charnière* in the political Centre – the joint initiative of Edgar Faure (ex-Radical and ex-RPR) and Maurice Faure (ex-MRG) begun in 1983–4 was in anticipation of such a situation. The presence of such small groups in the Assembly could of course signify the end of the bipolarisation which has existed in that forum since 1973–4. But even without them, the degree to which the close cooperation between coalition partners of Right and Left (which has been the basis of that bipolarisation) has evaporated will be an important factor.

Even allowing for these uncertainties, further potential outcomes can be suggested:

Possibly in the President's favour:
5 The President reaffirms his authority as the source of decision making by asserting his powers of political command; he appoints as government ministers, and especially as Prime Minister (Article 8-1) people who are in broad sympathy with his policies, and relies on an uncertain parliamentary situation (and possibly international tension) to avoid an Assembly vote of censure which would require his Government to submit its resignation (Article 50). This is analogous to the 1958–62 period. Such an outcome would be in the President's favour if he was seen to be an example of constancy in a time of uncertainty; he could even resign at an opportune time before the end of his term of office and gain a clearer popular mandate in the ensuing elections. The presidentialist logic of the Fifth Republic system would be even further reinforced.

Possibly in Parliament's favour:
6 Parliament is dissolved by the President (Article 12) after a period of confusion, in an attempt to force the electorate to see the error of their ways and return a majority favourable to the President. This is a different reason for dissolution from that of 1981, where it was necessary to complete the *alternance* of Mitterrand's election by that of a Left Assembly majority. It is akin to the dissolution of 1962 and 1968, in that it asks the people to decide in a conflict between the President and groups opposing him – most political parties in 1962, and some students and workers in 1968. But the difference is that the conflict would be between the President and the people (or the majority of them). Unless there is a significant derogation from the Republican principle of Parliament as the incarnation of popular sovereignty, it is likely that a dissolution in such

circumstances would lead to a reinforcement of the prestige and powers of Parliament. The analogy would be with the strong reactions in May–June 1958 'in defence of the Republic'.

If in the event there is no significant effect from uncertainties stemming from economic and social problems, a difficult international environment, and a weakening of bipolarisation in the party system, then a likely outcome is some kind of balance:

Balance between the President and Parliament
7   The President has already declared before the election of a hostile majority in the Assembly that he will carry on until the end of his term, just as Giscard announced in 1977 in anticipation of a possible Left victory in March 1978. It is perfectly in keeping with the presidentialist interpretation of the Constitution, adopted by successive Presidents. The new majority in the Assembly is a clear one over the Opposition, and shows every sign of internal cohesion – the characteristics, in varying degrees, of majorities since 1962. In such a situation, the fundamental balance in the 1958 Constitutions is decisive. The President cannot appoint a Government which is politically close to himself, because the Assembly has the means to require its resignation by passing a 'spontaneous' motion of censure. But the Assembly cannot follow the logic of this power and oblige the President to appoint a Government which is politically close to itself. This is not only because the President holds in reserve the power of dissolution (though not during the year after elections occasioned by a previous dissolution), but also because the President and the Government need to cooperate to ensure the effective functioning of the process of government. The President signs ordinances and decrees drawn up in the Council of Ministers (Article 13), and the Prime Minister or one of his colleagues has to sign Presidential 'acts', with the exception of those mentioned in Article 19.

It is in these circumstances that the Government assumes a pivotal position. It remains responsible to Parliament in accordance with Article 20-3, but its entrenched effectiveness in relation to Parliament, by means of the whole range of constitutional provisions designed to prevent Parliamentary domination, is reinforced by its virtual autonomy in relation to the President. No longer obliged to occupy an inferior position in the decision-making process, it recovers that function within the institutional structure which the Constitution allots to it, namely that *'le gouvernement détermine et conduit la politique de la Nation'* (Article 20-1). The President is obliged to curtail his role as initiator of policy, and reverts to the function outlined in Article 5. In theory, and for as long as Presidential and Parliamentary majorities do not coincide, distortions introduced into the Constitution by several decades of custom are corrected, and the text of the 1958 Constitution is subject to a literal interpretation.

We have seen that one result of the unique nature of the Fifth Republic regime, neither classicially presidential nor overwhelmingly parliamentary, is that the President who is elected by a majority sector of opinion, in order that his Prime Minister and Government can apply his policies, needs that same sector of opinion to elect a majority which will support the Government to the Assembly. A constitutional reform which would make such a coincidence of support extremely likely would be to have the same number of years for a Presidential term as for the life of a Parliament. This was first mooted in the 1960s, and, though not a burning issue, has surfaced on both Right and Left since that date.

The Fifth Republic kept its predecessor's provision of a five-year maximum for the National Assembly, and continued the much longer tradition, dating from the 1870s, of a Presidential *septennat*, but made it indefinitely renewable – hence the description *'monarchie élective'*. This arrangement suited de Gaulle since it fitted in with his view of the President as looking after, like his predecessors, the higher and more enduring interests of the State, removed from the political conflicts of which Parliament was the arena. But when de Gaulle became the inspirer (even *'le leader clandestin'*) of a Gaullist parliamentary majority elected in 1962 and confirmed in 1967 and 1968, the rationale of a *septennat* was considerably weakened. Proposals were made during the 1960s, by the Left-wing *Programme commun de gouvernement* in 1972, and in 1973 by President Pompidou, to reduce the President's term of office to five years (*quinquennat*). Pompidou was conscious of the fragility of the balance between two separately articulated expressions of popular sovereignty – President and Parliament –and feared, as a Gaullist, that it might degenerate into an Assembly-dominated regime. To solve the problem, he set in motion a constitutional revision using Article 89 of the 1958 constitution. It was accepted by a majority of the National Assembly and the Senate, but, faced with the probability that it would not get the required three-fifths majority of both Chambers sitting together, Pompidou withdrew the plan. Such proposals, and similar suggestions since, did not envisage that President and Parliament would be chosen in the same election, but a system might well have emerged of Presidential elections being very closely followed by Parliamentary ones, as happened in 1981.

In July 1981, Mitterrand suggested either a five-year term renewable once or a non-renewable *septennat*; this latter might inhibit younger candidates but it would preserve the existing approach, and be a step back from the idea of a virtually automatic coincidence of Presidential and Parliamentary majority. On the other hand, a Presidential *quinquennat*, more or less coinciding with the life of a Parliament which would have, unless the electorate was perverse, a supportive majority, would emphasise the notion of a 'contract' between President and Parliament. It would also make *alternance* easier, and obviate electoral intervention by Presidents in the name of 'stability', which has tended to be a feature during the Fifth Republic of all parliamentary elections held while a Presidential term still has time to run. It would however represent an increase in the presidential flavour of the regime, as would the election of a Vice-President, first suggested in 1962, to carry an interrupted *quinquennat* through to its full term. Moves such as these towards the virtual establishment of a presidential regime would make the President less a national leader than a political leader. It was Giscard's realisation after 1976 that he did not have the means to be a political leader, as Gaullist support in Parliament became more and more grudging, which made him accept the institutional wisdom of having, as a deterrence and a last resort, the Presidential power of dissolution.

President Mitterrand's predilection for a non-renewable *septennat*, in preference to his other suggestion of a once-renewable *quinquennat*, may indicate a French distaste for a President as the overt leader of a political faction, indulging in crude attempts to gain popularity (*démagogie*) towards the end of his term of office; and conversely a profound attachment to the idea of a President who, while holding firmly the reins of executive power, can nevertheless act if necessary as the framers of the Fifth Republic Constitution envisaged – to save the State from a nation in crisis. Although future constitutional change towards a presidential regime cannot be ruled out, it seems that the French people is content with the traditions, adapted to modern society, of parliamentary republicanism.

Bibliographical guidance

On the Constitutional Council:

L. Favoreu, and L. Philip, *Le Conseil constitutionnel* 2nd ed. (PUF 1981)
Pouvoirs no. 13 (1980) number devoted to 'Le Conseil constitutionnel'

On rights in general, the following are recommended:

R. Errera, *Les libertés à l'abandon* 3rd ed. (Seuil, 1975)
B. Maligner, *Les fonctions du médiateur* (PUF, 1979)
J. Rivéro, 'Libertés publiques et institutions judiciaires' in *Rapport général de la Commission du bilan*, vol, 5 (La Documentation Française, 1982)
G. Soulier, *Nos droits face à l'Etat* (Seuil, 1982)

On specific issue-areas:

J.-C. Allanic, *Consommateurs... si vous saviez* (A. Moreau, 1982)
C. Angoujard and J.-D. Tortuyaux, *Le pouvoir des consommateurs* (Hatier, 1982)
G. Cas, *La défense du consommateur* 2nd ed. updated. (PUF, 1980)
P.G. Cerny (ed) *Social movements and protest in France* (Frances Pinter, 1982)
CFDT, *Nucléaire – tout ce qu'on vous a caché* (CFDT – Comité régional d'information et de lutte anti-nucléaire de Saint-Lô, 1984)
CFDT, Groupe fédéral énergie *Le dossier de l'énergie* (Seuil, 1984)
B. Charbonneau, *Le feu vert – autocritique du mouvement écologique* (Karthala, 1980)
J.-P. Clément, *La participation dans l'entreprise* (PUF, 1983)
O. Corpet, 'A propos de quelques autogestions à la française – esquisses prospectives' in J. Chevallier *et al. L'Institution* (PUF, 1981)
A.G. Delion and M. Durupty, *Les nationalisations 1982* (Economica, 1982)
R. Kuhn, 'Broadcasting and politics in France' in *Parliamentary Affairs* (Winter, 1983)
B. Lalonde, S. Moscovici and R. Dumont, *Pourquoi les écologistes font-ils de la politique? – entretiens avec Jean-Paul Ribes* (Seuil, 1978)
D. Mothé, *L'autogestion goutte à goutte* (Editions du Centurion, 1980)
P. Rosanvallon, *L'âge de l'autogestion* (Seuil, 1976)
C. Villeneuve, *Les Français et les centrales nucléaires* (Sofedir, 1980)

On future prospects in the light of current developments, see:

R. de Lacharrière, *La Vᵉ, quelle république?*(PUF., 1983)
J. Fourastié and B. Bazil, *Le jardin du voisin – essai sur les inégalités en France* (Livre de Poche, 1981)

A. Fourçans, *Pour un nouveau libéralisme – l'après-socialisme* (A. Michel, 1982)

M. Gallo, *La troisième alliance – pour un nouvel individualisme* (Fayard, 1984)

G. Mandel, *54 millions d'individus sans appartenance* (R. Laffont, 1983)

Pouvoirs, no.1 (new edition, 1981) number devoted to 'L'Alternance'

Pouvoirs, no.5 (1978) number devoted to 'Le Consensus'

M. Vaughan, 'Persistent cleavages in a changing society' in M. Vaughan, *et al.* (eds), *Social change in France* (Martin Robertson, 1980)

Illustrative texts and linguistic exercises

Texte 9.1 Juristes et politiques

Mise en situation

Le renouvellement de 1983 du Conseil Constitutionnel fut effectué par la publication des noms des trois nouveaux membres. Désigné par François Mitterrand, M. Daniel Mayer succéda comme Président à M. Roger Frey. Le Président de l'Assemblée Nationale, Louis Mermaz, choisit M. Pierre Marcilhacy et le Président du Sénat, Alain Poher, désigna M. Jozeau-Marigné. Voici le commentaire d'un journaliste du *Monde*, Philippe Boucher.

*   *   *

Pour n'être pas des nominations exactement politiques, au sens le plus partisan du terme, la désignation des nouveaux membres du Conseil constitutionnel était attendue non sans intérêt par *la classe politique*. C'est dire que quelques flèches étaient prêtes du côté de l'opposition si celle-ci avait jugé que les nouveaux gardiens de la Constitution n'offraient pas de suffisantes garanties personnelles.

Aucun des soupçons qui avaient, à tort en fin de compte, accompagné la désignation de M. Roger Frey ne pourrait aujourd'hui avoir sérieusement cours à propos des trois nouveaux élus.

Tous juristes, de formation ou d'expérience, tous familiers et même pratiquants de la vie politique, ils réunissent la double qualité dont il paraît reconnu, à présent, par les deux moitiés antagonistes de la nation, qu'elle est nécessaire à un bon examen des évolutions constitutionnelles.

Il est donc bon que l'âge, commun à ces trois nouveaux – soixante-treize ans – n'ait pas empêché qu'ils fussent désignés. Il est donc bon qu'on ait écarté, cette fois-ci, la limite de soixante-cinq ans retenue lors de la composition de la Haute Autorité de l'audiovisuel. A croire que, dans ce dernier cas, la règle administrative venait au secours des autorités de nomination (les mêmes que pour le Conseil constitutionnel) afin d'éliminer quelques candidats de qualité difficiles à écarter sans les blesser, afin qu'on pût se borner à les dire trop âgés.

Agés, assurément ils le seront en fin de mandat, puisqu'ils atteindront quatre-vingt-deux ans. Mais ils ont neuf ans devant eux pour, avec le concours des six autres membres du Conseil, faire prospérer les observations et *les réflexions* qu'ils ont tirées de leur vie politique et, plus simplement, de la vie tout court.

Dans ce domaine, l'itinéraire de M. Pierre Marcilhacy, grand bourgeois libéral, qui en vint à *ferrailler publiquement* contre des lois et des décisions qu'il jugeait *à bon droit* scélérates (ce qui lui coûta certainement son siège de sénateur en 1980), justifiait qu'on fît appel à lui. La riche expérience de M. Jozeau-Marigné, aussi. Il renonce ainsi à son poste de président de la commission des lois du Sénat, qui pourrait revenir à M. Jacques Thyraud, lequel, à son tour, pourrait renoncer à la présidence de la Commission nationale de *l'informatique* et des libertés. Mais c'est aller trop vite vers un futur pourtant proche.

Curieusement, c'est M. Daniel Mayer qui est à la fois le plus évident et le plus étonnant. Evident, il l'est en ayant occupé durant de longues années la présidence de cette 'Ligue des droits de l'homme' que créa le sénateur Ludovic Trarieux en 1898 pour défendre la cause du capitaine Dreyfus. On y verra peut-être l'indice des nouveaux soucis que se donnera le Conseil constitutionnel, peut-être même, sait-on jamais, de nouvelles compétences ou de nouvelles procédures.

Mais, pour anecdotique que cela paraîtra avec le temps, la nomination de M. Daniel Mayer est, au même degré, étonnante. Car l'éclat de sa promotion ne peut faire oublier qu'on venait, il n'y a pas trois semaines, de renouveler ses fonctions de membre du Conseil supérieur de la magistrature. Comme il paraît peu vraisemblable, sinon constitutionnellement impossible, qu'un même homme siège aux deux seuls conseils de nature juridictionnelle prévus dans la Constitution, on est enclin à s'interroger.

L'actuel président de la Fédération internationale des droits de l'homme a-t-il été un élu de dernière heure, pour occuper un siège finalement refusé à un autre qui le voulait fort et menait grande campagne? Ou bien doit-on accorder foi à l'explication que laisse fuser l'Elysée et selon laquelle la première nomination était destinée à cacher qu'on se préparait à la seconde, afin de faire taire les rumeurs?

Là n'est pas l'essentiel, mais dans la confirmation ainsi opérée du credit reconnu au Conseil constitutionnel, par la qualité de ceux qui y sont appelés. Une confirmation qui est aussi le *bénin désaveu* de ceux qui avaient *jeté feu et flammes* contre lui, lorsqu'il jugea contraire à la Constitution *l'indemnisation* prévue par les lois de nationalisation.

C'est aussi pourquoi il ne serait pas heureux que M. Daniel Mayer réitérât les propos tenus lundi peu après sa désignation, et selon lesquels *le droit se lit compte tenu des orientations du suffrage universel*. Ce serait par trop rappeler ce parlementaire de la majorité, M. André Laignel, pour qui, lors du débat sur les nationalisations, l'opposition avait 'juridiquement tort' parce qu'elle était 'politiquement minoritaire'. Ce qui était permis à l'homme politique est évidemment interdit au président du Conseil constitutionnel. Sauf à se faire *vertement* rappeler qu'il est 'du parti du président', comme on en fit, en son temps, le reproche à M. Roger Frey. Celui-ci sut le faire oublier. *L'exemple est à suivre.*

SOURCE: Article paru dans *Le Monde*, 23 février 1983.

Exploitation du texte

1   Expliquez en quelques mots le sens des expressions en italique.

2   Faites une étude textuelle générale, en vous appuyant éventuellement sur l'approche suggérée dans l'Annexe A (p. 23).

3   A partir de cette étude générale, faites une étude plus détaillée de l'emploi du subjonctif dans ce texte.

4   Précisez quels sont les événements qui menèrent à la création de la 'Ligue des droits de l'homme' en 1898.

5   Donnez les arguments pour et contre le propos de M. Laignel, cité dans le texte, selon lequel l'opposition parlementaire a juridiquement tort parce qu'elle est politiquement minoritaire.

Texte 9.2   Une démocratie forte et paisible

Mise en situation

Valery Giscard d'Estaing, Président de la République de 1974 à 1981, naquit à Coblentz (Allemagne) en 1926 dans une famille de la haute bourgeoisie. Sorti de l'Ecole Polytechnique et de l'Ecole Nationale d'Administration il devint inspecteur des Finances et fut élu à l'Assemblée Nationale en 1956. Fondateur des Républicains Indépendants (RI) en 1962, son ascension politique fut très rapide jusqu'à la Présidence de la République, mais il fut battu par François Mitterrand aux élections présidentielles de 1981. Valéry Giscard d'Estaing est l'auteur de *Démocratie Française* (1976), de *L'Etat de la France* (1981) et de *Deux Français sur trois* (1984) où il expose les grandes lignes de sa réflexion sur la politique en général et sur la situation politique en France.

*   *   *

La vie démocratique est, certes, un débat et une compétition. Mais ce débat et cette compétition autour du choix des équipes et des politiques peuvent laisser intact un accord fondamental sur les principes d'organisation de la vie sociale ou se présenter, au contraire, comme le heurt entre deux conceptions opposées de la société.

Dans les démocraties au fonctionnement le plus régulier – aux Etats-Unis, en Grande-Bretagne, en Allemagne fédérale et en Europe du Nord –c'est la première situation qui prévaut. Certes les élections partagent apparemment ces pays en deux parts égales, et c'est le résultat habituel de tout scrutin majoritaire. Mais ils ne se croient pas coupés en deux pour autant, car les principales *familles politiques* ont en commun une même conception de l'organisation sociale. Leurs divergences se situent à l'intérieur de cette conception. Chacune des équipes reconnaît à l'autre l'aptitude à maintenir l'essentiel.

Leur rivalité n'est pas une guerre, mais une compétition. Leur alternance au pouvoir ne représente pas une suite de bouleversements chaotiques, annoncés comme des drames et ressentis comme des révolutions, mais *une suite d'inflexions* dans la progression de la société. En confiant alternativement la conduite de leurs affaires à deux équipes opposées, mais partageant la même philosophie de base, ces pays concilient les nécessités de la continuité et celles du changement.

L'alternance est le propre des sociétés démocratiques avancées, dont l'organisation pluraliste n'est remise en cause par aucune des principales tendances qui les composent. Elle est le mode de régulation politique des démocraties paisibles.

L'état de divorce idéologique qui caractérise la société française, seule parmi les nations comparables, s'oppose, à l'heure actuelle, à ce qu'elle connaisse cette forme d'harmonie. Tout se passe comme si le débat politique n'était pas la compétition de deux tendances, mais l'affrontement de deux vérités qui s'excluent. Son style n'est pas celui d'une délibération de citoyens décidant ensemble de leurs affaires, mais celui d'une guerre de religion, à peine tempérée par la cohabitation.

Cet état de choses trouve son origine lointaine dans notre tempérament et notre histoire. Notre vie politique a toujours été exaltée par la passion méditerranéenne et l'absolutisme latin. Le cri de Voltaire, *bassissant* l'intolérance, reste clamé dans le désert.

Or cette situation ne répond aujourd'hui à aucune *fatalité sociologique*. La réalité française, nous l'avons vu, n'est pas celle d'un pays divisé en deux classes sociales opposées, mais d'une société déjà avancée sur la voie de l'unification. Il n'y a pas identité entre les limites des groupes sociaux et celles des familles politiques. Nos divisions politiques proviennent moins de *déterminismes sociologiques*, parfois invoqués, que de traditions historiques et de tempéraments individuels.

La direction dans laquelle il faut rechercher le progrès de notre vie politique apparaît alors clairement.

Il faut d'abord que soient préservés avec soin *les acquis* de notre démocratie: ses institutions, ses règles politiques et institutionnelles fondamentales, mais aussi la neutralité, au regard du débat politique, de la justice, de l'armée, de l'école et de l'administration. L'introduction de la lutte politque, de ses intolérances et de ses exclusives, au sein de ces institutions essentielles ne constituerait pas un progrès démocratique, comme certains le prétendent, mais une dangereuse régression. Toute tentative dans ce sens doit être combattue.

De même doit être écartée l'assimilation du combat politique à une sorte de guerre civile menée par d'autres moyens. C'est pourquoi la '*décrispation*' de la vie politique française constitue une dimension essentielle de la modernisation de notre démocratie.

La dramatisation de la vie politique et le durcissement des attitudes *font le jeu* des adversaires du pluralisme. En accréditant l'idée que ce qui divise la société française est plus fort que ce qui l'unit, ils tentent de justifier l'excès ou l'injustice de leurs attaques. A l'inverse, souligner auprès des Français qu'ils doivent s'habituer à vivre en commun en respectant leurs opinions mutuelles, c'est préparer dans les esprits le pluralisme démocratique.

Ici apparaît la tâche historique qui incombe à tous les partisans sincères du pluralisme: celle de rendre irréversible l'option du peuple français en faveur d'une structure pluraliste des pouvoirs et de la société. De leur détermination et de leur persuasion dépendent nos chances d'affermir les institutions de la Ve République et d'engager définitivement notre pays dans la voie d'une démocratie moderne. C'est pourquoi nous appelons une majorité qui soit soudée par une ardente conviction, comme à l'aube de la Ve République, pour assurer le succès de l'option décisive.

Alors le vrai débat politique *s'inscrira*, chez nous comme chez nos voisins, à l'intérieur d'une même conception de la société commune à la grande majorité des Français, tolérante, ouverte, respectant la séparation des pouvoirs et le droit à la différence: une conception pluraliste.

Le débat ne sera plus ce combat mythologique des Gorgones et des Méduses, celui du bien et du mal, qui colore encore notre vie politique d'une violence primitive et dangereuse, mais la compétition d'hommes et d'équipes pouvant oeuvrer tour à tour pour le bien commun.

Et la France connaîtra une démocratie forte et paisible.

SOURCE: Valéry Giscard d'Estaing *Démocratie Française* (Fayard, 1976) pp. 154–7.

Exploitation du texte

1   Expliquez en quelques mots le sens des expressions en italique.

2   Quels éléments linguistiques confèrent à ce texte la clarté de son argumentation?

3   Relevez toutes les phrases qui contiennent la conjonction 'mais'. Peut-on établir un lien entre la fréquence relativement élevée de celle-ci et le contenu global du texte?

4   Dressez deux listes qui gravitent autour des notions de (i) "pluralisme" et (ii) "division politique". Comparez ces listes en les mettant en rapport avec les attitudes de l'auteur.

5   La démocratie dépend-elle du pluralisme?

Texte 9.3   Le consensus en France

Mise en situation

'Existe-t-il un consensus en France aujourd'hui?' 'Dans l'affirmative, quel est son contenu?' En 1978, la revue *Pouvoirs* adressa un questionnaire établi autour de ces thèmes à un certain nombre d'hommes politiques. Voici les réponses que lui fit parvenir Jacques Delors, ancien collaborateur de Jacques Chaban-Delmas, membre du Parti Socialiste depuis 1974, figure de proue de son aile 'sociale-democrate', et Ministre de l'Economie et des Finances dans les gouvernements Mauroy de mai 1981 à juillet 1984.

*   *   *

1 *Le terme 'consensus' est devenu d'utilisation courante. Lorsque vous l'utilisez ou lorsque vous le rencontrez, que signifie-t-il pour vous?*

Le terme consensus signifie généralement un accord quasi général sur certaines valeurs vécues par une société, ou bien sur certaines orientations fondamentales.

Mais on l'emploie aussi, et de plus en plus, dans une acception plus restrictive et opérationnelle. C'est alors une base sociale élargie pour accepter, explicitement ou implicitement, une certaine discipline économique. Tous les gouvernements rêvent de pouvoir y recourir pour affronter la présente crise. Certains y parviennent, d'autres pas.

2 *Dans le domaine politique, existe-t-il un consensus sur les institutions de 1958–1962, le pluralisme, la règle de la majorité, l'unité nationale, l'indépendance?*

Si l'on accepte la définition la plus courante du consensus, et aussi l'idée que la France fait preuve apparemment d'un faible consensus par rapport à d'autres pays européens, on peut constater une évolution générale vers davantage de consensus dans les domaines cités dans votre question.

Ce constat est indiscutable, me semble-t-il, en ce qui concerne l'acceptation de *la règle de la majorité* et l'unité nationale. Il doit déjà être nuancé en ce qui concerne l'indépendance, si l'on veut bien aller au-delà des mots et des déclarations. Autrement dit, la finalité est proclamée par tous, mais les forces politiques divergent grandement sur le style et les moyens de l'indépendance . . . ce qui ne manque pas d'influer sur son contenu même!

Pour ce qui est des institutions de 1958–1962, les vents de *la contestation* certes s'apaisent. Mais l'ambiguïté fondamentale de la constitution risque de faire rebondir à tout moment la querelle sur les pouvoirs respectifs du Président de la République, du Premier ministre et du Parlement.

Là où le progrès est plus fragile, c'est bien en matière d'acceptation profonde du pluralisme. Il y a toujours eu, il y a encore, en France, des hommes politiques, à gauche comme à droite, qui, par leurs attitudes et leurs discours, contestent aux autres le droit de s'occuper de l'intérêt général. Autrement dit, ils refusent, sauf sous la pression des faits, le compromis qui est l'essence même de la démocratie pluraliste. Et ensuite, ils le remettent continuellement en cause.

Ce climat est nourri, en profondeur, par la place omnipotente de l'Etat et des administrations dans la nation. A tel point que les citoyens, groupés en associations volontaires, se voient refuser l'accès aux tâches d'intérêt général. Ainsi, puisque tout doit passer par l'Etat, se trouve accentué *le caractère nominaliste*, quasi religieux, artificiellement dramatisé du débat public.

3 *Voyez-vous des valeurs de la société française illustrant un consensus permanent, ou, au contraire, une évolution: l'intolérance, la contestation, l'initiative privée, les inégalités?...*

De ce point de vue, les impulsions les plus fortes ont été conduites par les changements profonds intervenus dans *la société civile* et dans les moeurs. Nous sortons d'une longue période marquée par les représentations et les attitudes dérivées d'un 'christianisme conventionnel', c'est-à-dire la projection purement sociologique de croyances et de pratiques religieuses sur une société qui les a intégrées, puis adaptées . . . pour ses commodités, depuis la mentalité petite-bourgeoise jusqu'à la ritualisation de la vie privée.

Cette mutation s'est traduite, au travers de bien des secousses, par plus de tolérance envers ceux qui ne pensent pas et ne vivent pas comme les autres et par une certaine accoutumance à la contestation, considérée comme un mode d'expression, parmi d'autres. Mais encore une fois, la mutation est loin d'être achevée et le consensus fragile: la soif de sécurité et une certaine lâcheté peuvent conduire à des flambées d'intolérance.

Pour ce qui est du champ économique et social, un certain rapprochement doit être objectivement constaté. A l'époque des économies mixtes, aucune grande formation politique ne réclame plus ni la suppression de l'initiative privée, ni le retour à *l'Etat-gendarme*. Sous la pression d'un fort courant d'opinion que l'on observe dans toutes les sociétés industrielles, tous les partis préconisent la lutte contre les inégalités. Mais de là à parler de consensus! En France, plus qu'ailleurs, les inégalités sont fortes et tenaces, la lutte des classes est une réalité, fortement ressentie par les travailleurs. Les puissants et *les nantis* ne deviennent un peu raisonnables que sous la peur, comme par exemple après mai 1968. Mais la sagesse les quitte vite!

4 *Quelle place le consensus doit-il, à votre avis, occuper dans la société? Et dans les préoccupations d'un homme politique? Les affrontements sont-ils inévitables? Le consensus est-il toujours souhaitable? L'homme politique doit-il s'insérer dans les divisions existantes ou provoquer d'autres consensus?*

La transition avec la réponse précédente peut paraître simple et logique, à la fois. Seul un changement de rapports de forces peut créer les bases d'une politique plus solidaire, plus équitable, plus fraternelle. Les affrontements sont donc inévitables dans la société française, avec les virages brusques et parfois les excès qui s'ensuivent. Notre histoire est ainsi faite. Je suis le premier à regretter qu'il en soit ainsi, mais le réalisme commande d'en tenir compte.

Ceci étant rappelé, je voudrais souligner combien cette situation spécifique ne m'amène pas à renoncer à la recherche obstinée d'un plus grand consensus.

En effet, je considère que lorsqu'une majorité de Français vous porte au pouvoir, vous devez ensuite gouverner pour tous les Français. C'est une exigence absolue de morale politique. L'esprit de revanche n'a pas de place dans cette conception. Pas plus que le renoncement opportuniste aux orientations qui vous ont porté au pouvoir.

Certes, la voie est étroite, mais elle est au surplus la seule réaliste dans *nos sociétés à 50/50*, où par conséquent l'écart est infime entre la majorité et l'opposition, dans nos sociétés caractérisées par la puissance des groupes organisés, *ne serait-ce que* pour empêcher de faire. Pour changer profondément la société, il s'agit de n'épargner aucun effort pour convaincre, pour élargir sa légitimité. Il s'agit aussi de prendre le temps nécessaire à la *pédagogie du changement*, d'amener les groupes organisés à s'exprimer *sans fard* et à prendre leurs responsabilités dans le cadre d'une vie contractuelle à développer, au lieu de ne se fier qu'à l'action unilatérale de l'Etat.

C'est en ce sens que je considère la recherche et l'élargissement du consensus comme un élément fondamental d'une action politique s'inscrivant dans l'esprit d'un pluralisme authentiquement vécu et dans le perspective d'une profonde mutation de notre société, pour la mettre en mesure de sortir de la crise, de répondre aux défis de civilisation . . . et surtout de demeurer une collectivité nationale vivante et debout.

SOURCE: *Pouvoirs*, no 5. 'Le Consensus' (1978) pp. 37, 42–4

Exploitation du texte

1 Expliquez en quelques mots le sens des expressions en italique.

2 Dans quelle mesure le forme et le contenu des questions dictent-ils la forme et le contenu des réponses données? Est-ce que J. Delors esquive certaines questions ou fait des digressions?

3 Relevez dans ce texte les références plutôt 'socialistes' et les références plutôt 'sociales–démocrates'.

4 Résumez en 200 mots les arguments contenus dans les réponses de J. Delors aux questions 2 et 3.

Exercises de comparaison et d'application

1 Comparez globalement la structure des phrases des Textes 9.1 et 9.2. Est-ce que les différences linguistiques renvoient à des différences au niveau des buts des auteurs et des conditions de production des deux textes?

2 En vous inspirant du Texte 9.3, formulez plusieurs questions propres à sonder l'opinion sur les idées énoncées dans le Texte 9.2.

3 En vous référant aux Textes 9.2 et 9.3, rédigez une dissertation de 500 à 750 mots sur l'acception du concept du pluralisme dans la France contemporaine.

4 Quels seraient, selon vous, les 'défis de civilisation' auxquels la France contemporaine doit faire face?

5 La France peut-elle connaître 'une démocratie forte et paisible'?

General Bibliography

Chapters 1-3

The following might usefully be consulted for a general background to present-day France:

G. de Bertier de Sauvigny, *Histoire de France* (Flammarion, 1977)

J.P.T. Bury, *France 1814–1940* (Methuen, 1969)

A. Cobban, *A History of Modern France* 3 vols (Jonathan Cape, 1962–4; Penguin Books, 1965)

J. Friguglietti and E. Kennedy (eds) *The Shaping of Modern France* (Macmillan, 1969)

F. Goguel, and A. Grosser, *La Politique en France* 9th ed. (A. Colin, 1981)

D. Johnson, *Twentieth century France 1914–1983* (Fontana Books,1984)

R. Magraw, *France 1815–1914 – the bourgeois century* (Fontana Books, 1983)

R. Mettam and D. Johnson, *French History and Society : the wars of religion to the Fifth Republic* (Methuen, 1974)

Nouvelle Histoire de la France Contemporaine in eighteen volumes, (Seuil, 1972 onwards)

J.M. Wallace–Hadrill and J.M. McManners, *France : Government and Society, a historical survey* 2nd ed. (Methuen, 1970)

The more explicitly 'social' aspects of this background are dealt with in:

E. Cahm, *Politics and Society in Contemporary France (1789–1971)* (Harrap, 1972)

G. Dupeux, *La Société Française 1789–1970* (A. Colin, 1972)

Y. Lequin, *Histoire des Français XIXe–XXe siècles – la société* (A. Colin, 1983)

J.F. McMillan, *Dreyfus to de Gaulle – politics and society in France, 1898–1968* (E. Arnold, 1984)

Y. Trotignon, *La France au XX Siècle* 2 vols (Bordas, 1972–8)

T. Zeldin, *France 1848–1945* 2 vols OUP, 1973–7)

T. Zeldin, *The French* (Fontana Books, 1984)

Chapters 4–7

P. Avril, and J. Gicquel, *Chroniques constitutionnelles françaises 1976–82* (PUF, 1983) a collection of the entries appearing in the journal *Pouvoirs*

P. Avril, *Le régime politique de la Ve République*, 4th ed. (LGDJ, 1979)

R. Barrillon, *Dictionnaire de la Constitution*, 3rd ed. updated (Cujas, 1983)

B. Chantebout, *Droit constitutionnel et Science politique*, 3rd ed. updated (A. Colin, 1982)

J. Chapsal, *La vie politique sous la Ve République* (PUF, 2nd ed. 1984)

F. de Baeque, *Qui gouverne la France?* (PUF, 1976)

P.M. de la Gorce, and B. Moschetto, *La Cinquième République* (PUF, 1982)

M. Duverger, *La république des citoyens* (Ramsay, 1982)

J.E. Flower, (ed), *France today* 5th ed. (Methuen, 1983)

J.E.S. Hayward, *Governing France – the one and indivisible republic*, 2nd ed. (Weidenfeld and Nicolson, 1983)

D.-G. Lavroff, *Le système politique français: la Ve République* 2nd ed. (Dalloz, 1979)

N. Le Mong, *La Constitution de la Ve République – théorie et pratique 1958–80* 2nd ed. (Editions STH 1983)

F. Luchaire, and G. Conac, (eds) *La Constitution de la République Française* (Economica, 1979)

D. Maus, (ed) *Les grands textes de la pratique institutionnelle de la Ve République* (La Documentation Francaise, 1983)

P. Pactet, *Institutions politiques, droit constitutionnel* 5th ed. (Masson, 1981)

D. Pickles, *Problems of contemporary French politics* (Methuen, 1982)

Pouvoirs no. 4 (1979) 'Vingt ans après – la Cinquième République'

J.-L. Quermonne, *Le gouvernement de la France sous la Ve République*, 2nd ed. (Dalloz, 1983)

S. Sur, *La vie politique en France sous la Ve République*, 3rd ed. (Montchrestien, 1984)

S. Sur, *Le système politique de la Ve République* new edition. (PUF 1984)

V. Wright, *The Government and Politics of France, 2nd ed.* (Hutchinson, 1983)

Chapters 8–9

The following books are recommended as surveys of aspects of the contemporary political scene in France, but with future prospects in mind:

C. Debbasch, *L'Etat civilisé* (Fayard, 1979)

M. Druon, *Réformer la démocratie* (Plon, 1982)

M. Géraud, *Nous tous la France* (J.-C. Lattès, 1983)

V. Giscard d'Estaing, *L'Etat de la France* (Fayard, 1981)

P. Rosanvallon, *La crise de l'Etat-providence* (Seuil, 1981)

L. Stoléru, *La France à deux vitesses* (Flammarion, 1982)

A. Touraine, *L'après-socialisme* (Grasset, 1980; Hachette, revised and enlarged edition, 1983)
A. Touraine, *Le pays contre l'Etat* (Seuil, 1981)
A. Touraine, *Mouvements sociaux d'aujord'hui* (Editions ouvrières, 1982)

In addition, the following essays, sociological studies and collections are recommended:

M. Albert, *Le pari français* (Seuil, 1982)
B. Cathelet, *Les styles de vie des Français 1978–1998* (Stanké, 1977)
J.-M. Domenach, *Lettre à mes ennemis de classe* (Seuil, 1984)
J. Donzelot, *L'invention du social – essai sur le déclin des passions politiques* (Fayard, 1984)
M. Vaughan, *et al. Social Change in France* (Martin Robertson, 1980)

Journals and periodicals
Publications under the following headings are recommended for the student who wishes to be informed on current developments in the politics of Contemporary France:

Daily newspapers:
on the Left – *Le Monde, Le Matin*
on the Right – *Le Figaro, Le Quotidien de Paris*

Weekly journals:
on the Left – *Le Nouvel Observateur*
on the Right – *Le Point, L'Express*

Specialised journals:
Revue Française de Science Politique – as well as its articles, useful for book reviews and surveys of current research.
Revue du Droit Public et de la Science Politique en France et à l'Etranger –a constitutional law approach
Projet – very useful on up-to-date developments

Publications usually covering single themes:
Pouvoirs – not always on a French theme, though each number contains a 'Chronique constitutionnelle' on France
Après-Demain – the voice of the Ligue des Droits de L'Homme
Notes et Etudes Documentaires – surveys by the official *Documentation Française*

252   GENERAL BIBLIOGRAPHY

Journals in English with frequent articles on French politics are:
Contemporary French Civilization
European Journal of Political Research
Government and Opposition
Parliamentary Affairs
Political Quarterly
West European Politics

Notes to Chapters

2. Ideological Conflict

1.   Maurice Duverger, in his book *Les Partis politiques* (Seuil, new ed. 1981) pp. 250 ff.

2.   François Goguel, *La politique des partis sous la IIIe République* (Seuil, 3rd ed., 1968)

3. Political Culture

1.   C. Camilleri and C. Tapia, *Jeunesse française et groupes sociaux après mai 1968* (CNRS, 1974)

2.   Presented to the Munich International Congress of Psychology, 1978.

3.   See *Les Cahiers de la Communication*, vol. 1. no. 4–5; a special issue on television and the 1981 elections.

4.   See, for example, the article by Jean Stoetzel (who founded IFOP in 1938) on 'Les élections françaises de 1981 et les sondages', in *Revue Française de Sociologie,* vol XXIII.

5.   Over half of the deputies in the 1978 and 1981 National Assemblies were also mayors.

4. The Presidency and Executive Power

1.   The notion of a 'domaine réservé', which first surfaced at the end of 1959, was a product of the inchoate nature of constitutional practice in the early stages of the Fifth Republic. It amounted to no more than an attempt to build conceptual bridges between the majority of Gaullists who were willing to give virtually unconditional support to de Gaulle as President, and opponents who already feared a 'personalisation of power'.

2.   Olivier Todd's book on Giscard's career up to 1974 is called *La Marelle de Giscard* (Laffont, 1977)

3.   Mitterrand said on television in February 1984: 'Je compte mener à bien la politique dont je suis responsable, qui ne peut pas plaire à tout le monde. Mais je veux aussi que sur l'essentiel, la défense, les grandes lignes de politique extérieure, peut-être aussi – du moins je l'espère – la défense

des libertés fondamentales, enfin la justice sociale, là je voudrais vraiment rassembler les Français.' (In July 1984, he began the process of trying to enlarge the scope of Article 11, so that he could legitimately put questions concerning basic freedoms directly to the electorate.)

4.   Figure given by Pierre Joxe, Socialist parliamentary leader, on 'France Inter', 19 January, 1983.

5. Government and administration

1.   Chirac was leader as Secretary-general from December 1974 to June 1975, and then informally acknowledged leader until he transformed the party, and again became its head, in December 1976.

2.   Pierre Birnbaum, *Les Sommets de l'Etat – essai sur l'élite du pouvoir en France* (Seuil, 1977)

6. Political Parties and Interest Groups

1.   See D. Colard, 'Réflexions sur le renouveau des clubs politiques après l'alternance du 10 mai 1981', in *Pouvoirs,* no. 25 (1983)

2.   See, for example, J. Capdevielle *et al., France de gauche vote à droite* (Presses de la FNSP, 1981) pp. 52-3, and the table on p. 259. Also J.M. Colombani 'Qui est à droite de qui?' in *Pouvoirs*, no. 28 (1984)

7. Parliament

1.   Only fifty special committees were set up in the National Assembly between 1959 and May 1981, though in 1981–2 they were used for the media and nationalisation questions.

2.   It has been argued that after a Constitutional Council decision in 1982, the strict separation between the *domaine de la loi* and that of executive orders was replaced by a more fluid situation, more in keeping with political reality, where the Government could allow Parliament to legislate even in the area of executive orders (i.e. effectively to extend the *domaine de la loi*), by refraining from using its powers under Articles 37-2 and 41. The Constitutional Council remains, of course, the final arbiter.

8. Politics at the Local Level

1.   J.-F. Gravier, *Paris et le désert français* (Flammarion, 1st ed., 1947; 2nd ed., 1972)

2.   Parti Socialiste, *La France au pluriel* (Editions Entente, 1981) p. 57.

9. Rights, Issues and Propects

1.   See, for example, J.-F. Revel, *La Grâce de l'Etat* (Grasset, 1981) esp. pp. 134–5.

Index